John Cunningham

CREAGH DHU CLIMBER

The Life and Times of John Cunningham

by JEFF CONNOR

THE ERNEST PRESS

Published by The Ernest Press 1999
© Jeff Connor

A CIP catalogue for this book is available from the British Library

ISBN 0 948153 54 7

Typeset from the author's disk by Stanningley Serif
Printed and bound by Colorcraft, Hong Kong

CONTENTS

DEDICATION

To all Weekenders: Past, Present and Future

ACKNOWLEDGEMENTS

This book would not have been possible without the help of many people, most of whom knew John far better than I, and grateful thanks must go to Alison Quatermass, Jimmy and Pat Cunningham, Bobby Cunningham, Mrs Faye Ogilvie, Bill Smith, John Cullen, Karen March, Willie Rowney, Tommy Paul, Davie and Mhairi Todd, Mick Noon, Jimmy Marshall, Frith Finlayson, Fred Harper, Allen Fyffe, George Shields, Reg Popham, Bob Smith, Jim Lyon, Dennis Gray, Mike Wright, Gibby Murray, Hamish MacInnes, Yvon Chouinard, Ian Nicholson, Jimmy Thomson, Des Oliver, George Kemp, John McLean, Ron James, Willie Baxter, Tom Price, Dougie Hay, Ken Wilson, Mike Dales, Jimmy Reid, John and Helen Kay, Ollie Crane, Mark Shrimpton, John Cleare, Kath Murgatroyd, Eric Langmuir, Jack Hool, Alf Gregory, Dennis Davis, John Amatt, Chris Bonington, Pat Walsh, Iain McMorrin and Walt Unsworth.

Mrs Nancy Connor and Tracey Lawson performed miracles with the transcripts and I received invaluable help from the Mitchell Library, Glasgow, Joanna Rae at the British Antarctic Survey in Cambridge, Stephen Rodgers at John Brown Engineering Ltd., Clydebank, the staff at Glasgow University Archives, the American Alpine Club, the Alpine Club, the Alpine Club of Canada, Banff Centre for Mountain Culture (Alberta), the Principal Sheriff's office of Banffshire, Anne Venables the Anglesey County Archivist and Dewi Pritchard-Jones, the Anglesey Coroner.

A special word for Mrs Maggie Lyon, who gave kind permission to quote from her late husband Chris's inspiring writings and to Noel Hulmston whose heroic efforts to produce a memorial slide show after John's death produced not only much-needed funds for a young widow and her three children but an archive of John's career which proved an invaluable source of reference.

Finally, this book would not have happened without the unseen but nonetheless powerful inspiration of Kirsty, Shauna and Paul Cunningham (with some help from little Natalie).

John left little in the way of prolonged writing and when I have quoted him the words come in the main from letters written to the author in 1974-75 and from his 'official' account of the 1953 Creagh Dhu Mount Everest Expedition. He did, however, carry a camera from his early days and the bulk of the photographs in this book are from his extensive slide collection. Where this is the case, they are noted *JC Collection* in the caption. All other photographs are acknowledged to their authors, when known. Every effort has been made to trace copyright and any shortfall in this respect comes with sincere apologies and the promise of later amendment.

AUTHOR'S NOTE

It may be useful to give a brief background to the history of this book, since it was first mooted as a 'ghosted' autobiography with John some 24 years ago and such dilatoriness deserves some kind of explanation.

On an evening in March, 1998, I was seated in the delightful home of Davie and Mhairi Todd in Vernon, British Columbia. Outside, powerful lights ensured that the gloaming couldn't cloak the view of the Todds' pampered garden and swimming pool while inside the remnants of some of the fine produce of the Okanagan Valley wine industry littered the lounge table. In the garage outside four pairs of skis still dripped from the day's sport on the slopes of Silver Star Mountain, 20 minutes up the road from the Todd residence in Barker Avenue. Davie Todd, you could say, has come a long way from a Cornwall Street tenement in rough, tough Kinning Park on the south side of Glasgow. Although over ten years younger than John Cunningham, Davie Todd was one of his closest friends and there are uncanny resemblances between the two, not just in their shared Glasgow backgrounds and wide mountaineering experience but in a quiet, understated authority, biting wit and unwillingness to suffer fools – gladly or otherwise. Both were born into humble circumstances and both chose the outdoors as a way of rising above those circumstances. Both worked in the shipyards of the Clyde and both were outstanding performers of the Creagh Dhu Mountaineering Club. Cunningham later attended college at Jordanhill in the west end of Glasgow, as did Todd, and both men spent time together in Antarctica. Ironically, while John was to suffer death by drowning, Todd came within minutes of a similar fate on a trip South.

Davie's Glasgow *patois* has been tempered by over 20 years in Canada but I could sense a lot of John Cunningham in the man seated opposite me. As if to prove the point, when I began to recall how I had first met his friend, I had reached the time, the place, the company and the initial introduction when Davie lifted his hand and said: "I can write the script from now on." And he did.

That first meeting was hardly laced with the promise of future

7

comradeship, but fairly representative for people making the acquaint-
ance of Cunningham for the first time. His formula for acceptance or
otherwise was well-tried and seldom varied.

I had done a few routes in North Wales with Bill March, Cunningham's regular climbing partner at Glenmore Lodge and while working at
The Outward Bound Sea School at Burghead, Morayshire, had run across
the ebullient 'Big Bill' again. When he invited me and a colleague to join
him for a day at Duntelchaig, a gneiss outcrop near Inverness, March,
then the deputy principal at The Lodge, appeared in the company of a
wiry, dapper Scot in his 40s with the look and demeanour of a cynical
hawk and a distinctive proprietorial air, and not just about Duntelchaig.
One sensed straightaway that this particular crag, the Cairngorms and
Scotland in general, were all a part of his fief. We were simply invited
guests. By way of introduction, March explained that he and I had climbed
Vector together in North Wales (even in those days it was considered by
some that the measure of a man was the climbs he had done and Vector
was still respectably difficult and preenworthy). Cunningham was unimpressed. He professed not to have heard of Vector, although Tremadog
sounded vaguely familiar. Since there is a Creagh Dhu Wall on Craig y
Castell, Tremadog (first ascent J Cunningham, W Smith and P Vaughan
in 1951) I should have seen the metaphorical garden path looming ahead.
But the trap was carefully baited, and by an expert. Seeming to suddenly
remember his duties as the resident expert Cunningham offered a guided
tour of the local testpieces. His *droit de seigneur* also involved, seemingly, deciding on who climbed with whom on what. He suggested a 'wee
route to warm up on' on the Main Crag. The offering was a green, evil-
looking and suspiciously unmarked groove leading to a large roof. I looked
disbelievingly at Cunningham; poker-faced, without a flicker of emotion
he gazed back then nodded expectantly at the rock. I sensed a challenge,
a chance to impress and, being young and foolish, jumped straight in.

An hour later I was still in the same place. Little else had changed
although the first five feet of the groove bore some signs of abuse and
Cunningham was now perched in an eyrie thirty feet above and to the left,
gazing sardonically down. Occasionally he would shout the odd piece of
advice. To no avail. When he arrived back to base there was a brief word

of none too sincere commiseration before, gazing up at the groove again a look of none too convincing apology came over his face.

"Och, I made a mistake, the route you want is further right."
There, round the next corner and until then out of sight, a line of well-marked hand and footholds led skywards.

A year later, in 1973, when I went to work as a short-term instructor at Glenmore Lodge, I came to learn that this was archetypal Cunningham; the debagger supreme of chancers, braggarts and earnest young aspirants, a man who had made the put-down into something of an art form. Todd, in fact, had a similar tale and as the research for this book progressed I began to realise that the select band who had been sandbagged by Cunningham could form an exclusive little club of their own. When I first got to know him he was 44, but on the hill showed little sign of flagging. Off it, he retained that wicked sense of humour and the philosophy that demanded that a man be judged for his achievements – not by the talking about them. His was definitely not a personality given to braggadocio so I was surprised when he agreed to a tentative suggestion that with the proliferation of first-person climbing books – particularly in England – he should consider embarking on his own. He was to dictate or write down his story and I would work it into manuscript style and sort out a publisher. Although an intensely private individual, Cunningham probably recognised that with impending marriage any proceeds from sale of a book would not come amiss and that overrode any other considerations, including his stated concern that he would 'have to check it out with the Boys'.

The Boys, in this case, were the Creagh Dhu Mountaineering Club, an even more mysteriously secretive – and, it must be said for an Englishman in Scotland – frightening body of men. In particular the former club president, Chris Lyon, a man I had never met but whose omnipresent, Don Corleone-like persona tended to colour any discussion of the Creagh Dhu. I remember thinking it odd at the time that someone of Cunningham's forceful personality and obvious independence should have to request permission to write his own life story.

Marriage and differing career emphases for both of us stalled the project and John's death in the seas off South Stack, Anglesey, in 1980 seemed to have ended it totally. Then, in 1995, I moved north to work as a journalist in Glasgow. The newspaper office in Albion Street was 200 yards from the start of Duke Street where John was born and every night on the way home to Drymen I would drive past Strathblane, Carbeth and the Whangie, names I recognised as the cradle of the young Cunningham and the Creagh Dhu: Ben An and the Trossachs were a 20-minute drive from Drymen; The Cobbler and Glencoe not much further afield; and the seed was sown again. Occasionally I would visit an old friend Ian Nicholson, a more contemporary member of the Creagh Dhu, and time and again he would insist: "You've just got to write it." To his encouragement and persistence this book owes much.

Many of the old club were still living in retirement in Scotland and, after what I later recognised as a discreet screening process, it was agreed that they would help all they could in the story of John Cunningham, Creagh Dhu climber. There were, however, a couple of codicils. As George Shields, a Cunningham colleague in the old Creagh Dhu warned me at the time: "You'd better make a job of it, mind," while Cunningham's most prolific climbing partner Bill Smith (73 years old in 1997, but still deep of chest, firm of grip and shining with health) informed me in his matter-of-fact way: "If we thought you were a chancer you'd be oot the door in no time."

I remembered the reputation of the Creagh Dhu, and, as they say in the north of England, thought on. I sincerely hope this biography does justice to the memory of their friend and finally updates the life and times of a man sadly underrated and undervalued, even in Scotland.

This is not a book about climbing as such, although climbing played a large part in the life of John Cunningham and provided the stage on which he stamped his remarkable personality. Those readers looking for detailed analysis of his and the Creagh Dhu's many first ascents may be disappointed, but this was a character shaped by a number of differing facets and circumstances of which climbing was only one. The addition of the subtitle 'Life and Times' on this book's front cover hints at a self-imposed brief that took in many other events and personalities away from rock and ice faces.

There was an upbringing in an elemental district of the East End of

Glasgow a city which itself in the 1930s was one of the most poverty-stricken blackspots in Europe, and where for the vast majority life alternated between long waits by the locked big gates outside the redundant shipyards, the dole queue or the nearest saloon bar. Those who escaped this grey world, the Weekenders, formed the background into which the Creagh Dhu Mountaineering Club came bawling into life and John's story could not be told without a mention of these rough-hewn pioneers. His friends in the club – ruled by the sometimes iron hand of major domo Christopher MacGregor Lyon – played a pivotal role in his development as man and mountaineer, as did his experiences over a number of years in the lonely, lifeless wastes of Antarctica where his explorations, diligent leadership and occasional heroism earned him the Perry Medal and numerous citations from the British Antarctic Survey. As a teacher at Glenmore Lodge in the Cairngorms and later at IM Marsh College in Liverpool Johnny not only moulded mountain leaders of the future but gathered new experiences of his own, including a few tragically short years as a husband to Alison and father to Kirsty, Shauna and Paul.

Above all, however, this book is about a way and a philosophy of life that is no more. It is safe to say that the Weekenders of today and tomorrow, while still being driven by a love of the outdoors and the desire to look round the next corner or peep above the next cloud, are not motivated by the sort of straitened circumstances that existed in the Glasgow of the 1930s, 40s and 50s. A weekend then was a mad dash from the works gates, a shaky bus ride into the wilderness and a few lonely, glorious exploratory hours reaching out for a blue sky ahead of a single off-white rope.

Looking back over the last decade, I find it hard to recall an impoverished climber, there is little or no wilderness left and exploratory isolation, on the hills of Britain at least, is all in the mind.

PROLOGUE

On Thursday, January 31, 1980, a party of seven members of the Outdoor Education diploma course from Irene Mabel Marsh College in Liverpool drove the 60 miles of North Wales coast along the A55 to Bangor, crossed the Menai suspension bridge there and continued along the A5 to Holyhead and the cliffs of South Stack on the island's north-westerly tip.

The group consisted of six students – Stephen Miller, Michael Tonge, Stephen Poynton, Jack Inman, Narayanan Sreedharan and Ian Yarroll. In charge of the group was John Cunningham, a 52-year-old father of three and a senior lecturer in outdoor pursuits, who was driving the college minibus.

Cunningham's intention was to descend with the students to sea level and traverse, just above the ocean, a succession of the zawns that ate into the cliffs below the South Stack lighthouse, an activity that had become a popular, and regular, part of the college itinerary.

Holyhead is best known for the port linking it with Dun Laoghaire in the Republic of Ireland, but for climbers it means the spectacular sea cliffs falling from Holyhead Mountain into Gogarth Bay and which have became grouped under the generic title of Gogarth since their discovery in 1964.

In the 16 years since the first routes up those vast, unclimbed tracts of quartzite, the island had experienced one of the most remarkably condensed climbing booms in the history of the sport with, at its height, virtually a new route a day. South Stack itself boasts a fine collection of climbs, the best-known being Mousetrap, first worked out by Joe Brown and Peter Crew in October, 1966, which takes an improbable line up the fantastically folded strata of rock below the lighthouse steps. But Angle-sey had also seen the birth of a fashion for sea-level traverses, again with Brown as the front-runner, where the rock climbing was given added spice by the extra element of the sea and where technical climbing, interspersed with easy scrambling and the occasional complicated rope manoeuvre like a Tyrolean traverse, could be made in comparative safety. This new sport had the added attraction that, like its embryo sister on the outdoor pursuits curriculum, gorge walking, it was possible most of the year round – particularly in winter when most mountain crags were out of condition. It offered, in fact, adventure at a low-level of risk, as long as it was timed to take advantage of low tide, reasonable weather and of course the nesting season which in the case of South Stack runs from February 1 to July 31. And although some climbs in the Anglesey zawns are made more difficult by the one-way access, in the main by abseil, South Stack itself has a number of easy escape routes, usually via the Lighthouse steps. This comparative ease of access had been taken advantage of by I M Marsh and other outdoor bodies for some time. Cunningham himself had done the same traverse with his head of department at IM Marsh, Ron James, and knew the whereabouts of all the anchor points and the optimum amount of equipment needed. In this case, the party had two 150ft lengths of hawser-laid rope, one 150ft length of 11mm sheathed kernmantel and several shorter lengths for the fixed sections where students could use the rope as a handrail if needed.

The group had been late setting off from Merseyside because Cunningham had wanted to drop his car off at his home on the Wirral to avoid a double trip through the Mersey tunnel from the college campus on Barkhill Road in Aigburth. But although noon was a comparatively late start for that time of year, the nature of the traverse made it possible to call an early halt to proceedings almost anywhere. The forecast for the day was for strong winds from the south -west with rain at first and, possibly, heavy swells.

After parking in the carpark at South Stack, the I M Marsh group descended to the bridge leading across to the island on which the lighthouse stands and scrambled down to sea level and the start of the traverse.

Michael Tonge takes up the story:

"Ian Yarroll had stayed at the top because he had been injured on the dry ski slope so there was five of us, plus John. At the start we were quite sheltered from the prevailing wind and rain and we kept as low as we could. It was good fun and quite challenging although at times quite wet and slippery."

The group had been on the move for close to four hours when conditions began to worsen with occasional swells reaching high up the cliff. On some sections they had to judge a swell and time their next few feet of climbing in between the wave's arrival and departure, so much so that Cunningham was by then fix-roping every section, even the easy ones. Tonge again:

"It was obvious we weren't going to do the rest of the traverse and it was time to call it a day. But as Stephen Miller, the last man, was about to cross the final wall one big wave came in, lifted him off the rock and dropped him in the zawn where he was immediately whizzed away from the rocks. By this time we had coiled all the ropes up and we all looked at each other wondering what to do. Stephen panicked at first and tried to swim back but eventually he managed to relax and float on his back. Jack Inman and Steve Poynton set off up to the lighthouse to get help but it was obvious someone would have get to Stephen Miller because it was plain he wouldn't last long in that. I said to John that one of us would have to swim a rope out and John replied that he did not think he would be able to do that. I was a bit taken aback because I thought this was a guy who could do anything."

What Tonge did not know, in fact, was that Cunningham was virtually a non-swimmer and in any case his skills at rope-handling would be better employed on dry land, rather than going into the water and to what amounted to certain death. Tonge, a mature student at I M Marsh and a strong swimmer and life-saver, then bravely volunteered and descended to sea level belayed by Cunningham and Sneedharan where he "basically just waited for the next wave to sweep me off". He made good headway until within 20 feet of Miller where he managed to shout some encouragement, but by this time he was towing three lengths of rope tied together and they were proving more a hindrance than help.

"By now I could sense I was in serious difficulty. I had agreed with John that if I did get into trouble I would raise my hand and they would tow me back and I had to make that very difficult decision ."

The return trip proved an even greater trial with the rope tugging him through, rather than over, the waves.

"I had a job just to keep myself on the surface and by the time I got back to the rocks I was severely battered about and ready to come to terms with the situation. I was spending a lot of time under water. Stephen Poynton had arrived back to give a hand and as he and John were struggling to get me back in another big wave came in and knocked both of them in."

With three students and their instructor all in the water and in danger of drowning the situation was desperate. Poynton managed by a supreme effort to regain the cliff, but Cunningham was too far out to do the same and as Inman returned with reinforcements he saw his instructor being pulled slowly out to sea. Between swells Cunningham could be spotted waving both hands above his head, in all probability in one last effort to pinpoint his position. It was the last time he was seen.

Poynton, Inman and one of the lighthouse keepers who had arrived lifted the exhausted Tonge out of the water as a Sea King from RAF Valley lowered a winchman to rescue Miller. Neither Poynton nor Inman when they went to raise the alarm was aware that Cunningham was in the water and the helicopter was looking for only one person – another turn in the spiral of misfortunes that was to cost John Cunningham his life. Both Miller and Tonge were taken to Bangor General Hospital suffering from hypothermia. A sweep search for Cunningham, in what was now virtual darkness, proved fruitless, although the helicopter crew believed at one point they had spotted what looked like a blue anorak under the water close to the mouth of the zawn.

Over the next three days the RAF and Holyhead coastguard made further exhaustive trawls of the area until, finally, the search was called off. Cunningham's body has never been found; the sea, in this case, never gave up its victim.

News of the death stunned Cunningham's family, friends and contemporaries in the world of climbing. Most believed him indestructible, although there was a recognition, too, that water was an alien environment to him. Swimming lessons were not considered a priority for children brought up in Glasgow during the 1930s and '40s and the man who had climbed and explored at the highest standard within his own, considerable safety margins for 35 years had never actually learned to swim properly, although he did hold a canoeing and life-saving qualification. As James, his senior at I M Marsh, put it: "It was the closeness of the two

elements. John was so competent on rock but really, well, quite uncomfortable in water." For one of the few times in his life Cunningham was
not in control of his own destiny.

An enigmatic and almost secretive man throughout his 52 years,
this anonymity extended beyond death. The obituaries in the specialist
climbing magazines did him scant justice and there was nothing to mourn
his passing in the national press. Even his 'local' newspaper the Glasgow
Herald, instead of their usual fulsome tribute for a personality born within
three miles of its office, managed only a tribute from his friend Hamish
MacInnes, compiled some time after the death.

Neither, for reasons that will be explained later, was there an official
inquest nor even an inquiry by the college, with everyone accepting that
it was just an unfortunate accident.

John Cunningham, it appeared, had slipped out of life almost as
quietly as he had come in.

EAST ENDER

The second son of William John and Mary Cunningham was born on November 23, 1927, at Number 1252 Duke Street in the East End of Glasgow. The straightforward birth was aided by the local midwife in the Cunningham kitchen of the house, only emergency arrivals necessitating hospitalisation for expectant mothers in those days.

The boy was christened John Crabbe, the John after his father, the Crabbe being his mother's maiden name. An elder son, James, had arrived in September of the previous year while after John there was a sister, Faye and the youngest brother, Bobby. Another boy William, between Faye and Bobby, succumbed to scarlet fever in Bellshill Hospital at the age of four, a not uncommon occurrence in the Glasgow of that era.

These days Duke Street is a nondescript, if busy, road lined by tatty shops and pubs with the inevitable faded tenement frontages rising three floors above; the only sights of any note being the massive complex of Tennents Caledonian Brewery, the Glasgow Meat Market and the be-shuttered and redundant Duke Street Hospital. In reality, Duke Street is a shadow of the thoroughfare it once was. Drive two miles down there from the city centre now and just past the railway bridge and the junction with Carntyne Road the buildings vanish and the street runs out into open spaces and a large roundabout on Shettleston Road filtering traffic into The Forge Shopping Centre, a vast supermarket complex christened by the then Home Secretary, Malcolm Rifkind, in June 1987.

Most older residents would find it difficult to recognise Duke Street today, but the shopping centre's main entrance, where Rifkind climbed gingerly aboard a mechanical excavator to perform the laying of the first sod at The Forge, is less than 50 feet from what was once Number 1252. In 1927, when John Cunningham first saw the light of day, the street and its heavily-populated tenements stretched all the way from Glasgow's High Street close to George Square to Parkhead Cross within sight of Celtic Park and its football ground.

Put down in 1794 and intended as a route from Glasgow to Falkirk via Cumbernauld, Duke Street took its name originally from the Duke of York, of grand old fame. By 1837 the road was lined by close to three miles of red and white-fronted tenements housing in the main the labour force of the ironworks at the massive, steaming complex of Parkhead Forge, whose machine shops, smithies, gas plants and stores covered a site of some 80 acres between Parkhead railway station on Shettleston Road in the north and Parkhead Cross to the south. Parkhead Forge had been built originally by the Ironmaster, John Reoch, but when he became financially embarrassed and unable to keep the plant going, the site and its machinery were sold on to the equally underfunded David Napier in 1841. By 1863 it was in the hands of William Beardmore and his family who, with their other, later, works at Dalmuir in Clydebank, soon became the biggest employer in the West of Scotland.

Like much of the heavy engineering industry on Clydeside, Beardmores and its labour force owed a large debt to the two world wars: from 1910 the family firm, headed by Sir William, thrived on the Government rearmament plans and when the war broke out their contribution to the war effort consisted of a seemingly endless supply of guns, howitzers, aero engines, shells and even an airship. Ironically, in the light of a nearby resident's long and later association with Antarctica, they also produced equipment for Sir Ernest Shackleton before his epic attempt to reach the South Pole in 1908, including a one-off, prototype sno-cat. In January, 1906, in the later manner of politicians and their non-executive but lucrative directorships, Shackleton had been given the sinecure of secretary to the research committee at Parkhead with a salary of £30 a month. He responded gratefully two years later by naming the massive glacier which later proved to be the key to the plateau leading to the Pole – and where Petty Officer Edgar Evans later perished on Captain Scott's ill-fated-trip of 1912 – the Beardmore Glacier, thereby transplanting, metaphorically at least, a small part of the East End of Glasgow to the most desolate continent on earth.

By 1921 when the postwar boom collapsed, Beardmores, like every employer, large and small, in the West of Scotland was descending swiftly into a financial abyss and when the Wall Street crash came in 1929 they were another small, suffering statistic in a worldwide epidemic of recession and unemployment. All that changed in 1936 when rearmament re-started in earnest and from the massive Parkhead presses rolled new instruments of war: guns for warships, armour plating for other vessels and tanks, 25-pounder artillery breech mechanisms and the carefully-milled barrels for 3.7 inch AA guns. Work for locals, too, was abundant.

In the midst of this elemental mass of smoking foundry chimneys, clanking railway engines and pounding steam hammers was Duke Street and, at the corner of Duke St and Croydon St, Number 1252 a four-storey corner tenement block made up of 11 houses and flats.

With Beardmores No 2 melting shop 200 feet to the east and the forge's hammer bay two blocks to the south along with a steady flow of Glasgow Corporation trams up and down the street, Duke Street's new-born arrived in the world to the lullaby provided by the biggest, and noisiest, employer in the west of Scotland. Pre-teens became immune to the racket; it was a part of their upbringing. As Bobby Cunningham, the youngest in the family, recalls: "The steam hammers were going 24 hours a day; when they stopped, that was when you woke up."

Glasgow was, and still is, the city of tenements. In Victorian times their polished walls of red and white stone fronted large and comfortable accommodation for mill owners and merchants; but the acute housing shortage caused by the flood of munitions workers into the city before the Great War produced, first sub-division (making-down) by a despairing local government and greedy landlords, and from that the chronic over-crowding that gave Glasgow its image of the Slum City. For 28 shillings a week, inclusive of rates, a family could rent a two-roomed house with a shared outside toilet from Glasgow Corporation; the more affluent could buy one at a cost of between £289-£370.

The Cunningham home was fairly typical: a corner building with a large back close and a spiralling stone staircase leading to the three landings with the front doors leading off these. John and Mary Cunningham's, on the first floor, consisted of one living room, a kitchen and a scullery. The three boys shared the large room, Mary and her husband had a double bed in the kitchen and Faye slept in a bed chair alongside them. Unlike many tenement dwellings, however, the Cunninghams had the luxury of their own inside toilet. Once a month either Mary or, later, Faye walked along to London Road to the offices of Sharp Fairlie, the factors, to pay the rent and report the frequent breakages or leakages.

Before the Great War, John Cunningham Senior was a fireman with British Rail, "a good job with good prospects in those days", according to Bobby. But in 1915, and at the age of 17, the newly-enrolled Private Cunningham, W.J., had marched with the rest of the Highland Light Infantry down a crowded, respectful Sauchiehall Street before embarking on a troopship to Europe. He returned an invalid a year later, having taken a bullet in the right leg during action in the Dardanelles. Gangrene later set in and amputation midway between knee and ankle followed, along with the supply of a wooden leg from the Ministry of Defence. For his pain and suffering in the cause of his country he was awarded a war pension of 10s a week. Because he was so young – still growing in fact – when he was maimed John had to return to hospital once a year to have the bone shortened and the artificial leg refitted. The National Health Service later supplanted the wooden limb with an aluminium one. John, ever practical, preferred the wooden version as he could stick drawing pins in it to keep his stockings up.

The crippled soldier married Mary Crabbe from his home district of Bridgeton in 1924 and the invalid's pension and a part-time cleaning job for Mary helped the couple through his several years of unemployment before he managed to find a job as a labourer at Rolls Royce in Hillington just before the start of the Second World War. Even with an artificial leg he could decorate, climb ladders, and get around fairly well, although once a year, when the man from the Ministry of Pensions came round, the artificial leg had to give way to crutches to prove he was still disabled and in this way remain qualified for his allowance.

Mary, a large, cheerful woman, was a typical Glaswegian housewife in a 'working poor' household, her life revolving round the family and the home, scrubbing the linoleum floor until it gleamed, black-leading the kitchen range, cooking, washing, seeing the children off to Newlands Primary School and, later, taking young John back at lunchtime after he had run away. Faye, as the one sister in the family, was her mother's apprentice; the boys, as in every other Glasgow household, were never asked to help around the house. It was accepted that their turn as breadwinners would come later and young John's one and only attempt at domesticity had ended disastrously when his mother had left him to keep the fire burning while she went shopping. Father arrived home from work late to find the fire out and, naturally blamed his wife, John explaining quite truthfully that he didn't know, and had never had a reason to find out, where the coal was kept.

But for all the straitened circumstances in which they lived it was a happy upbringing for the four Cunningham children. Tenement life, as it did for so many before the vast clearances of the 1950s and 60s destroyed whole communities and imprisoned them in tower blocks on the city's peripheries, imposed its own basic values. James, after a spell at the Loch Sloy hydro-electric scheme and several years at sea in the merchant navy, emigrated to Australia in 1953. His Glasgow accent has long gone as he recalls:

"I measured out where we lived at Duke Street once and there were 18 families in two tenements in an area 100ft by 100ft and 200ft high. Where I live in Victoria now I own and live on a place the same area. Duke Street in those days was a tough place and one of the roughest areas of Glasgow at the time. There were some terrible characters around but it was self-regulating in many ways and no one tried anything, although later on there were some odd looks when we were heading out to the hills with boots and rucksacks. If you came home from school early and dad was out working and mum out shopping there was always a family to take you in and look after you until they got home."

For Faye, who now lives with her second husband Bill Ogilvie in Greenhills, East Kilbride, tenement life offered the best kind of upbringing:

"Duke Street was a very busy place in those days because Beardmores, right next to us, was one of the biggest works in Scotland. It was a very, very friendly place. We were brought up in the same close with another family and I know them to this day. It was a rare place to live. There was very little vandalism or crime because the gangs only fought with each other, there was no graffiti on the walls, anything like that. Even the football crowds were different in those days. We had a window looking right into Duke Street and my mother and I used to sit there and watch the crowd going past. There was the odd rowdy one, shouting and bawling at us, but no vandalism, it was just good fun. The Rangers fans would go down one side of the street and the Celtic fans the other. You don't get those sort of childhoods now, the kids are too busy wanting everything. We didn't have the money for anything so we just accepted what was there. When it came to Christmas time my father used to make the boys toys – he was good at that – and my mother used to do dolls and dress them up and things like that. It was a good life, I enjoyed it. I just wish children would have the same life nowadays, without looking for drugs and all that."

Brother John, according to Faye, was "a terror" although he suffered as a child from bronchitis – the tenements cough – and bow legs which together with a slight physique gave him a misleadingly frail appearance.

The two Johns, father and son, co-existed in an atmosphere of mutual animosity.

"John and my father never got on, probably because they were too alike, sarcastic and a bit dour at times, very hard to live with," says Faye.

"When my father died in 1965 I remember going into the room where the coffin was – you brought the body into the house in those days – and there was John writing letters on it. When I asked him what he was doing he just said: 'This is the only place I can get some peace and quiet.' I don't think John had much time for my father. He was my mother's favourite, though, no doubt about that. As a wee boy he didn't want to go out to play so she just used to put him out and one of the neighbours would bring him up and say: 'Is this yours?' because they had found him asleep on the stair. But once he got the idea that there was a bit of adventure outside he used to go and do everything. He had the kind of mind that had to be doing something, whether it was bad or good didn't matter to him. When the wagons used to come round with the coal he used to dance under the horses' bellies, he'd take a shower under the water carts and he'd fight with anyone. When he was five mother took him to Newlands School, where we all went, and he was crying because he didn't want to stay at school. To stop him crying the teacher gave him her keys to play with and he hit her with the keys. At playtime they used to open the door and let him out for a wee and John would disappear up the road and away home. My mother had to take him back again but at lunchtime he'd be off again, the same at playtime in the afternoon.

"Later when he went to Riverside Secondary he was the same. If John didn't want to do something he just wouldn't do it. I remember my first day at Riverside arriving there and finding John lined up for a strapping from Mr Page the form master. He would never go straight to school, either, he'd always be exploring up the Clyde somewhere first. But mother was always on his side. One of the neighbours used to wash the big flag stone outside her house, wash it then decorate it. John would wait till she finished and then go and wee on it. The woman came to my mother and said: 'What are you going to do about this?' and my mother would say 'Nothing. It's not your stone, it belongs to the street so why should I chastise him?' She wouldn't do anything to John. He was very, very small and he had these bow legs. They wanted to break them to straighten them, which was what they did in those days, but my mother wouldn't let them. She just put boots on him and that straightened them. But it was just mischief with John, he was never in court because my father would never have tolerated that. If the police had come to our door he'd have knocked John from one side of the house to the other."

The East End, as John Cunningham pointed out to the author in 1975, was indeed a rough place. It had its villains, its gangs and Friday night wife-beaters, but much of this was simply a metaphor for the straitening circumstances of the depression. It certainly was not as bad as some, usually uninformed, commentators from outside Glasgow painted it.

If a city could sue for libel or defamation, probably the first on the list for Glasgow would have been the authors of *No Mean City*, the best-selling collaboration between Alexander McArthur, a former baker from the Gorbals and the English journalist, H. Kingsley Long. *No Mean City*, reprinted some 30 times, paints an apocalyptic vision of Glasgow with razor gangs battling each other amid filthy slums in a city of containing nothing but foul-mouthed drunks equally divided into Prods and Tims. Alongside the 'Miles Better' metropolis of today, the rediscovery of its Victorian architecture and renaissance as the city of culture, *No Mean City* is no more than a crude fiction. The authors had made the worst of life in the slums appear as the whole. McArthur himself, perhaps justly, died after taking an overdose of disinfectant in 1947, but the image he had painted proved far more difficult to erase. There were gangs, certainly, but most would-be tearaways in the 30s and 40s were helpless in the face of the city's most organised and ruthless 'wild bunch', the Glasgow Constabulary, a body well organised and trained in the art of pre-emptive warfare by the then Chief Constable, Sir Percy Sillitoe.

Sillitoe's brief to his bobbies was simple: if you find a small gang, wade in and give them a good hiding; if there are bigger gangs, wait till they have exhausted themselves by fighting each other, then wade in and give *them* a good hiding. John Cunningham, who was by the age of 17 a member of the most exclusive gang in the country, the Creagh Dhu Mountaineering Club, had no need of such company and as Faye points out anyway: "We had a big bobby at Parkhead Cross and he'd just take villains up an alley and give them a doing and they never got in trouble on his patch again. He'd give John the odd kick up the backside. It got to the stage when John used to be going to school and every time he got to the Cross, he'd walk across there with his eyes shut."

Cunningham himself noted: "I was brought up in the very rough East End of Glasgow where people thought you had to belong to a gang just to survive. At school, if you were academically inclined, you became an object of ridicule, the hard men ruled. I was very glad to leave school at the age of 14 in 1942 and became an office boy at Beardmores, which was useful because there wasn't much travelling involved to get there."

In fact a clamber over a wall and a short walk led to the factory where John's main task was to run errands to the shops along Duke Street and fetch back bottles of soda water or the making of constant brews to slake the overwhelming thirst of the workers in the Beardmore furnaces. Such was his diligence, according to Faye, that when the Christmas collections came round John always had the fullest box.

He was following a well-worn path. In the Glasgow of the 20s, 30s and 40s, a male of 12 was a boy just left school; at 14, he was a working man. James the eldest brother was also employed by Beardmores (Bobby served an apprenticeship as an electrician) which by the time John Cunningham went to work there in 1942 were working round the clock on war products and James says:

"I got 13s 5p a week at Beardmores and gave my mum five bob. Then I would have to borrow it back because I was broke. My mother was the greatest person you could imagine, a marvellous personality with a super outlook on life. Dad was mean and miserable and John never got on with him. John was a leader and when he set his mind on something he would just go ahead and do it and never change his mind. He was a pretty good fighter even then and I was always getting a punch on the nose 'for your brother'."

Bobby Cunningham remains convinced that the apathy between father and John was down to the old, traditional ways of the East End – John Snr was a member of the Bridgeton Orange Lodge – and John's refusal to accept those ways, never once throughout his life evincing the slightest interest in religion or politics. Bobby says:

"My father was brought up in the old ways, Catholics and Protestants and all that sort of stuff. John wasn't even political. I don't know if he ever voted and religion he wasn't interested in at all. But he did have some old East End values. If there was bullying at school he would sort it out. He was that type. He was a quiet boy but he didn't like bullies so he just fixed them."

Not that it was all one-way traffic, as Faye remembers:

"John worked in the Forge as a boy and I had to laugh. He came home one day and they had painted the heels on his shoes white without him knowing; they would send him for a left-handed screwdriver, a pail of blue smoke or tell him to go for a long stand, things like that. The same thing happened at John Browns when he went to do his apprenticeship there until of course he was old enough and he started pulling the same ones on the other apprentices."

For a working-class teenager looking for a career in the Glasgow of the 1940s the choice was relatively simple; an apprenticeship in either heavy engineering or one of the 37 bustling shipyards that lined the Clyde. John chose the yards, mainly because much of the work was outdoors, and he began his apprenticeship as a shipwright at John Browns on the 5th of January 1944, at the age of 16 years and two months. Starting pay was £89 a year, rising to £256 when his time was served on January 21,

1949, at the age of 21. He was also told that he would be allowed to keep his tools if he served his full five years, this a measure of Browns designed to discourage apprentices from defecting to other yards. John, in fact, kept the same tools all his life and his close friend Tommy Paul has them in his garage today, several years ago employing them to build his house at Boat of Garten in the Cairngorms. Although an apprentice was notoriously lowly-paid, a state of affairs that prompted a succession of strikes including one in the early stages of the war, overtime from 1939-45 was virtually unlimited, John using these to finance his weekend trips and holidays. In November 1945 alone, he clocked 47 hours extra, hoping to spend a Christmas in the hills.

"I used to do his shopping for him on a Friday night if he was going away for the weekend, his sausage, his eggs and bacon," says Faye. "John didn't spend a lot of money, he was never a bloke that went out and blew his cash. He kept it, he was very, very thrifty. I never knew John to be short of money, not even from an early age. I remember one day when he was tiny and he was going to the pictures just down from school. A man came down Springfield Road on a bike and knocked John over and John was actually dying on the street. So the man says: "Oh, I hope he's all right, here I'll give you 3d if you don't tell anyone'. Next minute John jumps up, grabs the 3d and he's off, not a scratch on him. John always seemed to have money, but he was very generous, too. When my first husband died in 1966 I was living in Johnstone at the time and John arrived to see I was all right. When he'd gone I found a blank cheque on the settee. That was John."

At 6.30 am every weekday and most Saturdays, John would leave the house in Duke Street, walk down to Parkgate Cross and down Springfield Road to Parkgate Stadium on Whitby Street where a train would take him straight into Clydebank. A typical working day involved starting at 7.45 am, working nonstop to 12.45, an hour for lunch then straight through again to finish at 5.45. Tea breaks were illegal and punishable by a fine.

Mick Noon, later to become a regular climbing partner of Cunningham's in the late 50s, worked as a painter in the yards and he recalls the strict regime of places like Browns: "The thing I remember is that if you didn't get there by a certain time they locked the doors, you couldn't get in in the morning. If you were late, too bad. And at night they'd all pile up before they'd open the door and there was a great big mad rush for the tram cars ... and if you fell, that was it, you were a goner."

The first week at John Browns soon opened John's eyes to the facts of life there; Browns employed mainly from Clydebank and intruders from the East End were not welcome. The 'Bankies' had their own filial demarcation system and liked to keep it in the family. When he first requested directions to the stores, he was told "I dunno Jimmy, I've only just started here". Later, John found out the man in question had been employed there full-time for four years. On another occasion, John was on his way home to Parkhead when the ticket-collector asked for his weekly pass and it was only then he discovered a workmate had sewn up his top jacket pocket ... with the pass inside. The price of a workmate's prank was a ripped jacket. Cunningham soon became just as streetwise and too sharp, worldly and quick-witted for most. The workmate with the needle and thread arrived to clock on one morning to find his overalls strung up to scaffolding with high-voltage electricity cable, although Cunningham did resist the temptation to connect it to the mains. Even in those days, he tended to have the last word.

"There was this ancient carpenter he worked with," says Davie Todd. "Every day they would go to lunch together and Johnny would buy these two cakes, one of which was always better than the other, one had cream, the other didn't and of course Johnny always took the best one for himself.

This went on for ages until old Sanny got fed up and says one day: 'Did your mother never teach you manners?' Johnny asked what he meant. Sanny said: 'It's not manners to just go and take that. You could have asked me what cake I liked' and Johnny said, 'Well what would you do?' and Sanny said: 'Well I'd have given you the cream cake,' and Johnny replied 'Well, I took it'."

'Clydebuilt' was once the metaphor for all that was best in the ship-building industry. From trawlers to massive ocean-going liners this was the capital of the world. In the Clydebank yards of John Browns alone – birthplace of the Queen Mary and both the Queen Elizabeth and QE2 –

400 ships rolled down the slipways between 1899, when the Sheffield steel firm of John Brown took over from the ailing J and G Thomson's Clydebank Shipyard, and 1971 when the formation of Upper Clyde Shipbuilders and the unions' work-in signalled the end of a once proud industry. Clydebank was 'Tamson's Toon' and at the outbreak of war in 1939 Browns kept an average of 9,700 working men on their books, while in all some 24,000 were employed in all the yards that lined the massive rolling river between Govan and Greenock. To some like Chris Lyon, who began at John Browns as B5276, Lyon C, in 1945 when he left Singers (Sing-Sing) and retired as Mr Christopher MacGregor Lyon, manager, in 1982, the romance of shipbuilding was overpowering; it was a way of life, a social club, a sporting club and something that defined a shipyard worker even more than his family.

In his unpublished manuscript, *Thoughts, Poems and Reflections of an Elderly Patter Merchant*, Lyon wrote: "I was only in the shipyard five minutes when I knew this was my true vocation. These steel-tough, proud men who defied wind, weather and tide and with skill and strength and a few hand tools fashioned things of majestic power and beauty. The proud, arrogant little men who launched 50,000 tons of steel into the River Clyde and knew it would float. I was hooked."

At one time about 25% of the world's ships were made on the Clyde but what tickled Lyon and others was the proletariat concept that the men in charge of these epic enterprises, leviathans of 80,000 tons like the Queen Mary and the QE2, not only had never been to university but had received the humblest of formal education. Their education was the fundamental upbringing of the tenement, the burning tawse of the head teacher at school and a five-year apprenticeship that turned callow boys into shipbuilders. That five years was a qualification for anything the world could throw at them.

Hull 534 may have eventually turned into the Queen Mary but it began when a John Brown carpenter bolted the first frame to the keel plates. To the carpenter and the plater who followed him and the riveter and painter who came later it was a number, the next job. Whatever fancy name they gave it subsequently, they knew it was going to float. And, maybe later, that same joiner or riveter would be in the cinema on a Friday night when flickering footage of the Queen Mary or Queen Elizabeth bearing royal dignitaries to a foreign land would appear on screen and the man from Browns could turn, dig his neighbour in the ribs and say with pride of ownership: "Ah built that."

It was a tough environment. Cunningham and his mates worked in all weathers, and falls and serious injuries were common in winter when ice plated the hulls and men's hands were blistered by the freezing steel. The minds of management and their concept of the relationship between masters and workers remained rooted firmly in another century. When Fairfield's yard decided to recruit women during the Second World War the problem arose about finding separate lavatories. One director suggested the men's could be subdivided ... until someone pointed out that even the men didn't have lavatories. Industrial disease was common, too. Like Chris Lyon, Davie Todd thought it was the best job in the world when he followed his father into Alexander Stephen's at Govan – until reality set in. He can recall with appalling clarity the day his father came home stricken by the doctor's diagnosis that he had irreversible asbestosis; a hard man, a streetfighter who once punched Todd unconscious for a climbing escapade, reduced to a muted, head-shaking wreck by the news. Sam Brown, who opened Glasgow's first climbing shop on Dalmally Street, Maryhill, and Sandy Cousins, the doughty be-kilted battler for Scottish mountain access, were killed by the same disease from the same yards. Todd, who as well as his father's job, also inherited asbestosis and only keeps the symptoms at bay by prolonged exposure to the fresh air and open spaces of Canada, remembers:

"I thought it was wonderful at first; the camaraderie, the teamwork, the thought you were building something worthwhile. It was exciting, uncomfortable and dangerous. Then it palled. You went into a hull and saw the asbestos streaming down from above, the basic working conditions, the daily bombardment of deafening noise, flames, sparks, gases and dust that cut out the sun, it was appalling, Dantesque."

There was also the latent sectarianism with a hint of what was to come on the first day of an apprenticeship. Todd says:

"They asked on the indenture form if you were Catholic or Protestant and I soon found out when I wrote down Catholic that I was one of the

Great Untouchables. On the surface, they seemed all right, the bosses and foremen were sharing things with me but they were devious with it. When I finished a ship I wasn't given the deserved rest, a week of sea trials off Arran with 24 hours a day of double wages; instead, they sent me off to another new skeleton of another new ship on the stalks."

Work in the yard could be the ultimate in casual labour with often only two hours' notice of lay-offs. The completion of a vessel may have meant a day of celebration when it careered down the slipway into the Clyde but it also signalled mass redundancies. When work on the Queen Mary was stopped for two and a half years in 1931 after Cunard ran into financial difficulty, 3,000 at John Browns lost their jobs on the spot. Cunningham, too, with his sharpness and cynicism, was quick to recognise that for all the solidity of the end product and the men who produced it, the yards and the ships they produced always had an air of the ephemeral. As he told the author:

"Everyone served an apprenticeship and it was a means to an end. I enjoyed the joinery and the crack was good in the yard but a lot of the time I knew that all these great hulks were going to finish up as scrap."

He was right, of course: the greatest floating advertisements of John Browns, like Todd's father and many of the labour force, came to premature ends. Nothing, it turned out, would stay afloat for ever. Of the Browns royal lineage, the Lusitania was torpedoed and sunk by the German U20 off Ireland in 1915, the Empress of Britain suffered a similar fate in 1940. The unsinkable HMS Hood was blown apart by one shell from the battle-cruiser Bismark in 1941, and the Lusitania's sister ship, the Aquitania, finished in a breakers' yard in 1950. The first Queen Elizabeth was gutted by fire in Hong Kong harbour in January, 1971 while the mighty Queen Mary, some would say the greatest of all liners and the symbol of everything Clydebuilt, finished up as a plaything for rich Americans on the waterfront at Long Beach, California. Certainly Cunningham never saw the yards as a long-term career; while his mates headed straight off to the pub after work on a Friday or to Ibrox or Parkhead on a Saturday afternoon, he had his sights set higher. There were other heights to scale.

Browns did have its uses. The apprenticeship there was one of the most technically-honed and thorough anywhere and it did teach one invaluable lesson; life in the yard required team-work. That team-work and comradeship extended to the moonlighting electricians and painters who would rewire a friend's house using not only the expertise taught them by their employers but also their cables, plugs, fuses, tins of paint and brushes. In a huge company like Browns these were seldom missed, although a routine check on employees leaving the yard at night would have produced some surprising discoveries – like the 60ft of electricity cable wrapped round a torso inside a set of overalls or half a dozen three-point plugs inside a sandwich box.

Cunningham had a fund of stories about the 'Clyde set' and said: "It was a really hard game, a really tough environment. Like climbing you had to look out for yourself, if you were doing something stupid or showing off or whatever you didn't earn any admiration, you were just an idiot who would come a cropper and deserved to come a cropper. You were encouraged to stand on your own feet and you had to fend for yourself."

There was another bonus; with its scaffolding, gangways and lumps or iron and steel lying around, Browns was as good as a home gymnasium.

The Yorkshire climber Peter Livesey is often given credit for overt training for the sport of climbing in the 1970s, but a 16-year-old shipwright from the East End of Glasgow was 30 years ahead of him. Bobby Cunningham had already caught his older brother traversing the gable end of one of the Beardmores machine shops, now John began to improvise with his tools of work at John Browns. By 1944 and his first year there he was also well into his apprenticeship as a climber and had won the regard of the yard's indigenous Clydebankers with his unabashed performances on narrow planking high above the ground. Then the iron and steel lumps became free weights, the high walkways used to hone his balance, the scaffolding employed for continuous pull-ups and the outside shell of the scrap metal disintegrator became an improvised climbing wall, all this to the understandable amazement of his fellow workers who were soon giving him the kind of respect that only eccentricity affords. The sight of 'Big John the Climber' skipping about in the skies above the yards or doing repetitions with 20 lb weights during his lunch hour while the rest of the gang tucked into their sandwich pieces, became commonplace; some even joined in. Willie Rowney, who was to become a Creagh Dhu protegé of Cunningham and Bill Smith, says:

"When John was working in the yard he used to climb about on the boat and if there was a ladder over there and if he could get up another way and the gaffer wasn't looking he would do it. It was a fitness thing and one day – he didn't like being caught looking stupid – he was practising his pull-ups and hanging from a scaffold and this bloke saw him and said: 'What are you doing?' Instead of sheepishly saying 'training', John said 'I'm trying to break the record for hanging by the fingertips'. The chap said: 'What's the record?' and John said: 'This guy from Manchester can do it for two minutes,' and the bloke scoffed 'Two minutes? That's not very long'. So John said 'Well, it's not as easy as you think.' That was the end of the conversation but you know 15 or 20 minutes later everybody looked and there's these wee men in boiler suits and bunnets hanging and shouting 'How long is that?' and then dropping off when their arms got tired. It conjures up a wonderful picture; all of them trying to beat the champion of Manchester for hanging from a scaffold pole."

John's formidable strength (many of us can recall to our costs the paralysing grips he could put on arm or neck) was also augmented on Tuesday and Thursday nights down at LMS Rovers Wrestling Club in Eglinton Street in the Gorbals. Originally, Cunningham saw this as useful training for his climbing but he soon became a canny and forceful expert. There were prizes available at Highland Games meetings and, perhaps more importantly, it also gave him an outlet for a mean streak that he was never to lose.

The usual mode of wrestling then was catch-as-catch-can, the forerunner of the Olympic style where an opponent had to hold both his rival's shoulders to the floor for a count of 'and one' with the best of three falls deciding the winner. Willie Baxter, now secretary of the Scottish Wresting Board and founder of the Celtic Wrestling Federation, remembers Cunningham's arrival at Eglinton Street:

"John and Hector MacDonald and one or two other Weekenders would go down to the Eglinton Street gym which is now the site of a petrol station. In all we'd probably have 15-20 there. John was immensely strong in the legs and if he put a leg hold on that was it. He got very good

over the years and he won the West of Scotland Lightweight championship at Rothesay Highland Games in 1952. He also made a comeback and
won the British Student Championship in 1967 at the age of 40 when he
was a student at Jordanhill. He did have a mean streak, I know. John Duff
was our heavyweight, about 5ft 8ins and 18 stones, and one night John
buttocked him, threw his legs in the air and landed on his chest, breaking
Duff's collar bone: Duff told me later: 'That was one reason why I carried
on wrestling because I wasn't going to let a wee skinny bugger like that
get the better of me'."

"John loved the wrestling because it gave him the strength he needed
for climbing," says Faye Ogilvie. "They called him Killer Cunningham
and the trainer was a wee bloke called Jock Rose. He says to me one
night: 'I'm wrestling John, I'm gunna murder him', and of course they
carted wee Jock off to hospital with a cauliflower ear where John had
thrown him off the mat and on to the floor. He loved it – it was something
for him to go away at night, away along to the gym and do his bit. He
even ate for it. Mum couldn't afford steak but when John got working he
would buy odd bits of steak to build himself up. They were a great crowd
of boys and of course the wrestling and the climbing was what kept them
off the street. He used to frighten the guys when he walked on, he used to
put on this face. I used to travel with him round the country for his con-
tests and one night this lad came up to him and said 'Ah'm fighting Killer
Cunningham, do you know who he is?' and of course John says: 'Never
heard of him and I don't think much of that name'. Then when the bloke
came into the ring there's John looking at him with that face and he nearly
had kittens. He'd lost before he started."

Cunningham, according to Tommy Paul, was probably the best
wrestler at his weight in Scotland at the time, although he was never
Scottish champion.

"There was this guy in Edinburgh who wasn't in the same class but
he was John's bogey man. Always beat him. John couldn't understand it."

And Bill Smith remembers the sadistic element which never quite
disappeared: "When we were out in New Zealand in the early 50s there
was an Inter-Club match and they 'd put Johnny in with this chap who was
quite simple and the only thing he knew was a headlock. It was pointless

because he wasn't going to pin Johnny like that but it was painful and the guy knew it.

It was based on three submissions so Johnny shook his head and submitted but he was a nasty so-and-so in things like this. The second bout started and Johnny got into a thing they call the grapevine and the chap's legs are like this and Johnny's legs are there and he is squeezing as hard as possible with an arm up there and stretching it. Well, the guy pretty soon starts foaming at the mouth and he's trying to get his arm through to tap for a submission and Johnny just hung on and wouldn't let him. I had to step in and tap for him. That was Johnny. He wouldn't be content with pinning someone he'd get a little tweak in to let them know who was really boss."

"He could quite happily crush you," says Willie Rowney.

One night Cunningham was wrestling in a club competition at the police gym in Beith Street, Glasgow, when he noticed a woman intently watching the action from the edge of the mat.

"She was called Margaret Morris," says Tommy Paul, "and she was having trouble getting men in her ballet class at the Baillie School; plenty of women, but no men. Johnny and a couple of others went up and she was giving them some stretching exercises and stuff like that, basically to beef up her ballet school."

This brief flirtation with dance later gave rise to one of the more popular Cunningham myths: that he took up ballet to improve his movement and balance on rock, but as Paul insists: "It didn't last long. As soon as she asked them to get into leotards that was the end of that."

The work in the shipyard, the improvised climbing walls and the wrestling had given Cunningham an awesome power to weight ratio and at around 5ft 10ins and 10 1/2 stones, the perfect build for climbing. Narrow shoulders and chest were reinforced by strong arms and powerful legs. He was, in fact, already a formidable athlete with the genetics that would probably have made him a success at most sports requiring physical strength. Certainly his body responded to exercise and Helen Kay, who emigrated with her husband John – a well-known Weekender and later Scottish Organiser for the Scottish Communist Party – from Glasgow in the 1950s, can remember Cunningham arriving back in New Zealand from the Himalaya in 1954: "I have never seen anything like it, with all that walking and load-carrying his legs were bursting out of his trousers."

And if the young Cunningham was a perfect physical specimen, the motivation for outdoor sport was there, too. Duke Street and John Browns were places to escape from and not too distant was a promised land of green hills and black crag. The playground was on his doorstep; all he needed were the right teachers and like-minded companions.

BONNIE FECHTERS

Slack Dhu is the nearest thing to the traditional concept of a crag that the Campsies can muster amidst their rounded sprawl from Kilsyth close to Cumbernauld in the east to picturesque Killearn, the stockbroker belt bolt-hole of Glasgow, on the A825 in the west. Subdivided by winding B roads into their geographical subordinates of the Touch Hills, Kilsyth Hills and Fintry Hills, the Campsies offer fine walks of easy gradient below the 2,000 foot contour – and all within a bus ride of Glasgow. But their crumbling dolerite outcrops and vegetated gullies are virtually worthless to the man with boots and rope.

Not that that deterred Andy Sanders when he set out from his home in Clydebank on a spring weekday in 1930. First he first took a tram ride to rural Milngavie north of Glasgow then, with a companion tramped – clinker-nailed boots ringing on the tarmac – along the remainder of the A87 to the village of Blanefield above which Slack Dhu and its conical outpost of Dumgoyne do their best, in their own modest way, to tower. It was a fine day and although in the past Sanders had used his thumb to hitch from Clydeside out into the hills north of the city, he and his mate were in no hurry; like some 120,000 other unemployed Glaswegians of that year, they had time on their hands. At Blanefield the two mountaineers turned right along the Campsie Dene road, hastened on tiptoe past the gamekeeper's cottage – Slack Dhu like most of the Campsies in those days was on private land – and then struck up the hillside towards the cliffs, just on the 1,400 foot contour. Sanders had been here before and the gap in his broad and often employed grin was the legacy of an earlier attempt on Coffin Gully, the deep black cleft in the centre of the crag, when a loosened rock hit him full in the face and removed a front tooth.

This time his target was the two-tiered outcrop on the right of the escarpment and a route directly up its face which, after a struggle with loose rock, vertical grass and vegetation, eventually succumbed to the determination and bloody-mindedness of the two Clydesiders. It was as they were coiling their manilla line at the top that they noticed they had company: two doctors on their way south along the track from Earls Seat.

36

Astonished to see two bodies clad in ill-fitted, buttoned corduroy lumber-jackets and with baggy trousers tucked into puttees, emerge from the depths below, the gentlemen hikers hastened over and there followed something approximating the following conversation :

First doctor: "Good heavens, man, have you just climbed up there."

Sanders: "Aye, that's right, Jimmy, no' as hard as I thought."

First doctor: "But that has never been climbed before, it's a first ascent!"

Sanders: "Aye, well, that's as maybe, but it was good fun an' a' and anyway I dinnae even ken the name of yon crag."

It was then that the other doctor, who had remained silent until then but who was obviously a local expert, interrupted.

"It's called the Black Crag," he said, "although some locals know it by the Gaelic name, Creagh Dhu ..."

If the Creagh Dhu Mountaineering Club saw its birth on a scruffy crag in the Campsies, its roots were embedded deep in Clydeside and in the depression of the late 1920s and 1930s where life for most revolved round the dole queue or the local saloon bar. Those years and their ability to brutalise bodies and souls bred a host of iniquities for the former working man of Glasgow, a man in the main with a strong work ethic, but whose pride and hopes were damaged, sometimes irrevocably, when the shipyard or heavy engineering factory gates closed for what seemed the last time.

The Great War of 1914-18 had produced near full employment, end-less overtime, good pay and, crucially in an effort to keep ammunition workers and their colleagues safe at work in the afternoon, restricted licensing hours. There was money in the pocket and bread on the table but all this relative prosperity made the crash of 1921 even more punitive.

By 1922, there were 90,000 unemployed in Glasgow, a decade later 131,000 or a third of the work force. As if this wasn't enough the gods, seemingly, had also chosen Glasgow for more perverse experiments in suffering with mass overcrowding and teeming slums adding to the penu-ries of the slump. At the height of the depression years, there were close to 1,400,000 people living in what was, and still is, a small city in terms of breadth. It amounted, in fact, to 60 heads per acre and with poverty endemic it took a strong man to keep that head above water. Staple diet became potatoes, bread and dripping, and with the dearth of vitamins in that diet, rickets and other symptoms of poverty and deprivation were rife. A succession of governments unblessed with socialist principle – including it should be said Ramsay McDonald's Coalition Government of 1933 – had also steadfastly maintained the iniquitous means test. This decreed that if a single member of a family had managed against all the odds to find employment – no matter how menial – the benefits of the other members of the family were reduced accordingly. The dole payment for a single male was the princely sum of 15/- a week. The means test in its turn produced a new breed of lowly Glaswegian, the Lobby Dosser who, to avoid detection by the social security watchdogs and avoid even more suffering for his family, would sleep rough in a friend's hallway, often for a small fee, then creep away at first light.

It was an era that scarred Glasgow almost permanently. The image of the Slum City has been hard to live down and even now the place names of the Gorbals, Govan and the Garngad conjure up visions of grey closes, shared outside toilets, children in bare feet and comatose bodies who had chosen to escape the blankness of the days via Red Biddy and screwtop bottles (with the bottles forming useful additions to the armoury of warring street gangs).

It was into this unwelcoming world that the founding fathers, later the stalwarts and, later still, the young bloods – including John Cunningham – of the Creagh Dhu were born. That they managed to rise above the greyness was not only down to the philosophy espoused by the likes of Chris Lyon – that in any group of humanity lumped together in a uniform mass the best will eventually percolate to the top – but the beckoning vision of green rounded hills on the horizon to the north.

Your average Glaswegian, apart from an independent streak and large measures of pride and determination, has his curiosity, too, and the chance to indulge all of these qualities, and escape the privations of the city, lay in a one-penny tram ride from the city centre where the adventurers would disembark in the promised land of rural Milngavie, the village in which the city's northern suburbs ran out into green fields and rolling hills. There, all Scotland lay before them.

This was a chance for exploration, for sniffing the fresh air, and the welcoming beacon for all with time on their hands was the Fire at Craigallion, the headquarters for hundreds of wanderers who would gather to drum up over the flames, talk revolution – the general mode of thinking was tinged pink or blood red – and sing the nights away. It was here that the rural version of the Lobby Dosser would spend weeks at a time, returning to the city once every seven days to sign on and collect his dole money from the 'Buroo' – the Labour Exchange. Legend had it that the fire would never go out, since there was always someone there to feed it from the provenances of the surrounding woods, and with the local landowner Allan Barns-Graham, for a time at least, turning a blind eye, the Craigallion Fire became the focal point for the despairing, the dreamers and mere down-and-outs. For a Scottish landowner, Mr Barns-Graham was a remarkably benevolent soul. On his 1,000 acre estate he presided over the erection of wooden shacks at Carbeth used as holiday homes for the war wounded of Clydeside and approved a semi-permanent, tented camp close to Craigallion where Ruth Kerrigan, wife of the well-known Clydeside Communist Peter Kerrigan, organised prenatal classes for expectant Glasgow mothers. Mr Barns-Graham, who died in 1990, turned out in fact to be far more accommodating than his antecedents, with his grandson embroiled in a bitter legal battle during 1998 to evict the Carbeth Hutters from the ancestral land.

Chris Lyon described one of his first visits to Craigallion graphically:

"The nights were drawing in as I hiked along the Stockie on to the Bracken Pad that followed the course of the Allander water. It had been many long hours since I had seen another soul when I smelled the pine wood smoke of the Craigallion Fire. The welcoming warmth of this fire attracted hundreds of wandering men. From this developed the Scottish outdoor activities enjoyed today: walking, rambling, scrambling, climbing, skiing, boating and sailing. The group who dominated around this fire were left-wing philosophers who spoke a new language, Dialectical Materialism, Proletariat, the Masses. They seldom spoke of Scotland's plight but offered Russia as the latter-day Paradise. As schoolboys out for a walk we were tolerated ... as long as we sat silently in the background.

"That evening I strode boldly through the pine wood, dumped my pack at the fire, picked up the ever-boiling big drum of stewed tea from the fire, filled my can and sat on a log and took my ease. A hundred eyes sized up this brash boy, then the conversation flowed once more, plotting a new revolution. I was accepted as a WEEKENDER!"

The generic title of 'Weekender' covered a multitude of sinners and saints; from the man with the simple urge to explore, to escape the gloomy uniformity of his urban privations, to the poachers who saw the hare, deer and fish of the land as useful income support and a proletariat two fingers at the landed gentry. John Kay went out for his first weekend in 1939 at the age of 14 and only an arthritic hip stops him carrying on today at the age of 73, although "I did manage a walk up in the Campsies recently which quite pleased me".

Kay recalls his Weekender days with wit and style:

"My mate was Alec Caldwell and he had this theory that the skin was waterproof so we were out in all weathers stripped to the waist and usually in our kilts, which mode of dress was a bit passé by then. I also had this wee soft hat I'd borrowed off my father and stuck badges on it and on the summer holidays we joined the hostels and then planned our route in great detail. We caught the bus out to Kirkintilloch, walked over to Fintry then on to Aberfoyle. Because of the distance we were hardly stopping to eat anything and then at Aberfoyle it was over the Dukes Pass and we tottered into the hostel sick with no eating. No-one, of course, believed we'd walked from Fintry. The hostel was packed but they found us a three-tiered bunk and we were on top with Alec on the outside. In the morning after waking from the sleep of the dead there's Alec lying on the floor. He'd fallen off – and it was a hell of a long drop – during the night and not even woken up. This became a very famous tale and I even told it at Alec's funeral."

Kay, for all the severity of his expedition, soon discovered that this adventure was fairly typical and indeed paled into significance alongside some Weekenders' padding exploits; scores of others were also heading out of the city come Friday night, a tattered army of young explorers drawn by the unexplored mysteries of the countryside.

"We were soon heavy into Weekending, my big mate Jimmy Bennett and me would buy weekend gear in Milletts and basically we just got hooked on it. Friday night in Glasgow the haunt of the Weekenders was the Bath Hotel in Bath Street. The beer was bloody awful but they had tables, chairs and a lounge which was a bit of a rarity in a Glasgow pub and it made for a good atmosphere.

"If you didn't have money for the beer you just drank the lousy coffee in the Café d'Ore at Killermont Street bus station. That's where I met most of the people I got friendly with over the years. Most of the groups had names, like the Gnomies, all with their own places to go but we just went under the title of 'the lot who went with JB.' Eventually Jimmy Bennett introduced me to Ben An which of course by this time from all these stories I imagined as some bloody great mountain; Jimmy Bennett's crowd had the bottom glade and someone else had the top glade. Even in those days it was *de rigeur* not to have a tent so ours was the tarpaulin off the top of ammo and flare dumps from the war which was damp and smelly but with permanent poles made a really good dry doss. Jimmy could climb but never took it seriously and was a great droll character and he would decide who was going first at rock climbing, all easy stuff, by saying: 'Whoever has read the most books can take the lead' and other strange qualifications like that which really quite appealed to me. When I was about 15 or 16 Weekending became quite a cult thing in Glasgow and you'd go out with no gear at all, no tent and no idea where you were going to doss. Alec and I used to knock around the ice cream parlours, the Tallies, and there were a couple of older guys in there who knew this place out by Balmaha.

"The government had commandeered a couple of big mansions there for 'Weary Women War Workers' so all these young women went up there for the weekend whether you were a war-worker or no' so of course that encouraged hundreds of young men to do the same. They all went to the dances at Drymen on a Friday or Saturday night. Can you imagine it? All these village halls were jam-packed and they'd all troop down the road to Balmaha because the Young Communist League had a camp on Inchcailloch and all night these guys would be taking boats back and forth to the island. The amazing thing about Inchcailloch was that you'd be there late on a Saturday night and they'd have this enormous fire and the YCL used to run these political lectures and everyone listened, maybe 60 to 100 people round this fire and there would be this guy telling you about his adventures in Spain with the International Brigade. You're 15 or 16 years of age and you just sat there. There was a cemetery on Inchcailloch which added to the dark mystery of the place. There were plenty of posers there, too. If it was a warm Saturday night there'd be guys running about naked and all these women there pretending to be horrified. Some of it got in the papers and the locals were scandalised. Another time Hector MacDonald and Postie Leitch [uncle of Donovan, the 60s folk singer] and a guy with a colostomy bag were at Ardlui for New Year and they had got a boat. Oh, the carry-on. They were well and truly drunk and the boat overturned and they all fell out and the cry went up: 'Rescue us first, that other guy's got a built-in life-jacket!' "

With regulars gathering at Craigallion and other open fires and dosses like the Shelter Stone and the Pines at Arrochar and Glen Lyon, the raggedy band of Weekenders became like a feudal clan in their own right. They tended to look after their own, too and the hills and glens of Scotland are covered in the ashes of deceased Scots returned to their places of youthful memory by their friends. It still goes on today. Jimmy Marshall, the Edinburgh architect who became one of the most influential Scottish climbers of the 50s and 60s and a weekender by inclination rather than by circumstance, went to one such sending-off in the Trossachs and says:

"One of the old boys had taken ill and basically the doctor had told him not to bother buying a new suit. So he thought 'Well I'll go out in some style' and splashed all the money he had left on a party. This party went on for five days and cost him thousands but all his pals turned up and enjoyed it and 10 days later he was away. They decided to scatter his ashes up by Loch Achray and we were all sat round outside the tinker's loan on the fine bit of grass there. Throughout the day they all kept turning up in ones and twos and the fire got bigger and bigger, some had guitars and we all sat round singing the old bothy songs. And all the time the box of ashes is perched alongside. Then there was a sort of drunken arousal and someone decided they would say a few words. Then there was another song before they opened the box and flung the ashes ... all over someone's passing Alsatian. The dog was covered in the guy's ashes. It was all very funny but very touching, too. We were all familiar with the Craigallion attitude, you see. Even the climbers, while keen on climbing new rock, would all disappear into the moors from time to time; they had a great respect for the outdoors. They were not just crag rats."

"A lot of the boys who emigrated to Canada or Australia and died out there of course always wanted to come back," says John Kay. "They had it written in their wills, which is a terrible trial for the poor old widows who have to trek up Ben An and places to scatter the ashes. I would think a lot of these hills have actually grown in height over the years."

In the van of this wide-eyed invasion of the wilds in the 1930s – although climbers were looked down upon as frivolous chancers by real Weekenders; they were "sneered at for their aggrandisement" according to Marshall – were Sanders and the like-minded spirits of his newly-formed club, the Creagh Dhu. Chris Lyon, later to follow Sanders into the club presidency – and remain there for 15 years until succeeded by John Cunningham – was, like his friend John Kay, the archetypal Weekender and his introduction to climbing was fairly typical. He began his outdoor life as Big Chris the Rambler until he graduated to become Big Chris the Climber under the stewardship of Sanders just before the Second World War when the depression was starting to ease off to just hard times. Along with Sanders and Cunningham he was to dominate the history of the Creagh Dhu Mountaineering Club.

Chris Lyon was born at 36 Crown Avenue, Radnor Park, Clydebank on October 1, 1922, Crown Avenue being a traditional tenement of 12 apartment houses in which survived "a close-knit community of 94 souls, 12 racing pigeons, eight mongrel dogs, seven pet cats, three thorough-bred greyhounds and a tortoise – Oor Close". Lyon went to Radnor Park School where with the name of Christopher he soon graduated to become the best fighter in a place full of Jocks, Willies and Tams. In the holidays he humped coal off McFarlane's wagon ('Nae Tick' it warned on the side) up tenement steps in Clydebank and at 14 he was a working man in Singers and later, like John Cunningham, a shipwright in John Browns. His life, as recounted earlier, was dominated by the shipyards and his upbringing on Clydebank where, as they say, 'you can always tell a Clydebank

man, but you'll no tell him much' . Lyon learned a fierce independence
from an early age, although much of that independence was forced un-
willingly upon him. On March 15, 1941, on the morning after the night
when a young Bill Smith and the rest of the Rolls Royce night shift had
sat shaking in the factory air-raid shelter, Lyon returned home to find
most of Crown Avenue and Radnor Park gone, along with his family. His
sister survived but both mother and father died later from injuries received in the Luftwaffe's Blitz of Clydebank. Hitler's targets had been
the munitions factories, Rolls Royce and Singers, but instead his bomb-
ers took out a large part of the town, with over 1,000 citizens killed. It left
Lyon, at 19, an orphan, but his strength of character saw him through this
and virtually everything else, including long, debilitating illnesses late in
life. Most remember him as a man with whinbush eyebrows and massive
hands, and even as a pensioner, according to Ian Nicholson, one of the
leading lights of the Creagh Dhu of the 60s and 70s, he was definitely not
a man to argue with. Davie Todd recalled that whenever Lyon's time for
reselection of president came round he would take a knuckle-duster out
of his pocket, place it on the table and ask, perhaps only half-jokingly:
"Right, boys, who's voting fur me?" Cunningham, too, told of the confrontations Lyon would have with the local bobby at Drymen close to the
southern end of Loch Lomond to decide whether a club member caught
poaching would go free or be detained in custody before an appearance in
front of the local beak. Villagers would form a square and lift the policeman back to his feet whenever he was knocked down, which was fre-
quently. Lyon's strength was legion. Bobby Cunningham remembers
going to see his brother in John Browns on some Creagh Dhu business
and John telling him to go and see Chris Lyon.

"I asked John how I would tell Chris Lyon from all the others in the
yard and John said: 'It's simple, Bobby. You'll see men with jacks working. Most of them will use either their left or right hands on one jack.
Chris is the one with both hands working two jacks.' It was true, that was
how I recognised Chris. He was an iron man and I think we were all a bit
afraid of him."

But behind that formidable exterior was a multi-layered personality.
Lyon, although a traditional Glasgow hardman, a 'bonnie fechter' quite

willing to settle an argument in the time-honoured manner of a square-go, was also a formidable troubadour with a rich way with English; a poet and sage in the tradition of old Viking, Irish and Scottish clans. Like Patrick McGill, the poet tramp of the 30s who wrote of the lives of the navvies building the Blackwater Dam on Rannoch Moor and later, Davie Clark the mountaineering bard, Lyon had a rare gift of capturing the philosophy of the outdoors and the Weekenders in words. According to John Kay, another man of intellect, he was a man with a varied outlook on life, widely-read and with an interest in classical music, the theatre and a devoted follower of the Scottish National Orchestra as well as a habitué of the justly famous Citizens Theatre in Glasgow's old Gorbals. Kay says: "Chris definitely did not have a narrow outlook of life. On Friday nights if we were working on Saturday and unable to climb we would quite often go down to the Citz to see Donald Wolfit and people like that."

Lyon's passion for the outdoors and his literacy – an envious descriptive gift that could vividly paint the spirit of the explorer of the depression years – can be found in the account of the day he received his first big pay packet at Singers and will strike many chords, even today.

"I purchased a stove, a sleeping bag and a bargain rucksack. Every Saturday afternoon I slung my pack and journeyed into the wilds, following a track that began at Craighton Moors and led to the North Face of the Matterhorn. As schoolboys we had wandered every track and lea-rig in a radius of 12 miles from Clydebank. With weekend gear the horizon expanded to 40 miles. The autumn winds blew my fair weather chums away and I walked on alone. I saw my first peak, the Gartocharn Dumpling, and conquered it. Resting on its lowly summit I saw Loch Lomond spread before me. The islands drew me but my woefully inadequate education made me ill prepared to find words to express the tremendous magnetic pull of that backdrop of mountains, Vane, Vorlich, Oss and the dark silhouettes further and further away. This first enchantment lay buried deep inside me for many years."

The haunting imponderable of 'why the outdoors?' was also explained by another weekender, Robert Grieve, born in a tenement in Maryhill, later a renowned urban planner and chairman of the Highlands

and Islands Development Board and later still, Sir Robert. A young TV
reporter once posed him the question: "Why is it that a man born and bred
in the tenements of Maryhill came to have such a fanatical love for the
Highlands?" To which Grieve answered: "If you stand on the pier at
Balmaha and look up Loch Lomond the Ptarmigan shoulder of Ben
Lomond sweeps down in the loch forming a corner. I have always wanted
to see what was round the next corner." When Chris Lyon peeked round
his next corner it was to find Andy Sanders and the embryo Creagh Dhu
waiting there.

At the start of Glasgow Fair fortnight in 1936 Chris, in the company
of a formidable padder known as Big Mac, who scorned both public transport and the new-fangled mode of travel known as hitch-hiking, had walked
the 35 miles from Glasgow to Arrochar – all along the road – for his first
sight of the Arrochar Alps and the Cobbler. By 7 am on the Sunday morning Chris and his friend were atop the South Peak, then:

" ... as we jogged over the ridge and began the descent into Sourmilk
Burn we were stopped in our tracks. The three peaks of the Cobbler and
the Spearhead of Narnain stood in the bright morning sun like islands in a
billowing sea of white cloud. An arm breeze crept up the burn bed from
Loch Long, rolled the cotton wool mist into a neat ball and gently nudged
it over South Peak. A small village of tents clustered around two massive
boulders. Big Mac spoke: 'That's the Shelter Stone and Narnain Boulder,' he said. 'Those tents will be rock climbers.' Before a tent a boy of
my own age sat hovering over a big black tea drum balanced on a primus
stove willing the water to boil. He glanced up, 'Ullo boys' then turned his
attention to the can. 'Bile, damn you, bile!' I recognised the boy from the
Singers factory. Here he looked different. Yellow pigskin climbing boots
clinker-nailed, corduroy lumber-jacket. A manilla rope sling crossed over
both shoulders and another sling was tied in a reef knot round his slim
waist. The sun shafted into the dark maw of the Shelter Stone and eight
men staggered blindly out into the morning with bare feet, baggy pants
and semmits. Big Mac whispered to me as if in the presence of some
wrathful god: 'That fella is Andy Sanders, president of the Creagh Dhu
Mountaineering Club'. Everyone on the road had heard of this man's exploits, a legend in his own lifetime and the pioneer of new standards of

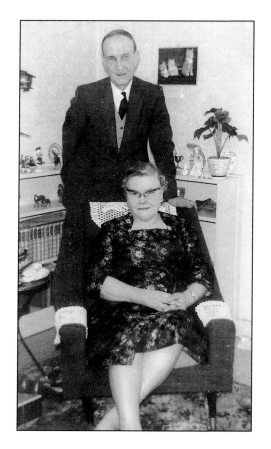

Left: John's mother and father

Above: John, James and Bobby Cunningham

Below: Beardmores Foundry in the 1950s, from the south. Carntyne dog stadium at top left; Duke Street runs east to west across middle of picture; Shettleston Road lower right.

Photo: Glasgow University Archive

Scottish Lightwieght Champion, Rothesay
Highland Games

Photo: Cunningham coll.

The first ascent of Chimney Arête, The
Cobbler, in 1947

Photo: Cunningham coll.

Above & left: Punsters, first ascent by Cunningham and Bill Smith in 1949, on the Cobbler's North Peak. Jimmy Gardiner is the belayer at the top in the left picture.

Photos: Donald Bennet

Below: HMS Tiger in John Brown's yard. The 'bonus boat'.

Photo: Glasgow University Archive

The Cobbler with – in the insert – Cunningham showing the Creagh Dhu how to climb Crucifix on the
Narnain Boulder

Photos: Cunningham coll.

Above: The 'Norwegian' hut, Glenmore in the late '40s. Seated; Chris Lyon leftmost, Cunningham second from right, Postie Leitch third from right. Standing; Bob Clyde fifth from right, Blondie Cameron just right of chimney.   *Photo: John Kay*

Below: The Café d'Ore

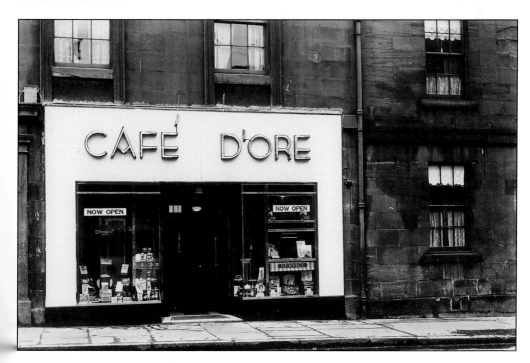

Above: Chris Lyon on the train to Martigny

Below: The Creagh Dhu at Ullapool. From left to right; Tommy Paul, 'Sunshine', John McLennan, Frith Finlayson, Willie Rowney, Bill Smith. *Photos: Cunningham coll.*

Right: Cunningham on the first ascent of Crow's
Nest Crack, Buachaille Etive Mor, 1946
Photo: Cunningham coll.

Below: Cunningham on Engineer's Crack, Buachaille
Etive Mor
Photo: Cunningham coll.

Above: In the Himalaya: Cunningham hunting for game with the ·22

Below left: Base camp at Thyangboche
Below right: Load carrying after the first ascent of Pingero

Photos: Hamish MacInnes

rock and ice climbing.

"Few below the 2500 ft level ever saw him but we all knew him as Tiger, a Giant, a God. I stared in disbelief for he was a small, wiry man with curly hair, hooked nose, strong overlapping front teeth and arms that hung down to his knees. Surely this wasn't the legendary Sanders of the Creagh Dhu?

"The god spoke. 'Jesus Johnnie, look what the wind's blew up, Big Mac!' Turning to the others he said: 'Now here is a boy that can hike. If some of you layabouts could clim a hill like big creaky knees here you could pile in a lot more rock climbing.' Turning to me he roared with laughter: 'Mac, what nest did you steal this wee scuddie burd frae?'

"There was I, tackety boots, socks and swimming trunks and sweat glistening from every pore thinking I looked like Tarzan Almighty Junior. The wild mountain men laughed good-naturedly. Sanders, seeing me redden beneath my tan, held me with the gaze of his steel blue eyes then stepped forward and crunched my hand in a vice-like grip: 'Sonny, if you can keep up alongside the king of the padders you'll do just fine. Hey, blackboy, what's happened to the char? Pour out two cans for two iron men, Big Mac 'n' Wee Scuddie here.' "

Lyon made his first climb that day in the company of Bill Howie the blackboy, later to become a regular partner. It was Recess Route, far less polished in those days than the classic severe of today and a route first climbed by Jock Nimlin, the equally formidable climbing partner of Sanders, the year previously.

"On the climb up the series of cracks and chimneys I made every mistake; skint knees, leg trembles, rubbery wrists, upbraided every now and then by Bill's scolding tongue: 'Aff yer knees. Hing oot, no in. Don't hack a' the grips off wi yer big tackety subs.' Howie, Sanders trained, was a master in the art of belaying and rope handling and I enjoyed every inch of that 300ft climb."

It was then, in what was typical Creagh Dhu style, that Howie thanked an incredulous Lyon for his company and informed him that Recess was his first lead. It didn't matter; Chris was hooked: "The 35 miles road walk home I slogged in silence with Big Mac, my mind still up there in The Fold, The Sentry Box, the Last Chimney." A year later, in 1937, Chris

Lyon was invited to join the Creagh Dhu. He was 15 and the youngest member ever.

Entry was, and still is, by invitation only and then as now, the club had the minimum of rules. No-one could ask to join and those wishing to gain entrance were first invited to hang around with the members until they demonstrated the relevant qualities. For some this could mean a period of weeks, others waited for years without success before the magic day when the earnest aspirant was informed that a meeting of members (and it had to be a 100% per cent vote) had decided he was made of the right stuff.

The right stuff, in this case was an indefinable trait of character which most Creagh Dhu members struggle to explain even today. Usually the potential member had to be a competent climber, but non-climbers have been members and some very good climbers refused entry and it seems more likely that qualification depended more on an aspirant's ability to mix in, his reliability, whether on the hill or in a bar-room rammy, his gift for patter and his background. Perhaps the best definition of the Creagh Dhu as a whole was the Scottish *gallus* – an edged compliment applied to a man touched with mischief and, metaphorically at least, bound for the gallows. George Shields, one of the unlauded stars of the Creagh Dhu and a man many rank the equal of Cunningham in technical climbing ability, explains: "It was a macho sort of club. If your face didn't fit you could not join. There were a lot of guys in the Creagh Dhu who weren't really climbers but you had to have other qualities, a sort of character. If you were obnoxious you stood a good chance of getting in."

Most successful entrants, as it turned out, were working-class Glaswegians, but neither was this a hard and fast rule. At one time there was a Dundee Section of the club, Shields was from Dunfermline and later members like Willie Rowney, Hugh Currie and John Cullen worked in an office. Later still, Rab Carrington was born in England and Jimmy Marshall, the club's one honorary member, came from Edinburgh. Hamish MacInnes, closely associated with the club for many years, never joined, however, although whether this was through his choice – the Groucho Marx principle that "I don't want to belong to any club that will accept me as a member" – or the whim of others remains unclear. Frith Finlayson,

Maryhill-born, hard climber, hard drinker and still one of the most high-profile ski teachers in Britain, was never invited to join either, although on the face of it he was archetypal Creagh Dhu. So strict were the guidelines for membership that John Cunningham refused to vote in his young brother Bobby – James was already a member – until he was persuaded otherwise by Bill Smith. Bobby, however, was a competent climber and in fact made an early ascent of Cemetery Gates on Dinas Cromlech, when it was still a forbidding Brown-Whillans extreme, on a trip to Llanberis Pass with Patsy Walsh. Bobby reckons in his case big brother was just being-bloody-minded, but in fact Cunningham, along with another member, Peter Ferguson, blackballed virtually every membership application that came up. His philosophy, according to Davie Todd, was simple: that if he kept the same lofty standards of qualification it would force an enduring legacy of trustworthiness and reliability. He could go away to Antarctica for years at a time, return and climb with a Creagh Dhu from any generation and know they were out of the same, trusty mould. Smith himself laughs now when he recalls:

"The club wasn't just all about climbing although I think Johnny blocked his brother because he didn't think he was doing enough. It was a social club, too. I think Frith applied but started making too many demands. He'd borrow climbing ropes and tents and then he told someone he wanted a tent so he was going to join the Creagh Dhu and get one and we were thinking: 'Oh, aye?' Same as MacInnes. You had to be invited and of course you put that to MacInnes and he doesn't want that." Willie Rowney, however, insisted of MacInnes "he was not club material" while of Finlayson, Tommy Paul says: "Frith blotted his copybook too many times."

This SAS-like exclusivity and selection procedure meant that the total membership from 1930, when the club was founded, to 1967 when Lyon stepped down as president, numbered just 137 and took the club to the edge of extinction on more than one occasion. Marshall recalls going to his first annual meeting in 1988, the year after his induction, and finding just three members present: "sad and a bit pathetic," he says. Apprentices, in those pre-Politically Correct days, were known as blackboys and served a humbling indentureship. Their duties included fetching the

water for brews, the provision of kindling for the fire and carrying of
ropes and rucksack to the foot of climbs. Above all, however, they listened and learned and were encouraged to climb within the safety proce-
dures set down by Sanders and Lyon years earlier. Rowney was blackboy
to Cunningham and Smith and he says: "The three of us would share a
tent but they never did a stroke. I got the water, I worked the primus, I
only did as I was told."

When Chris Lyon joined in 1937 the normal subscription was £1,
but the unemployed paid nothing, and the fees went towards the purchase
of the best equipment available and the annual dinner, a notoriously rum-
bustious affair never held in the same place twice; like the piper in battle,
the Creagh Dhu dinner had to stay continually on the move to avoid retribution.

Somewhat incongruously for a body that eschewed rules and regu-
lations and built its reputation on nonconformity, members were also entitled to a brass or cloth badge depicting a rope and ice axe, and inscribed
CDMC.

Early members, apart from Howie and Goldie, included Jimmy
Wynne, a Glaswegian who also mixed and climbed with Nimlin and the
Lomond and Ptarmigan clubs, Rab Syme who served in the International
Brigade in the Spanish Civil War, Tommy Jolly, a boxer who plied his
trade in the travelling booths during the depression years and whose party
piece was to bite mouthfuls of glass from pint pots, and Tom Craig and
Willy Clark, who it was said, timed every expedition so that it terminated
at a pub doorway precisely at opening time. Many were unemployed but
had in some cases perfected elaborate ploys to travel into the hills away
from Glasgow and still collect the 'burroo' money. This could usually be
done by informing the clerk at the labour exchange that he had an interview for a job up in Kinlochleven/Fort William/Inverness/Skye but that it
would take a week to walk there whereupon they were issued with a travelling dole card allowing the collection of the 17/6d a week wherever.
This did, however, rebound in spectacular style on Wynne. Said Lyon:

"Jimmy was the last of the depression boys and had succeeded
through the years in steering clear of the time-consuming, obscene, four-
lettered word W-O-R-K. At the Glasgow Fair Holiday of 1938 the club

were encamped in Glen Nevis and Jimmy, too, felt he was in need of a holiday. Experienced in all angles of the Burroo system he reported to Glasgow Labour Exchange and told an excellent story of a promised job in faraway Fort William and received a travelling dole card allowing him to uplift his dole money without the inconvenience of hitching back to Glasgow each week. Come dole day in Glen Nevis and Jimmy bade a cheery farewell to those around the camp fire, saying: 'Cheerio, wage slaves, I'm away doon to Fort Bill to see the man and collect my holiday pay.' Shortly after a shocked and sadder Jimmy returned and informed us he had been instructed to report for an interview at the British Aluminium factory the next day to take any job offer and be struck from the dole records. The morning after a group drumming up in the camp were surprised to see approaching the first negro mountaineer in Scotland. As he neared the fire the boys guffawed as they saw that 'the wage slave' beneath the dark skin was, in fact, Jimmy. It took three dooks in the river and the combined effort of every drum, dixie and tea can to provide sufficient hot water to scrape Jimmy clean. He then explained: 'I landed a job on the smelting furnace but believe me boys I won't stick that for long'."

Jimmy Wynne, did in fact stick it and was later promoted to foreman at BA and became a respected citizen in Fort William, an authority on Ben Nevis and the Mamores, leader of the local mountain rescue team and founder member of Lochaber Mountaineering Club.

The Creagh Dhu was an extremely social club, although not renowned in its early days for the spate of hard new rock routes of the Cunningham era of the late 40s and 50s. Sanders himself did few first ascents, most of his climbing being done as second to Nimlin, the shipyard crane driver who became one of the most influential figures in the working-class climbing movement. Like most successful partnerships they were an unlikely couple: the gnome-like Sanders with his ill-proportioned physique and the handsome, blond and blue-eyed Norseman, Nimlin. This pair, according to Chris Lyon, set the pattern for all great climbing duets since: both rugged individualists, both employing different techniques and styles to tackle rock problems and both with complete confidence in each other. Nor, observed Lyon, were they particularly fond of each other.

But Sanders proved an invaluable teacher and motivator. Like Lyon later, he ruled the club with an iron hand and was explicit that aspirants had to learn their climbing trade thoroughly. Miscreants who stepped out of line and over the limits of safety earned a severe dressing-down and time and again he hammered home his message: 'Staying alive is an art.'

With the outbreak of the Second World War and the return to full employment, conscription and every other symptom of war, Sanders, Lyon and the rest of the Creagh Dhu reverted to becoming Weekenders. But overnight, people disappeared off the face of the earth with 22 out of 25 members of the club being called up. The rest, like Lyon, James Cunningham and others were too young to fight although Chris had to be dissuaded from setting out to confront Hitler in person after his parents were buried in the rubble of Crown Avenue.

The four Cunningham children were evacuated for 18 months to Wilson's Farm at Moffat in Dumfriesshire where Farmer Wilson, along with his sheep and cattle, found he had problems of the two-legged variety in young John. Faye says:

"If you were evacuated you were supposed to help out on the farm, milking cows things like that, but of course if you told John to do something he wanted to do exactly the opposite. All he wanted do was go off on his own and climb trees and explore. Unfortunately for him, Mr Wilson proved a lot stronger than him."

The two older boys returned to the city in 1942 just in time to find that Beardmores had become one of the Luftwaffe targets. They bombed nearby Allen Street but while there was an air raid shelter in the Forge itself, John Snr had the theory that they would be safe in the smallest room in the house.

"Just like John, you see," says Faye. "No-one could tell either of them anything. When the sirens went the whole family would be in the toilet together."

For most Glasgow teenagers under the age of conscription, however, the war was nightly blackouts and the occasional bright light in the sky accompanied by the distant thump of a bomb. James Cunningham recalls lying in his sleeping bag at Balmaha watching the Heinkels and Junkers drone over on their way to Manchester and Coventry, Loch Lomond by moonlight apparently offering a useful bearing for them on their bombing run.

When the war theatre moved from Europe to Asia and restrictions on petrol and transport relaxed, walking and hitching for the Creagh Dhu and other clubs, gave way to more luxurious means of travel.

The Club Bus, not just for the Creagh Dhu, was to become a much-loved institution and even today provokes misty-eyed nostalgia among survivors of the postwar climbing and rambling groups who poured joyously out of Glasgow, Edinburgh, Manchester and Leeds after VE Day. To most it remains the rock on which club solidarity and friendships, lasting in some cases in the Creagh Dhu for 50 years or more, were built. The acknowledged pioneers of the Club Bus were the Lomond Club, another working class, but less anarchic group, founded in 1933. The Lomonds' original form of transport was a canvas-covered truck 'borrowed from a friend of a friend'. Travelling on this broke every rule in the book, not least the numbers of members piled illegally under the canvas in the rear. The Lomond truck era came to an untimely end when it broke down at a busy intersection on the way out of Glasgow and had to be given a push by two members of the Glasgow police force and a crowd of football fans while the 20 Lomonds under cover – including a member who happened to be an inspector in Strathclyde constabulary – held their collective breaths in the back. When the first hired Club Bus appeared the Lomonds invited some of the Creagh Dhu in to make up the numbers and offset any financial losses, an arrangement that worked perfectly until, on a trip to Langdale in the Lake District, half the Lomonds were inadvertently left behind in Cumberland after the bus was commandeered by the Creagh Dhu and, thereafter, the Lomonds decided they could do very well without their rough Glasgow cousins.

Not to be outdone, the Creagh Dhu hired their own club bus and, usually with the same apprehensive driver, the rickety old vehicle – usually after a prolonged trawl of the surrounding pubs for tardy members followed by a scramble for the back seats for the dice and cards schools. – would belch away from St Enoch Square in Glasgow at 2.30 pm prompt on a Saturday.

Non-gamblers or the merely broke were offered their own in-house entertainment on the journey up to Arrochar, Ben An or Glencoe with a selection of songs conducted by the Creagh Dhu choirmaster, Bob Harper, better known as 'Haps'.

"Bob would have us all organised and we would all have to sing our separate bits. It was quite a high standard really, great arrangements with close harmony," recalls Bill Smith. The standard entertainment was light opera, Irish rebel songs or bothy ballads and anyone who missed a cue or performed out of tune was likely to suffer banishment for the next two or three performances by the martinet perfectionist standing at the front of the swaying wagon. Although not a great contributor of original material, Harper did have a famous party piece, sung to the tune of 'Thanks for The Memory':

Thanks for the memory,
Of stalking red deer quarry, of lifts on Bryson's lorry, of clappie
    doos, wild Creagh Dhu and nights in Cobbler corrie,
How lovely it was.
Many's the night we spent boys
Down in the Bath Hotel,
We got inebriated, what the hell, what the hell
We'd stroll down Bath Lane
And in accent loud and clear
Sing the Bar-room Mountaineer
Then stagger to the Clarion
To meet the ladies so tender and so dear
How lovely it was.

The first stop on the road up to Glencoe was invariably a tall Wellingtonian pine close by Luss on Lomondside, the average club bladder after a few drinks round St Enoch Square before departure being only good for a distance of some 15 miles. "Oi, driver, stop at the Big Tree" was the shout, a call that became a universal plea for relief wherever the club travelled although it did cause some confusion for the occasional change driver who would peer vainly into the wilds of Rannoch Moor looking for a pine, an oak or even a gorse scrub. The Club Bus, too, did produce two rare Creagh Dhu club rules. After the owner complained about the effects on his paintwork, and in particular his eponymous sign on the side, no peeing was allowed out of the bus door. And later, after a drunken gamekeeper, seeking retribution for some alleged poaching, blew out the back window with a shotgun, it was decreed that henceforth no fishing poles would be carried on board.

John Kay recalls the Club Bus with relish: "The Lomonds bus was drab, unexciting thing but on the Creagh Dhu bus you might see a gun or a net or something. In fact, and there's no argument about this, half the people on the Creagh Dhu bus weren't climbers at all. There would be the odd ·303 rifle and Haps had made these silencers for them. Not perfect by any means but they would take away that crack of the weapon on the moor. Some of the conversations were quite interesting, about films or books and not just Smythe and Shipton. Many could quote piecemeal from the *Grapes of Wrath* and the great poets and at times it got quite serious. I can remember an argument between Hugh Currie and Blondie Cameron about the words of *Gray's Elegy* and it got very bad, they were coming to blows. There were some classy posers, too. John Young used to have a double-breasted suit as his outdoor gear. He did the Aonach Eagach ridge in winter in it along with a pair of sandshoes and of course this was only because he couldn't afford any gear from Milletts or wherever. Then we saw a party coming the other way and John stuck his hands in his trousers and sauntered along looking casual which of course greatly impressed the other party. John was no climber but he was a great patter merchant and hilarious company. He'd shirrack the serious climbers and give them a hard time and before long Cunningham, Smith and the others began to think it wasn't all that good to be too serious."

By then the Creagh Dhu, even outside their own territory had built up a reputation for anti-establishment behaviour and there is no doubt that many of the members were not averse to lifting a fish from the river or a stag off the land. Chris Lyon, who took the job very seriously, described the modus operandi of the traditional poacher – "unlike the professional poacher who is loathed by all, a well-loved character".

He said: "The main problem confronting the professional is transporting his kill in bulk to the market. The gamekeeper has only to watch for a strange vehicle parked in a lonely road, summon the police and the poachers and their equipment are caught red-handed. Our team survived because we carried our cargo on our backs, 150 lbs per man. Our equipment was mainly ex-army gear and could be jettisoned and re-purchased without any great loss. Mountain fit, few could outrun the team on the hill. If one keeper was particularly fleet of foot there was little he could do on his own, any member of our team was a match for any one man and as a fighting unit four of us were a match for any ten. When a well-organised campaign was mounted against the team with police cars patrolling the main roads and jeeps and Land-rovers patrolling the back roads and every able-bodied man and his dog on the high moorland, we took to the high places until night fell and by dawn we had force-marched 30 miles between us and our attackers. It was a good life: kill Monday, sell Tuesday, enjoy the city fleshpots; kill Wednesday, sell Thursday enjoy the city fleshpots and weekend with the Boys. Each stalk called upon the reserves of skill, ingenuity and tenacity."

There were, however, some narrow escapes and many trips into the wild turned into protracted battles with the appointed protectors of the land.

A group of members in a rowing boat were once pursued across Loch Lomond from Inversnaid by a band of armed American Army servicemen recruited by the helpless, and possibly craven, police at Luss; and Lyon remembers a soldier friend home from leave joining a poaching trip that went slightly wrong.

"A posse of keepers and bailiffs turned our team from hunters to hunted. In our flight we began to outrun the older men so they let blast at us with 12-bore shotguns. Later that evening, when we were dividing the spoils, our army mate confessed he had seen more action and had seen more guns fired in anger in two days with us than in his two years' service in World War Two."

W H Murray, the great Scottish Mountaineering Club pioneer of the 30s and 40s, and for all his hardiness on the hill definitely an establishment figure, recalls entering the lonely Ben Alder bothy late at night to find a sing-song in progress. Opening the door the notes died abruptly and a dozen young scruffs stared at him. Murray didn't believe they were climbers. "Fishing?" I inquired discreetly. "No" said one then with a roar the whole chorus, whistle and mouth organ, resumed at the note they had halted.

They were in fact the Creagh Dhu and Murray described them as 'like a band of robbers'. In a shed by the bothy he found a stag hanging from the rafters.

Kay, who was a member of the Lyon poaching cooperative, says: "We had some real epics, carrying vast chunks of meat on our backs through the snow. I think what saved us once was the fact that a herd of other deer had gone the same way before us and we followed their trail through the wastes. Chris would think nothing of wading into icy waters in the middle of the night to plant nets for the fish – that was his role in the combine. On another occasion he left his salmon in a case on the bus back home and then had to go and ask for it back at the lost property office in Dumbarton and there's all these guys behind the counter sniffing this case and looking at Chris and wondering whose body he had left inside it and whether they should call the police or not. Some of the boys would bury the guns in holes in the ground of the various dosses. A friend of mine, Wattie Hutton, last time he came over from New Zealand on a holiday said he had been up to the caves at Ben An and found all his guns in the floor of the cave, greased and wrapped in paper, from 20 years before."

In the youthful days of the club there was a lot of climbing done, although precious few new routes and much of this became entangled in the myth of marauding hardmen, the most colourful example of this being the Battle of Zermatt, an incident that gave the Creagh Dhu its definitive image of the Glasgow punch-up merchants, men for whom a rammy was as important as a rock climb. In the case of the Battle of Zermatt, like many legends, it is hard to separate fact from fantasy, but it is still a good story for all that.

After the war the club were among the first to head back to the European Alps; the usual modus operandi for many years after 1945 being to work and poach for nine months then spend three months climbing abroad.

The first Creagh Dhu Expedition to Switzerland was in 1947 and as well as a bunch of able climbers, the party included some of Lyon's beloved bonnie fechters, including Bob Clyde, later first manager of the Cairngorm chairlift, Alex Muir, a carpenter in the Highland hydro schemes known even to Chris Lyon as The Ironman, the fiercely aggressive Bill Bernard and Jack Thomson, a towering, rawboned handyman from Clydebank. These were the heavies. There was also the one-time Strathclyde policeman Bill Allen, 6ft 4ins and 17 stones ... but a hopeless pugilist, insists John Kay.

In a fighting sense at least, the 'fillers-in', according to John Cunningham much later, were Sam Smith, brother of Bill, Willy Wilkes, George Dixon, Bob Harper, the Club Bus choirmaster, and Kay. In all, the party numbered 12.

The first priority was equipment and the club called at their favourite outfitters in the open-air market of Barrowland close by Glasgow Cross, known colloquially as 'The Barras', where virtually everything, legal and otherwise, could be purchased – and indeed can today. For under £1 members treated themselves to a new cloth cap, 2 shirts, 2 pullovers, 2 pairs of socks, 1 pair of shorts, one long heavy pair of trousers, and a gaberdine cut to jacket length. Some of them had been given a supply of brand new postmen's trousers, courtesy of a friendly GPO worker, but the climbing gear was the best that money could buy, usually imported from Lawries the bespoke maker of boots in London. These were nailed with tricounis or shipyard-manufactured facsimiles, ice axes were prewar or home-made and snow-goggles were the kind used by shipyard burners.

Pitons and crampons were scorned as pansy gear although the travellers didn't hold back, either, with ropes and tents. Ropes were long-strand manilla, 120 feet in length and half an inch in diameter. Lyon reported that one sceptic, during field trials in Glencoe, was worried that the rope was too light and was told: "Och, dinnae worry. If you peel and yours breaks there's plenty more money in the club funds to buy you another." Money for ropes and tents came from subscriptions, functions and dances – after costs and damages had been taken out. There were also tarpaulin jackets bearing the bold legends of Wimpy or McAlpine and one dandy even turned up in a jacket made from trim black canvas, the effect of which was spoiled when viewed from the rear where it said 'Blackout Type No 1, Admiral's Cabin, HMS Vanguard'.

Zermatt was chosen as their base camp because many of the club had seen Alexander Korda's 1938 film, *The Challenge*, starring the mountain guide turned matinée idol, Luis Trenker, which most agreed had a doubtful story-line but did include some inviting footage of the Matterhorn and surrounding peaks. All of these appeared the logical next step up from Buachaille Etive Mor and the Cobbler, and Monte Rosa, the Liskamm and the Matterhorn were ascended in relative comfort by various members of the party, although Lyon and three others did have an epic on the North Face of the Matterhorn and were at one time given up for dead. Unfortunately, while the club's Zermatt Expedition found a great deal of favour with, in particular, the local innkeepers and many of the village females, including a large and formidable lady known as Madame Paulette, their appearance in the village did not go down too well with the local guides. After a long tradition of gentlemen British climbers abroad, they were more used to rich clients turning up to pay vast amounts to be towed up the Hornli Ridge, the *voie normale* of the Matterhorn and the Creagh Dhu's independence and self-reliance was something the Valais guides found hard to live with. One in particular, nicknamed Mr Five by Five by the Scots, proved exceedingly aggressive and before long grumbling resentment spilled over into something more physical.

The catalyst was the night of August 1 and the celebrations to mark the formation of the first three Swiss cantons, an occasion where even the most abstemious of Zermattese were inclined to forget the pledge. Coincidentally, the national holiday came round on the same day the Creagh Dhu, having decided to sell their ropes locally in anticipation of their return home, were flush with Swiss francs and in town in an equally thirsty mood of celebration. The first hint of trouble came when Mr Five by Five spotted some of the Creagh Dhu sketching out a route up the Matterhorn to a visiting English party. This definitely overstepped the guiding demarcation line in the eyes of the Swiss and Mr Five by Five and some cronies set out looking for redress. The first skirmish was up an alley, where a lone Creagh Dhu taking an enforced leak narrowly missed retribution. Later Wilkes, who had fought alongside Tito's guerilas in Yugoslavia, strayed into a private dance and was bloodily ejected by boot and fist. This was a language most of the club could understand and when Wilkes staggered back into the Creagh Dhu's favoured local, there was a general mobilisation and 12 good men and true strode, Wild Bunch style, out into the night and on to the street. A strong contingent of guides and local yobs were waiting. What happened next has gone down into folk-lore, although the true facts have perhaps become distorted in the mists of time. Suffice to say that there was a stramash, Wilkes exacted his revenge on Mr Five by Five who by all accounts talked a better fight than he actually performed and the Battle of Zermatt ended in high farce when a French tourist, busy trying to explain that he was on the Scots side and would fight alongside them against the Zermattese, was mistaken for the enemy and decked by Bill Allen, his first and last punch of the night. As Chris Lyon wrote later: 'Some say we won, some they won but one thing's for sure: the Creagh Dhu fielded a bunch of bonnie fechters that night.'

John Kay, however, one of the few survivors of the night alive to-day, has few doubts: "We were massacred, massacred. That story has grown and grown over the years. The truth of it was we were in the Café der Platz or something like that having a good sing-song and getting stuck into the Swiss wine. The guides were all drunk and so were most of us and everyone else in the town for that matter. Bill Bernard had already upset some of the guides on the way up the Matterhorn when one of them jumped the queue and Bill waited till he was six feet up then just grabbed his rope and pulled him off. So that hadn't made us too popular with them. We were all singing and the Swiss were all singing and everyone was having a great time. Then the proprietor's wife gets up and sings and she is singing operetta, very nicely, but then Bernard who fancied himself as a singer got up and wanted to join in with her. They're going to sing a love duet together. Some of the Swiss thought this was great, some of the Swiss didn't think this was very nice at all.

"Anyway, later on, some of us were basically lying around in al-leys in an advanced state of inebriation and someone got a good kicking. I was up a lane feeling terrible and I remember these two Swiss young-sters fumbling about with me and they put a firecracker in my jacket pocket. Then two of them dumped me in a horse trough and you can imagine the temperature in a horse trough at four o'clock in the morning high in the Alps. There was a bit of a rammy and Chris was actually trying to patch things up. One thing is for sure: we got the worst of it. It was a pretty battle-weary crowd that tottered back to the tents. Some of our lads never emerged for two or three days after, but I think some of the boys got quite friendly with the guides later on."

There is little doubt that stories like the Battle of Zermatt imbued the Creagh Dhu with an anti-social aura that has competed with the club's climbing prowess over the years and that its members since, while not actively encouraging the myths, have not sought to discourage them either. Various people, not even club members in some cases, have claimed to be at the Battle of Zermatt, although it doesn't take a degree in mathematics to work out that some must have been around three years old at the time when they stood toe-to-toe with the Swiss guides.

Because of its exclusivity and the mythical status membership of the club bestowed on the wearer – rather like the later hordes of territorial army irregulars who overnight became members of the SAS in the wake of the Iranian Embassy siege – there were also plenty willing to claim membership. A Scottish accent – and not even that at times – appeared to be the only qualification, although this had its risks. John Cullen, who joined the club not long after the war, admits the climbing reputation was justified, even if the fight stories were not. It was exciting being a member. Amusing at times, too.

Cullen, and his fellow members John McLean, Davie Todd and Alec Fulton were paying one of the club's periodical visits down to the Lakes in the 60s when a day's climbing on the traditional playground of Kern Knotts on Great Gable was followed by the traditional pint in the traditional Climbers Bar of the traditional Wasdale Head Hotel.

"It was one of the biggest laughs ever," says Cullen. "We were down in the pub afterwards and this guy at the bar who had been listening to us talking says: 'Are you lads from Glasgow?' Todd says 'Yes, I'm from Glasgow?'

'Oh, you'll have heard of the Creagh Dhu then?

'Oh yes, we have heard of the Creagh Dhu.

'Well, I'm an honorary member.

'Is that right?' says Todd. 'Tell us more about the Creagh Dhu.'

Well it was like a work of genius the way Todd led this guy on.

Todd said: 'Oh, you must know Black Bart then ?'

The guy says: 'Me and Bart ... like that.'

"And so on and Todd just upped the ante and upped the ante until, finally, the penny dropped and he had to beat a hasty retreat. I have never seen such a look of horror on anyone's face."

Even members with an overly high opinion of themselves could get their come-uppance, too.

"Stuart Fulton had spent a year in the Alps and he got involved with John Harlin and Haston and Hemming and people like that," adds Cullen. "A magazine had described him as the Finest Free Climber in Europe which didn't go down too well with some of the lads, particularly Stuart's brother, Alec. It was understood they were going to get him and we were on the way up to Great Gable from Wasdale to do Tophet Grooves and Alec was in front and the pace gradually got faster and faster and Stuart is puffing along, really struggling, behind. We were on the first pitch and everyone goes up and Stuart can't get off the ground. Patsy Walsh goes up and down solo once or twice to show him all the grips and he still couldn't do it. They had to pull him up, on a tight rope, the Finest Free Climber in Europe. There was no malice in it, it was just a way of putting him in his place."

Bill Smith says: "Some of the madcap things we were supposed to get up to ... it was crazy. One of the stories going about was that to become a member you had to go up to the top of Ben Nevis and throw yourself down one of the gullies. We'd just say 'Aye, of course.'"

There were the occasional formal initiations and some of these could be painful and occasionally embarrassing. Ian Nicholson first met John Cunningham at Dumbarton Rock in 1965 when:

" ... this guy I didn't know started showing me some routes. He was very friendly and very helpful and very good. Afterwards someone said: 'Do you know who that is?' and of course I didn't but it was Johnny. Later they encouraged us to go up to the Coe and places like that and we were climbing quite well and of course hoping to get the call, to become members. Then one day John McLean told Rab Carrington and me to meet them at the Alt-na-Craig in Aviemore, We thought this was it."

Nicholson, known universally and justifiably as Big Ian, went on: "We went in and saw a whole bunch of Creagh Dhu we knew from a distance. Then I was introduced to Hector MacDonald, an old guy, short and stocky. After a bit I gathered I was supposed to fight him but thought it would be no contest with me being so young and fit and him being an old man in his 50s, Next thing, I'm over his shoulder and on the floor much to everyone's amusement. I wasn't having this so I got up and went for him again, this time I was over the other shoulder and into a pile of tables. Third time lucky I thought, but then McLean stepped in and said: 'You're game, you're in'. I was delighted but then spotted Carrington drinking his Guinness at the bar: 'What about Carrington? I said. 'What about his initiation?' 'Och, you were fighting for both of you.'

"So that's how Rab and I got in the Creagh Dhu."

For all their hard climbing, hard drinking and occasional fighting, there was an unsuspected mellower side to the Glasgow heavies. Frith Finlayson's son Iain, later to ski for Britain in the Winter Olympics, spent a large part of his pre-teen days with the Creagh Dhu and at one time must have had more uncles than anyone else in Scotland. At Christmas 1955, Frith, his wife Jeannie, Chris Lyon and a number of others along with three-year-old Iain were in the ski doss in Glencoe, a crude rough, but functional shelter complete with bunks and potbellied stove. The doss served as lodgings and weekend headquarters for the operatives of the White Corries' one and only tow on Meall a' Bhuiridh beneath what was later to become one of Scotland's foremost skiing areas.

With snow storms raging outside the day was spent passing round a bottle and spinning yarns – until it came to Lyon's turn. He was midway through his tale of mountain derring-do when he was interrupted by young Iain. He wanted an apple. With his best punchline ruined, Lyon like all good storytellers did the next best thing and improvised. He picked up an apple core off the floor, popped out a seed and told the boy that if he planted that he would have all the apples he could possibly desire. Then he carried on with the story. Iain, however, persisted and calling the Lyon bluff, dragged him by the hand outside into the blizzard and insisted he plant the seed there and then. Lyon patiently complied and by way of guarding the plot from marauding animals erected a circular fence – of empty whisky bottles. That should have been that, but by this time Lyon was also getting carried away by the fantasy of a little boy, so he searched in his pocket, found some crumbled tobacco and biscuit and handing it to

Iain, told him: "This is magic dust, one pinch of this will make your precious tree grow."

Iain, content, was packed off to bed while most of the adults headed off to the pub. Next morning was Christmas Day and as the sun blinded through the windows of the doss whoops of delight from young Finlayson woke the weary mountain men. The boy insisted they all had to go outside.

Said Lyon: "Out we trekked, bleary-eyed, clarty semmits, long johns, bare feet stuffed into unlaced boots. And behold, there in the centre of the whisky bottle fence stood Iain's tree, five feet high and from every branch dangled a rosy red apple. A keen-eyed poacher may have spotted that the apple tree looked suspiciously like elderberry and the apples over-ripe. He may also have noted the traces of fish gut between branch and stalk but of course the three-year-old could not see this as his eyes were filled with tears of joy and delight."

Twenty-five years later Iain Finlayson went on to compete in the downhill and slalom at Saporro before dying tragically of a heart attack before the age of 40. It seems unlikely that of all the happy memories in his life anything could surpass that of the hoary-handed, blue-jowelled hard-cases from Glasgow who became the Magi of Glencoe one Christmas Eve.

By the late 1940s, Chris Lyon sniffed the air and detected a change in the climate of climbing, particularly in his own club, the Creagh Dhu. He said: "My generation had been so busy enjoying our Alpine junketings we failed to notice a new generation striding up the road. The new bunch, a mere twinkle in their mammies' eyes in the depression years, nurtured on cod liver oil and orange juice during the war years, had reached manhood as the doors of restriction were flung wide open. The world was theirs for the taking."

BIG JOHN THE CLIMBER

Climbing in the 20s and 30s was a sport of the privileged, a pastime for the upper and middle classes with time and money on their hands. Scottish pioneers like W.H.Murray and his colleagues in the Junior Mountaineering Club of Scotland and later the Scottish Mountaineering Club would drive up to Glencoe in their automobiles, head for the nearest gully or ridge and return to the lounge fire, hot water and clean sheets of the Clachaig Inn or the Kingshouse Hotel while the masses, without the time or wherewithal to travel far, dossed under boulders or inside makeshift tents at the Cobbler or Ben An.

Murray worked in a bank, while one of his regular climbing companion, Dr J.H.B. Bell, was an industrial chemist. They wrote as well as they climbed, although much of Murray's descriptions were highly coloured and almost metaphysical. Murray, in fact, was known to the Creagh Dhu as 'The Feather' because of his highly spiritual accounts of routes like Clachaig Gully, where he subconsciously left his own body behind and floated up the rock 'like a feather' while his anxious cohorts held the rope below. It was only when the depression came that an army of the working class with a similar amount of leisure time – but without the money – began to indulge en masse in the esoteric delight of hauling themselves bodily up lofty crag or snow gully, preferably where no man had trodden before. They discovered what the famous French mountaineer, Maurice Herzog, later defined as the five reasons for climbing: beauty, muscle, adventure, risk and escape, although in their cases the reasons were more broadly and less romantically defined.

"We used to call Murray 'WC Murray'," says John Cullen. "To be fair to the man he obviously had this great love for the mountains and that love was expressed pretty well, his books are classics but some of it was right over the top. Crowberry Gully acquired this tremendous aura of difficulty and it was nothing really. In 1948 me and two of the lads out of the office, not even proper climbers, went and did Clachaig Gully and it hadn't had many ascents then. We didn't find it unduly difficult, it had been blown out of all proportion. The absolute classic is Rubicon Wall on

Ben Nevis, which is written up in one of his books as a real gripper. When we went up there on a September weekend there would be Cunningham and Noon, the A team on the first summer ascent of Point Five and Zero and the camp followers, the no-users like myself, soloed up Rubicon Wall and we weren't even the B Team, more like the C or D team. It was nothing at all."

The Creagh Dhu had had its share of competent climbers in its first decade. Lyon was bold and strong and Kenny Copland – a man highly rated by Cunningham – was a superb balance climber, "one of the best around at the time". Copland excelled himself with his first ascent of Fracture Route with Bill Smith in 1946, a strenuous and awkward route on the north -east face of Crowberry Ridge on the Buachaille. But they had failed signally to move the standards on from the Bill Murray/Scottish Mountaineering Club era and this definitively establishment figure and his Junior Mountaineering Club of Scotland colleagues left the club standing in terms of pioneering in both summer and, in particular, in winter. Andy Sanders, as has been noted, did most of his new routes as a second behind Jock Nimlin while Lyon preferred to tackle established routes in both Scotland and on his trips down south to Wales or the Lake District..

Of many of the others, John Kay says: "A lot of them talked a good climb but a lot of it was all in their minds. There were a lot of posers around."

There was, in fact, a danger that the Creagh Dhu would become known simply for anti-social behaviour and a few well-embellished, time-honoured myths, until the appearance of John Cunningham and a group of like-minded young climbers who had set out independently from the city in a search for they knew not what. With horizons made limitless by their penurious backgrounds and the added strength and hardiness of the working-class, they were to change Scottish climbing irrevocably.

But, as the editor of Mountain magazine, Ken Wilson was to say much later in the case of the Creagh Dhu and the SMC: " It was almost as if a bunch of East Enders had taken up polo."

For Cunningham's emergence as one of the greatest of Scottish climbers, and indeed for the golden age of the Creagh Dhu, we should thank his mother, Mary and his brother James. In the summer of 1942, during Beardmores holidays, James was planning a weekend trip to Fintry in the Campsies.

"I was 15, John would be 14. I enjoyed walking and would go up to places around Milngavie until someone suggested a full weekend trip to Fintry which of course was high adventure for us. I was getting things ready when my mum said: 'Why don't you take wee John with you.' So I did. We took the double decker to Campsie Glen and we had army packs, a blanket and a borrowed tent because we had been told the youth hostel at Fintry was nearly always booked. When we got there we found the camping ground was booked, too, so we found a farmer who said we could stay. But then he said no fires were allowed and as we didn't have stoves we just had to plod on.

"Just near the Balfron Road we met four climbers in their clinkers and with proper packs, obviously purchased at great expense. Pop Lyons was the obvious leader. They asked where we were going and then told us to follow them. They were sleeping under this overhang on a rocky out-crop and just lower down there was a grassy patch where they invited us to pitch our tents. Later they invited us to the big fire and talked most of the night about climbing on Ben An and the Cobbler and John and I looked at each other and decided this was for us. They promised to introduce us to another group of novices and told us to meet at Dundas Street bus station the next Saturday. There we were introduced to Jimmy Young, Chic Wilson, Bill and Sam Smith and Sinclair Miller. We took the bus to Aberfoyle and headed for Ben An."

The three-tiered mica schist crags of Ben An lie in a spectacular position overlooking Loch Katrine in the Trossachs and had been used as a training ground for climbers in the west of Scotland since the 19th century. Short in length and without great technical difficulty, it is possible to solo many of the problems of up to 30ft while the longest route measures around 100ft. Nimlin had left his mark here in the 1930s with routes like the Last Eighty and Birch Tree Wall and in addition to the delights of the Trossachs Hotel, the numerous glades offered ample dosses and food for fires. The bus in those days, however, stopped at Aberfoyle and a lengthy hike was necessary over the Dukes Pass on the A821 to reach the climbs. With his young brother puffing alongside, James and his five new companions, resplendent in their triple-hobbed army boots, headed up through the forest to the lower tier.

"Our first climb was the Jughandle an easy climb on the First 30 and the seven of us queued up for it. That was the first of many happy days at Ben An," says James.

John proved a quick learner although a little headstrong and there was a minor setback on Jughandle, a 40ft difficult with the large hold that gave the route its name halfway up.

"John was soloing and just generally playing about when he came off and did a rapid descent of the Jughandle. He cracked his face on the rock and that accounted for the shape of his nose."

James Cunningham himself proved to be a fine, forceful climber although from the start the brothers studiously avoided tying on the same rope.

Says James: "You couldn't afford to have two breadwinners falling off together." With Smith going through a similar novitiate at the same time and with both he and Cunningham showing natural ability from the start it seemed inevitable that the two would gravitate towards each other.

"I read a lot of climbing books as a kid and started venturing out walking with James and kids from the youth club in the early 40s, before I started my time at Browns," said Cunningham. "At first it was just padding, but I had a great fancy for climbing. I left my rambling friends at the youth club and started going out to Ben An in the Trossachs which I'd read about. I would sleep out in the Tinkers Loan on Saturday night and do a bit of solo climbing on the Sunday. I had quite a few epics at Ben An before I became efficient enough to cope. All the routes I was doing I discovered later were graded about severe and I was in basic army boots nailed with triple hobs.

"After about a year of aimless climbing on my own I met up with a bunch of climbers who called themselves the Ben An Boys, among them Bill Smith. When I saw Bill for the first time I realised he was different from the rest, mainly because he didn't fall off. Now we had a team of six who met regularly at Ben An, climbing mostly solo as we still didn't have any ropes. We then decided that the best way of surviving would be to eventually climb with ropes so we decided to nick some from our various places of employment. Others in the group were Jimmy Young, Chic Wilson and Jimmy Sinclair and James my brother. Then after the war equipment started to trickle onto the market with War Department karabiners, the first tricouni nails, ice axes and lots of other stuff we wouldn't have had an idea how to use. Anyway, very little of this was available to us as we had no money so the lads like Bill in Rolls Royce started turning out their own trikes, krabs and ice axes. The trikes lasted for years because they were of monstrous proportions, as were the krabs – but at least we were equipped."

Clothing was just as basic. Says James: "My take home pay was 9s 5d as a first-year apprentice and John was on less so standard gear was army pack and boots, a blanket and a cutdown raincoat which served as an anorak."

After their apprenticeship in the Trossachs, the Ben An boys became more adventurous. All Cunningham's available time and money – helped by the overtime at John Browns – went into his weekend trips and one of these, to Arrochar, proved crucial, not only to Cunningham but the future of the Creagh Dhu Mountaineering Club. The Cobbler, rising above Loch Long, is one of the most distinctive mountain silhouettes in Britain and its three craggy tops had thrown out a challenge for mountaineers arriving at Arrochar since 1889 when W. W. Naismith had first ascended the south ridge of Central Peak. Easily accessible from Glasgow, its only drawback is the teeming hordes of trippers in Arrochar itself but a stiff walk from the pier head leaves these far behind, as Cunningham and his friends had found when they first arrived in the summer of 1945.

Sweating up from the Narnain boulders into the small corrie below the south face of the North Peak they were suddenly transfixed by the sight of three climbers spread-eagled on the face above, their shouts of encouragement and occasional curses echoing around the corrie. These were obviously real climbers and the big blond man in the lead was equally obviously the man in charge. It was Chris Lyon.

Cunningham recalled: "On our first time up there we had to take it in turns to climb with the one rope, then we met the hard men of the climbing world. We saw these three guys on Cat Crawl, a VS on the North Peak. Chris Lyon was in the lead with the Monaghan brothers, Jim and Chic, behind him. They were good climbers and, we found out later, hard fighting men into the bargain. That was it, we finished our climbing and just followed them round the crag. They didn't seem to object."

Far from it. Lyon, although not unaware of his status as the head man of the Creagh Dhu, was quick to recognise the juvenile talents of Cunningham and Smith. They seemed, in fact, ideal candidates for membership. The club needed new blood and Lyon realised at once that in the slight frame of Cunningham and his powerfully-built friend lay the future.

"Johnny from the start was obviously outstanding," he said. "I think we all knew we were about to be left behind. When John joined the Creagh Dhu at the ripe old age of 17 he immediately began his climbing career at the highest standard set by my generation and by the end of his first season had begun pushing those standards higher and higher beyond our reach."

Cunningham's invitation to join came in early 1945 and membership and use of the Club Bus spread his horizons even wider. Although he made his mark on the Cobbler with a total of ten first ascents between 1947 and 1955, his first recorded new routes on Scottish rock were on Buachaille Etive Mor, a mountain over 100 miles from his home in Glasgow but which was to become almost an exclusive preserve of both him and the Creagh Dhu.

The Buachaille is not only the most dramatic peak in the Pass of Glencoe but also the most accessible. Rising in the crook formed by Glencoe and Glen Etive, the foot of Crowberry Ridge on the summit peak, Stob Dearg, can be reached from the A82 by an averagely fit climber in under 30 minutes. The land between the road and the mountain is meadow-like in places and as well as the River Coupall, thirsty climbers are a short stagger from the Kingshouse Hotel, another crucial ingredient in most climbing days. As a base for the Creagh Dhu, there could hardly have been a more idyllic or practical location.

The fact that most of the club's activity was concentrated on the pink-brown rhyolite of the Buachaille owed much to the fact that most members were working on Clydeside and forays further down the Glen would have eaten into their all too brief weekend. The lucky ones managed to get away from Glasgow on the Friday night, many others – even after the advent of the five-day week – did a Saturday morning shift and their climbing and exploration was limited to Saturday evenings and Sunday mornings.

Bill Smith says: "On the Buachaille at the time there were virtually no routes, there was plenty of scope. The Club Bus wouldn't get there until Saturday evening and you might just have time to nip up and do a route. To get away from the Buachaille was difficult because you could spend half the day walking down Glencoe."

As it was, the Creagh Dhu became so fond of the Buachaille they eventually erected their own permanent club hut a few minutes from the road – without the formality of planning permission – and over the years from 1946, when Cunningham paid his first visit, literally plastered the mountain with routes. As with most cliffs, early exploration had followed the obvious lines of weakness, the main gullies and ridges, leaving the walls and cracks in between to a later generation. Cunningham soon began to fill in the gaps. He found Shattered Crack on the North Buttress of the mountain on June 23, 1946, followed the next day by Crows Nest Crack on the same crag, both of which significantly upped the prevailing standards. As with most of his early routes they were virtually solos with a rope trailing behind, and as well as technical ability required a very long neck. Both were seconded by Ped McGonigle and led by Cunningham in bendy, smooth-soled sand shoes; both at the time were graded 'severe in rubbers', an early example of masterly understatement from him. The new star soon discovered, however, that he was bound by the old club strictures on safety. Sanders' Creagh Dhu dictum that 'staying alive is an art' still applied and Cunningham's performance on Crows Nest earned him a severe dressing-down from Chris Lyon. He had looked on as Cunningham ran out 200 feet without a runner or a stance on Crows Nest, having asked McGonigle to untie and move up behind him. Lyon, who had hastened to the top with a rope in case it was needed, was furious. His main concern was for McGonigle, who was but an average climber, and as Cunningham pulled himself over the top onto High Ledge he was greeted by the formidable, and fuming figure of the club president.

Cunningham said: "I had been quite close to the top when this rope whizzed down with a ready-tied knot in it, but as it happened I was past the worst bit and it wasn't needed. When I crawled over the top Chris reached out his hand and I thought, great, he's going to congratulate me on a great lead but he started to crush my hand in his and basically told me it was the most stupid stunt he had ever seen."

In October that year the club were back on the Buachaille, Cunningham teaming up with Smith for the first time on a new route to climb Autumn Slab, now the first pitch of Whortleberry Wall. Curving Groove and the great classic of Grooved Arête, both on the magnificent, and virtually unexplored Rannoch Wall followed, all three first ascents being accomplished in the same weekend. Smith was on leave from his National Service at the time – he was with the Paratroop Regiment in Palestine – and it was only then he learned that Cunningham had avoided a call-up altogether. All the names beginning with CU in Glasgow had been fortuitously mislaid by the War Office – John Cullen, too, missed out. Smith discovered to his disgust that his new partner was to be granted 18 months' start in the race for new routes, while he drilled and patrolled in the dust and heat of the Middle East.

If England had its Joe Brown and Don Whillans, there is no doubt that their Scottish counterparts, many would say their equals, were Cunningham and Smith. A contrast in both build and styles, they made a formidable team and Smith, who is not given to boasting, insists: "I would say we were as good as anyone around in Britain at the time. It was a few years after that Brown and Whillans started in Wales and we used to go down there and do a lot of the routes they had done. I did the second ascent of Cenotaph Corner with Whillans and found it all right, we did Cemetery Gates, too, which was supposed to be big time just then."

Tommy Paul, who climbed with both and was a self-confessed member of the club's B Team, says: "Johnny was the one who really upped the standard, but he and Bill, they were a great team. Johnny had this natural balance, he was a beautiful climber but he could be impatient. Bill was more clever, he had the thinking ability. We met Jock Nimlin once and he was a bit unhappy about some of his routes being downgraded. But we explained to him: Jock helped raise the standard and it was up to other people to take it forward. It was just natural progression. You talk about John and there is no way you cannot mention Bill. Bill, there was something different in his make-up. In a tight spot I think Bill would get more people out. Johnny unfortunately didn't appreciate his natural ability. But they were safe, I don't think I ever saw Johnny overstretch himself. If you were going to climb with someone it had to be with someone who was not going to put your life in peril. I saw plenty of examples of that down south."

Smith, according to Hamish MacInnes, was "built like a tank and a tremendously powerful man" who excelled at virtually everything he tried. As well as his climbing ability he was also – unlike Cunningham – a skilful and fearless motorcyclist who would take on and beat the ton-up bikers along Lomondside on the weekend dashes up to Glencoe.

Before Davie Todd came on the scene, Smith also held the club freefall record, having survived, totally unscathed, a 500-foot plunge down Buachaille Etive Mor during an early attempt on Ravens Gully when after rocketing down the narrow walls of the gully he shook himself free of the snow in Great Gully and shouted up to the relief of a party that included MacInnes and the visiting commando climber, Mike Banks: "Come on doon, it's great!" Banks, who later marvelled at Cunningham's skill in Vibram-soled boots – no crampons – on a winter attempt on Clachaig Gully, was mightily impressed.

Like many, Smith's hardiness and determination can be traced back to his Glasgow roots. Born on the south side of the city on June 12, 1924, he was brought up in Shawlands and served his apprenticeship at Rolls Royce in Hillington, a time made hazardous by the Luftwaffe's assaults on one of Scotland's major munitions factory.

"We would be sat there in the shelter with everything shaking," he says. "And that included us. But they were awful shots, Clydebank got the worst of it. In the early days I was knocking about with a bloke called Jim Smith. We were actually cyclists and we would cycle over to the Trossachs, leave the bikes at the bottom of Ben An and just wander up. Jimmy sort of gave up and I started knocking around with Johnny and James. It was strain or bust to Arrochar. We worked on the Saturday morning and got the 1.30 pm bus from Glasgow. That was the hardest thing in those days, the transport out of town. We didn't own tents and it was a case of sleeping out in the open most of the time with sleeping bags we had made ourselves, there was a wee bridge at Brig o'Turk which came in useful. Boots you either got from Timpsons in Glasgow or wrote off to Robert Lawries in London, who made really good boots. When we started doing harder stuff we had sandshoes which were a bit slippy in the wet, this was long before PAs came in. Johnny I think acquired some sisal ropes from John Browns, not the best climbing rope because it used to get quite heavy and in winter just froze solid. Basically you made sure you didn't fall off. We didn't have our own transport of course, the motor bikes came later. During the war it wasn't worth getting one because there was no petrol for them. Most of the times to get out for a climb it was a case of getting on a bus. Food? Well, towards the end of the week during the war we would get the big tin of meat and veg, although you didn't find much meat in it. We met the Creagh Dhu at the caves at Arrochar and they were watching us climbing and they asked us to join. I agreed to think about it but when I went into the army for National Service I came back after 18 months in the middle east and found Johnny had joined me, although I had never been to any meetings. In those days Chris Lyon and Kenny Copland were the leading lights. We had heard of them but we found out that although they had quite a reputation they didn't really do an awful lot of climbing. Their reputation was for something else. But then Tommy Paul started coming round and John McLean, Pat Walsh and Bob Hope, that was the heyday of the Creagh Dhu. Pat Walsh was a very good climber, so was George Shields, although he tended to be off on his own a lot. Frith Finlayson came with us for a while but think he only lasted one season. I think he applied but started making too many demands, he was after borrowing ropes and tents and I think one day someone in the club heard that he had told someone 'I can get a tent, I'll just join the Creagh Dhu' so that did for Frith. When the Club Bus appeared the club got even more social, although some would say anti-social. There was a heavy card school on it and one or two of course were better than anyone else and were taking all the money. I didn't like playing cards, I couldn't afford to lose a penny and I certainly didn't like taking money off people who were my friends. We couldn't afford to drink either. Johnny was a joke drunk, no idea how to pace himself. We were in the Norwegian hut at Glenmore one New Year and Johnny appeared with this bottle of green Chartreuse, he would drink the bottle as if he was drinking lemonade and then pass out and he was lying there with the mug jammed in his hand and us trying to get it off. But he could climb all right."

As Lyon had recognised earlier, the world for the Creagh Dhu new boys was theirs for the taking. With Smith away in the Middle-East, Cunningham teamed up in the June of 1947 with another Creagh Dhu member, Ian Dingwall, for a climb that was to become a Buachaille and Glencoe testpiece and with a name many good climbers since have found totally apposite. Gallows Route on the east face of North Buttress takes a line up a series of thin scoops up the right-hand side of the crag and although only some 80ft in length was undoubtedly the valley's first extremely severe. Unlike the majority of routes of the time it did not follow a line of weakness and was climbed simply because there was a blank spot on that wall; a worthy precursor to today's modern horrors. Gallows was graded very severe then and for many years later, this being the upper limit in Scotland, and a native idiosyncracy that was to cause a number of major epics among visiting climbers from down south. Often compared in technical difficulty to Chris Preston's Suicide Wall in Cwm Idwal, unlike that route Gallows was climbed without the benefit of top-rope inspection and still holds a place in the upper echelon of E1s in the Glencoe guidebook. Cunningham led it in his ubiquitous sandshoes and without a runner, although even today it is hard to protect. The second ascent, in fact, had to wait several years until the appearance of Whillans on one of his frequent visits north and that purveyor of cryptic and occasionally caustic wisdom later offered to Cunningham; "Hey, Jock, where do you find these bleedin chop routes!"

The Buachaille became even more of a home from home for the Creagh Dhu later in 1947 when the club's first permanent doss appeared by the River Coupall midway between the road and the foot of the mountain. Jacksonville, as it became later, started life as an army tent covering an old sheep fank and was a far cry from the comparatively palatial mansion of today. As with many Creagh Dhu projects, Jacksonville was free and improvised.

"We were down in the Coe one weekend and the army were camped down at Coupall Bridge," says Bill Smith, "It was a terrible weekend and their tents got blown down. They were big tents with four poles and an outer cover and another one that hung down inside that. One or more were in the river and we fished it out and took it back to where Jacksonville is now because that was our regular camping ground. We used to leave it at the side of the sheep fank and we called it the Dent Blanche, after the mountain. Then we put a canvas cover on the sheep fank and it has gradually built up from there."

Jacksonville was christened by Bob Harper after another club member, Jimmy Jackson, although it could well have been Smithville or Cunninghamville. Over the years it sprouted walls and a door and a chimney and has remained inviolate both from intruders and the National Trust, on whose land it stands. The reputation of the Creagh Dhu ensured there were never any trespassers (the door is never locked) and the message would be hammered home by a fusillade of rocks and boulders drenching passing visitors as they attempted to cross the Coupall by the stepping stones, an ordeal that became almost obligatory for climbers on the way to the Buachaille in the 60s. Occasional half-hearted attempts by the National Trust for Scotland to enforce planning permission have all foundered over the years, although the traditional car parking space on the A82 has now been blocked off. Smith fended off an early National Trust sortie single-handedly: "I was sat inside once drumming up when I saw this chap and a woman coming across the stepping stones and next minute he is tapping on the door. He says: "Is there a Mr Jackson here?" and I told him "No, he's away in America, you'll no get hold of him." So then he starts muttering about permission to build the place and I put him off and suggested he go and see the police. Of course the police told him it was a good thing to have the hut there because if there were any rescues they knew where to find climbers who knew the area."

" I personally was involved in four different versions of Jacksonville." says Willie Rowney. "It was our doss, we built it and we didn't really like other people coming in. We got a very nice letter once from a young woman asking if the weather was bad if it would be all right if she and her friends used the place for shelter. She was told equally politely No. It was really very basic and at one time we had to put rocks on the floor to keep the mud level down. We moved on from there, rebuilt it and rebuilt it again, all on exactly the same spot. I was secretary of the club for a while and we got a note from the National Trust for Scotland to say that they had spotted this and it shouldn't be there. So I was sort of detailed to try and do something about it, partly because I used to go to Edinburgh from time to time on business. They were very good, gave me an appointment and my approach was that Jacksonville was close to the only off-road parking at that end of the valley and was used by the police and ambulances if there was an accident. Every weekend they could find a nucleus of very capable rescue people in the hut and it also gave people involved in rescues somewhere to shelter if the weather turned bad. He was very reasonable and agreed with me but said he couldn't give permission but if we undertook not to enlarge they would turn a blind eye. So that is how it stood and that situation has lasted a very long time."

Using the new, illicit base, Cunningham and Smith excelled themselves further with the first ascent of Guerdon Grooves on the west face of North Buttress, the intimidating crag overlooking Ravens Gully and christened Slime Wall even before the first climber had set foot on it. The club were there en masse on the weekend of June 12-13, 1948, and for Cunningham and Smith, happily liberated from Her Majesty's Service, it was to prove a productive couple of days.

"We climbed June Crack on the Saturday and I was allowed to lead this because it was my birthday, otherwise I wouldn't have got a sight of it. It was my birthday present, I suppose," says Smith. "The next day we went up to Slime Wall to see if we could find a line up there as there was nothing on it at the time but as with a lot of things with Johnny there was very little planning went into it. You never knew where you were going to end up. The first bit had very few places for you to get anything in and we had to borrow another rope. That would be two 120ft lengths of rope joined in the middle. We were heading for the big cave that's near the top but there was a bit of weep there and I remember I had to take my rubbers off but it was hopeless and we should have maybe tried to keep further left of the main groove. I reckon we made the mistake of going too far right and ended up in that groove with all the green slime running down. But we got up with a struggle and I remember there was a big bunch of the lads sat below jeering." (Guerdon Grooves was in fact an attempt on the line that was to become Shibboleth.)

Cunningham said: "When I did Guerdon Grooves I had one peg, one sling and a karabiner and I couldn't use any of them. I got half way and tried to bang in the peg with the karabiner which was useless and in the end I ran out 160 feet of rope without protection, it was more or less soloing. In comparison Gallows Route was harder, but far less serious."

Some of the watching members thought the epic on Slime Wall went beyond the pale and a small deputation met the descending climbers later to tell them just that. But as Tommy Paul, who was on Cuneiform Buttress on the other side of Ravens Gully the same afternoon and had a grandstand view, says: "I was surprised to see a lot of the old gang at the bottom watching. Johnny was on what looked like really thin stuff and I was trying to see if there was anything above for him. There was a lot of loose stuff around, too. Some may have thought it was unjustified but what was he supposed to do after he had run out 120ft? Reverse it? I was looking and watching and I thought they made the right decision. There is nobody going to give them a rope from the top because there is nowhere to go up, you would have to go up Ravens Gully."

Smith says: "I think some of the lads were more upset because they thought we had been deliberately undergrading routes but that wasn't right. Some of them were trying June Crack the same day after we'd done it and couldn't get up. They couldn't get over this bulge and while we were doing it the crack was full of grass and I was just throwing grass down. I don't know what they expected but things had to move on. Usually as soon as someone had done a route someone else would go and have a look what it was like but there were also routes that lay for years without anyone going near them. We also had some problems with the guidebook writers. When we did a new route we would send the details off to the SMC and this bloke called Bell wouldn't have it, he was always objecting to the names of the routes or something like that. It got so you wouldn't even bother sending them in. I think there's a lot more routes in the Coe that we did never got recorded."

While many thought the ascents of Gallows and Guerdon Grooves pushed the safety limits too far towards folly, Cunningham's nearest misses came not on rock but the road. Totally in control on rock, this did not apply to his efforts in the saddle. He had bought his first motor bike, an Ariel, just after the war and while Smith initially was happy to accept the pillion seat on this speedier transport into the hills from Glasgow it soon became clear to Smith that while Cunningham may have been a Diaghilev on the rock, he was no Geoff Duke on two wheels.

"A book about Johnny on his bike would be just as entertaining as a book about Johnny climbing." says Smith. "Before I got my first bike, a Panther which cost me about £60, I used to ride behind Johnny and I used to make sure I had a rucksack on my back because when I travelled with him he fell off that much it ripped the side pockets off. I think he designed the first rucksack with no side pockets. There is one bend on Lomondside and we always reckoned the woman in the cottage there got so used to him coming off the bike there she would leave a hammer outside her front door so he could straighten his footrest. We reckoned she used to have a cup of tea ready for him as well. He was so haphazard with bikes. I think I was driving a Thunderbird one time and Johnny had got himself a wee ex-army 350 Ariel. I used to travel behind him because you never knew what he was going to get up to. Anyway he stopped half way along Lomondside and I stopped alongside and asked him what was up and he said: 'Oh this bike's terrible, my arms are shattered.' The whole cylinder block was going up and down and he said he had just overhauled it but he hadn't tightened the nuts enough. You can imagine the vibration must have been something terrible. Another weekend we were down in the Lakes climbing. We went down on a Friday night and he crashed into the front of a car down there. We spent most of the weekend straightening his front forks. Anyway on the road back we were driving through Kendal and all sorts of traffic is coming towards us and he says: 'You'd think they would do something about this controller system.' I said: 'They have, John you're in a one-way street.' Further on, this is before they built the new bit of road by Beattock, there is a section of road with about a mile of straight and there's a lorry about a mile in front and I said to John: 'There's that lorry turning right for Edinburgh, the left fork is for Glasgow.' So of course he drove straight on into the back of the lorry. I asked him what happened there and he said: 'My foot slipped off the brake.' That was in one weekend. There's countless others I could think of."

Tommy Paul, too, was astonished by Cunningham's lack of coordination on two wheels: "You could watch him move over a rock face and appreciate the movement but if you saw him on a motor bike it was a completely different thing. He was something else on a motor bike. On Lomondside he had gone off three or four times on the same corner. We came back though Dumbarton once and I was in front for some reason or other and Bill was behind and Johnny was in between. There's a bit where you drop down to a right-hand bend and it was winter and we were sliding all over the place and there was a car in front of me that had skidded. I went round it and then ran back up the road shouting to Johnny: 'Slow down, it's like glass' and he stamped down into a lower gear and said: 'I don't see any grass' and just drove off and of course down he went. Maybe I should have shouted 'It's like ice' but then he would have just said 'No, I don't want any ice.' I remember going to visit him in the Royal Infirmary in Glasgow after he had put his foot-rest through his foot and I asked him how he had done it. He said: 'They all turned left and Big Bill said: Did you no see the autumn leaves ? Leaves are slippery things, John.' He didn't follow the same line as Smith. He'd swung wide and gone into these leaves and he just went and put the rest through his foot and ended up in hospital."

Willie Rowney remembers a more serious – in the light of what was to happen later – weakness: "Physically he was a very funny guy. He climbed so well and was very fit, very well put together and yet he didn't appear to have great coordination. You know anything that involved speed or formal sport and he never seemed to excel. We were in Skye about 1950 and we had 14 days of almost perfect weather, never had weather like it on Skye before or since and we climbed ourselves to a standstill. I could actually squeeze tiny drops of blood through my fingers they were so worn. So we decided to have a day off and Johnny suggested going down to Loch Brittle and we were messing about in the water and I noticed Johnny just sticking to the side. So I thought, oh no, he can't swim and I thought for goodness sake, he would be about 23 at the time and he had never learned to swim. So I just held his head up and we got him doggy paddling. Here was this chap, very athletic and all for the great outdoors and he literally couldn't swim a stroke."

Throughout the late 40s and 1950s, Cunningham's appetite for rock climbing remained undiminished, although made sporadic by his ventures further afield to New Zealand, the Himalaya and, later, Antarctica. Many were struck by his ability to return from long trips abroad and start again virtually at the same standard.

"People like Charlie Vigano would more or less have to start from scratch after a winter off the rock," says Rowney. "Johnny would just come back and start virtually where he left off. He would just appear without warning – there were no phones then – and away he'd go. He'd come back and start with a little bouldering and just burn everyone off."

In August, 1955, Cunningham made a rare excursion from Jacksonville westwards into Glencoe to find Boomerang with Mick Noon, the first climb on Aonach Dubh's lower North-East Nose. The following winter, there were abortive attempts on Zero and Point Five Gullies on Ben Nevis, travelling up for a weekend inside Noon's sidecar and usually ending carried back to the CIC Hut atop an avalanche. In the case of Zero, Cunningham's long campaign was totally fruitless.

Noon says: "Johnny, MacInnes and me tried Zero Gully together once and as usual and there was a huge avalanche came down and buried Johnny up above and it just continued avalanching all the time. MacInnes was saying, 'You're OK, keep going'. I was at the side, I don't think I'd even tied on, and I just figured, well, it's snowing like crazy and all this stuff's coming down, so let's get outta here. I shouted up to Johnny 'See you down at the hut' and I just jumped. Shwoooo! Then as I was getting close to the bottom I heard this Schwooo! behind me and looked behind and it's Johnny, he'd bailed out too. He'd had enough of it. But those avalanches could be pretty bad coming down there, sweep you right off, especially if you didn't have too much protection as far as ice pitons and that ... we had them but they weren't very good. And then we had to bail out of Point Five of course. We got up right below the crux ... the right wall was like a blank piece of rock, covered in verglas, Johnny was trying it and he said do you want a go, but I said 'No, if you can't do it how the heck am I going to do it?' So he took the little six-inch piton and hammers it and puts the sling on it and he jumps over and away he goes. The when it was my turn the heat off the piton had melted the ice and it was moving. Of course halfway down Johnny wants me to stop so he can take a picture which I wasn't too keen about but I did hold it for a minute to let him get a picture, all the while waiting for that piton to come out."

Noon, too, can recall Cunningham's chagrin when after another avalanche ended another attempt in the winter of 1957, MacInnes teamed up with Tom Patey for the first successful attempt on Zero.

"I think we would have got it eventually but we never had any luck on it," says Noon. "We had just been bombed out again when Hamish arrived and we had to get back to Glasgow that night. Johnny was a bit sick because conditions were almost perfect and I think he knew they would get it."

Cunningham's trip home was made even more miserable by the ride back, Noon's sidecar having a hole in the base through which water and sludge vented upwards almost continually.

"Johnny liked the sidecar – when it was dry. Leaving Meall a' Bhuiridh once, from the old ski doss, Ian Allen and Johnny had to spin a coin to see who would get the sidecar. It was winter and coming down in sheets. Johnny won, to his delight and Ian got on the pillion. By the time we got to Tyndrum and stopped Johnny was frozen solid and Ian was sat there dry as a bone behind my windscreen."

Not all the club exploring was confined to Scotland. The Creagh Dhu were dedicated travellers and trips in the early 50s down to Llanberis Pass in North Wales would see the club encamped in the roadmender's hut by the Cromlech Boulders, and most of the Peter Harding routes there climbed – at that time the upper limit of climbing down south. On a drive down to the roadside crags at Tremadog in 1951 Cunningham, Smith and Pat Vaughan (known as Fawin' Vaughan because of his lack of adhesive qualities) discovered and climbed the great classic severe on Craig y Castell named Creagh Dhu Wall; "and it wasn't us who carved the graffiti on the bottom" insists Smith.

Easter traditionally saw the club down in the Lake District, usually the Langdale Valley where locals awaited their arrival with some trepidation.

Jack Hool of Barrow Mountaineering Club remembers them appearing in the valley, driving down from Chapel Stile to the camp site by the Old Dungeon Ghyll in a 5-ton Bedford truck – complete with piper.

"At the camp site the piper would patrol around while the others put up tents. Word spread of course and a lot of people just packed up and buggered off. There were all sorts of rumours like that there had been a punch-up with the Wallasey Club and someone got killed but I must say that I saw them at dances at Chapel Stile and there was never any trouble although someone warned me that if you got into a fight with them you had to stay down and expect a boot. If you got up they would just do you, it was a total thing with them and probably had a lot to do with their very tough backgrounds."

In the Lakes, Cunningham led Central Buttress on Scafell and most of the other upper-grade classics like Kipling Groove (George Shields made the unrecorded and for many years unsuspected second ascent of Kipling Groove on Gimmer Crag along with Noon, then a young novice, in the early 50s). Says Shields: "We just went down, did it and came away again, no fuss. There was no question of going in a pub and blabbing all night about it as some did."

"We used to go down to Llanberis or the Lakes and climb and just come away again," says Tommy Paul. "You would go down, find out what had been climbed and then do it. Brown and Whillans weren't on the scene then. The difference was they had a sort of camp following. Up here in Scotland people were individuals in their own right. You are a climber – so what? You enjoyed it and that was it. As soon as you went down south the first question they asked was: 'What grade do you climb?' That didn't go down too well."

On their travels the Creagh Dhu mixed well with the English activists of the time; they were eventually to meet Whillans and the Rock and Ice Club in Langdale and Dennis Gray and the Bradford Lads, both working class groups with a similar philosophy to the outdoors.

"Johnny and Bill would earn their respect, just burning them off on the boulders," says Noon.

Whillans, the pugnacious Lancastrian with a fondness for a punch-up and hard new routes, was on the face of it a man with whom the Creagh Dhu could identify, although there were to be problems over the years.

"What a pillock he was," says Paul. "I met him years later and he was just as bad. Joe Brown was the best of that bunch, no doubt. When Whillans came up here on his honeymoon in 1958, he gave his wife a rotten time in front of us. I just thought, well, he may be a good climber but he is a right prick. He was trying to be the big-time climber but after that he never climbed with us."

Whillans also fell foul of the normally placid Bill Smith. "It was John McLean's stag party over in Aberfoyle," says Davie Todd. "It was really invitation only, Creagh Dhu only, but some people came over from Edinburgh, Haston and Elly Moriarty and of course Whillans. Whillans obviously decided he was going to stamp his personality on the evening and we were in the lounge bar and of course the public were in there and one of them complained about the language. Then there had been another guy there playing a guitar and trying to join in with our songs and the guys were getting fed up with him. The manager says: 'Is there anyone hear complaining, about the language?' and the guitar player says 'As a matter of fact I'm complaining'. But he really didn't like the fact that we weren't singing his songs so they did the obvious thing and threw him out. When that little fuss died down, Whillans piped up: 'I'm also objecting to this language' obviously prepared to see how far we would go. Smith is there as the best man, the guest of honour and obviously getting all these drinks bought for him and Bill, the mildest man you could think of, turns to Whillans and says: 'Well, the guitarist has gone through the window ... and you're next.' That was it. Whillans got up, left his drinks and walked out."

Smith can also recall the legendary reluctance of Whillans to stand a round: "Whillans arrived at another do where there was plenty of drink and he was helping himself until the drink ran out and we had to go out for more but there was no sign of Whillans putting his hand in his pocket, which to us was the worst crime you could think of. The next day we all go back, about 20 of us , and shout the drink up. I had a whisky and a half pint of beer, most of the lads had the same, and then we all stood back and said: 'He's paying'. He had a habit of that. I think he had been spoiled in the Lake District and Wales, people sucking up to him. It didn't work with us."

Whillans, as it turned out too, had reason to be grateful for Cunningham on more than one occasion.

"We were all in the Kingshouse." says Jimmy Marshall, "and Whillans was being Whillans and upsetting people. A great big fat guy, an infamous puncher, was going to knock Whillans all round the bar and Johnny just said very quietly: 'No you're not' and the guy backed off. It was a control thing."

Another visiting English climber also ran into problems at Jacksonville, in an incident that has gone down in climbing folklore. If Scottish rugby had Will Carling and Scottish football Jimmy Hill, Scottish climbing had, probably has, Christian John Storey Bonington as the embodiment of the snotty, arrogant English, the very name being sufficient to raise sneers and snarls north of the border. Bonington's ability to make a healthy living out of mountaineering, his high profile and his comfortable, southern, middle-class background certainly brought out the worst prejudices of the working-class Glaswegians, although Bonington's unpopularity probably owes more to envy than any other factor. Whatever the reason, the rank and file have looked on with jaundiced eyes as Sir Chris over the years has climbed, literally and figuratively, to the top of the world. But Bonington's close friends will defend him staunchly, often vehemently. Many swear there is no more entertaining company on the hill, as does the discriminating Ken Wilson, the former editor of *Mountain*. MacInness, never a man to follow trends, became a close friend and even Whillans, while sneering about Bonington behind his back, found their relationship mutually profitable. But while English rough diamonds like Whillans – a former plumber – were tolerated by the Creagh Dhu, Bonington's cut-glass accent, junior army officer background and obvious ambition could never be. He was definitely a man who had not come up the hard way, an unforgivable failing in their book. If any Englishman had to be sent home tae think again it was this one. Before the Jacksonville Incident the club had run across Bonington before and had tended to give him a wide berth since.

"If he appeared we would send him in one direction and head off in the other," says Bill Smith. "We spent a week once down in Llanberis avoiding him. He was a menace, he kept falling off routes and none of us fancied that. Mick Noon can tell you a tale about that. Ask him about the Bonington Scar."

"That was away back in the dark days," says Noon. "He turned out quite a climber too, didn't he? He'd a very high standard you know, people would be hiding behind the rocks when he came around. I was staying in a barn away down below in the Ogwen Valley on my own, this would be the early 1950s. I wasn't in the hostels at that time, you'd just go down and pay the farmer a couple of shillings to stay in his barn. Anyway this guy turned up looking for someone to climb with and I didn't even know him at that time. We finished up on the east wall of Tryfan on a route called Scars. We were off the route, well I thought we were off the route. There's a whole bunch of VS's there and he would lead one and I would lead one. Short climbs, we'd get down and go straight back up again. Anyway, it was my turn to lead this and it looked to me like a big snatch getting up. At that time we'd the sannies it wasn't PAs, so I reneged on it and came back down and up he went. I had seen him making a snatch, and he moved up a little bit and I could tell he was coming off and he did, he just came right off and the rope went round my neck. It was just as well I had a good belay. I was actually hung upside down on the ledge, and the rope came across and burned my face and my neck. I've still got the scar on my neck from it, I call it the Bonington Scar. Lucky I had my hand up, because I probably might have been choked. So anyway I held the rope with a bit of difficulty. I couldn't see him, where I was at, and I shouted, but there was no sound so then I lowered the rope down, tied it off and started going down to him, just slid down the rope. He was kind of knocked out and had a big gash on his knee, so I shouted to some people way up above and asked them to get somebody up, because I thought he was seriously injured. He had hit the ledge and bounced off, although he didn't actually hit the ground. In the end, he managed to recover and walk down and we met the rescue party coming up. .. they weren't too happy about that. Then we went with him to the doctors and everything and got him back to the hostel. I always did say he'd be a good climber, if he lived long enough."

Bonington had also rubbed the acerbic Tommy Paul up the wrong way: "We were in the youth hostel in Glencoe and it was just after New Year. The weather was bad and we were blathering away. Apparently Bonington had asked some of the lads if they had climbed in Wales and someone had said: 'No but Tom Paul has'. So then he interrupted the conversation I was having to ask what I had climbed in Wales and I mentioned a couple of routes near each other in the Pass, one of which I had gone up but couldn't remember the name and he said well it must have been such and such because the other one is hard, his assumption being that I would only manage the easier one. So I said: 'Well it doesn't really matter because I climbed up one and down the other.' That shut him up."

It was with this chancer's reputation painted by Noon, Paul and others that Bonington later turned up at Jacksonville looking for a climbing partner. As Cunningham said, however, "he went about it all the wrong way".

"We didn't have much time for Bonington," says Smith. "We had met him a few times before and this was in his early climbing days. It was his attitude that put us off. We were all sat around in Jacksonville and this bloke comes in announcing that he is looking for John *McLeen*, and of course it's pronounced *McLane*, so that didn't set him off to well with McLean who is sat there in his underpants eating his breakfast. 'My name is *McLane*' he says. Bonington just stood there watching McLean eating until McLean told him to push off. Then Bonington started to talk to Johnny asking him if he fancied a climb, I think he was hoping to do Red Slab or something, and Johnny says: 'Oh that's much too hard for me. Try some of the younger lads' and of course they just burst out laughing. Then McLean started to get annoyed so Bonington had to leave sharpish."

Ken Wilson, however, is convinced that it was six of one and half a dozen of the other and that the Creagh Dhu were as much to blame: "I thought they could be very narrow-minded and full of working-class snobbery. The incident with Bonington at Jacksonville was typical. OK, I know most people thought Whillans was great and Chris a stuck-up prig, garrulous and self-centred but he was incredibly keen and you would have a great day out with him. Apparently when they had thrown him out of Jacksonville, Chris had felt a sudden call of nature, dropped his kegs and crapped near their hut which absolutely outraged them. Amazing!"

Bonington himself sees the episode in a different light and looks back more in sorrow than anger: "Until the Jacksonville incident, I thought I had a really good relationship with the Creagh Dhu and a lot of good friends and memories. I first got to know them in 1953 when I made the first winter ascent of Agag's Groove. Hamish MacInnes with a young Creagh Dhu'er I think called Gnomie, led the first rope and I led the second with a guy called Kerr McPhail and John Hammond. I went on to do the first winter ascent of Raven's Gully with Hamish but also mixed and stayed with the Creagh Dhu in various barns. I think it was the following spring/summer that I climbed with the Creagh Dhu on the Cobbler – I remember crowding under an overhang with about six of them. I went home with one of them and we went climbing on the Whangie. It was as a result of this that I arranged to meet up with Mick Noon in Snowdonia – I was still at school at the time. That was when I fell off Scars Climb – my first leader fall. These were all good climbing days of a young lad who was made warmly welcome by the Creagh Dhu. The Jacksonville incident was sad. I went to Jacksonville with those memories of earlier climbs and friendship, hoping as a fellow climber to find someone to climb with. It was a later generation of climbers, none of whom, as far as I know, I knew. I suspect the fact that I was now well known and from south of the border, encouraged them to give me the brush off. I fell in with some of the 'Squirrels' later on the morning and had a great time. I hardly knew John Cunningham, though from everything I've heard of him, he was a really good guy and a great climber."

Other climbers found the club more tolerant. The late Paul Nunn recalled in a letter to Noel Hulmston in 1981 when Hulmston was preparing his memorial slide show for Cunningham: "I first met John at Jacksonville in 1959 when he was there with McLean. They spent the gaps between the Glencoe rain playing 'heid the ball' and allowed Richard McHardy and myself to stay in the hut, a privilege extended to precious few Sassenachs at the time – it was more usual to send them on the hill on some fool's errand or very hard route and then eat their food. Since we had neither food nor money they were rather kinder to us, although they punctured our climbing pretensions by sending us up a very wet

Ravens Gully as a 'recommended wee route'. I fell off twice and Richard three times before we packed in. When we got back to the 'Ville' they asked us how we had descended expecting us to say we had left a sling or something so we said the webbing belt in situ. Our meanness gained their respect I think and it also meant they did not have the opportunity to nip up and acquire one of our slings."

Cunningham teamed up twice to climb with Whillans, and Whillans came out the worse in both encounters. In June, 1958, the little Lancastrian arrived in Glencoe on his honeymoon with his new bride, Audrey, surely the longest-suffering climbing wife in the history of the sport – and there have been many of them.

"The shipyard was on strike over something or other, and that was too good an opportunity to miss," said Cunningham. "I hitched up to the Coe to find two tents pitched at Jacksonville. In one was Charlie Vigano and his wife and the other contained Whillans and his new wife on their honeymoon. Whillans and Vigano had been trying a new route on what was then the unclimbed Creag a' Bhancair but had abseiled off about halfway up. The Creagh Dhu had tried for some years to force a route up the face, starting more or less slap bang in the middle but Whillans had found a new way in by traversing in from way over on the left. But he had been having some trouble with a flesh-eating bird which wouldn't let him on to the ledge with its nest on so he'd driven down to Fort William and bought a catapult to bomb the carnivore into submission. Charlie was none too keen on the route, mainly I think because if the second came off on the traverse he was certain to hit the deck, and he asked me if I would climb with Whillans and although I wasn't climbing very well I agreed. But I had most of the gear and as Whillans was supposed to be on his honeymoon he hadn't brought much up with him. Next day we set off, without a carnivore in sight, passing an old sling left by Marshall on his one and only attempt. A long traverse right brought us to the first ledge, home of the bird, and it was covered in the skeletons of small animals.

"Then came another hiccup, the belay peg was in an awkward corner and I couldn't shift it. And then I discovered that every difficult to remove belay or runner was my gear and the easy ones were Don's. I was running out of gear fast so every time I found one of my pegs impossible to remove I helped myself to one of his. Eventually we were both stopped by a really nasty-looking crack and we decided to call it a day. Whillans whacked in another of my pegs, clipped into one of my slings and set off into space.

"When we got back to earth we put our gear in a little pile on the floor and Whillans was astonished to find he hadn't any pegs left. He said: 'Funny, Jock, I could have sworn it was all your gear I was banging in there.' The conclusion was that while I was roping off I saw a really good line wending its way through the final overhangs but of course didn't mention this to Whillans. Two weeks later I was back with Mick Noon and we finished the route off. What's more we recovered a load of the gear, too. Whillans and his missus took it pretty hard but he came back a couple of years later, climbed the nasty crack and produced the Villains Finish to Carnivore."

And Noon insists: "I don't know why he took it so hard, it was first come first served as far as we were concerned."

Whillans and Cunningham had also got together for an attempt on the Long Wait on the Etive Slabs, a much-attempted, and as the name implies, perennial problem. Tilted at an angle of 40 degrees but split into planes by several overlaps, The Slabs offer thought-provoking, normally runnerless padding with the added local hazard of the most voracious midges in Scotland. Eric Langmuir – later to become Cunningham's principal at Glenmore Lodge – and a Cambridge University Mountaineering Club party had made the first tentative breaches in the Slabs' granite armoury in June, 1954 with Sickle and Spartan Slab, but curiously the remainder of the crag remained untouched until April 1957, when Cunningham arrived with Smith and Noon.

After finding their way up the two main corners of Hammer and Agony and failing on what was to become Swastika, Cunningham departed for the Antarctic leaving the field clear for Noon, who didn't waste any time in finishing off the classic of the Slabs two months later.

"Johnny was a good pioneer, he could always pick those lines out there." says Noon. "After Hammer and Agony he wanted to have a go straight up the middle, that was his idea. On the third pitch we had been stopped by the overlap and Johnny was trying to go straight up without much success and so we had to bail out and come all the way down. Then Johnny went on one of his expeditions so I went back there with another guy, Eric Taylor, and went up, and instead of going straight up I traversed along the lip. I remembered I had said to Johnny: 'Why don't you go along there and try that?' because I could see these quartz bands higher up which looked as though they would go. Johnny, for whatever reason, insisted on trying the hard way but I managed to traverse along the moustache ledge as we called it, because it looked like a long moustache full of grass and vegetation, and then followed those two quartz bands up. It wasn't much of a belay either and it was raining and running with water. I got up the first band and by the time the second came across and up it was wet, and we were stuck there asking how are we going to get out this thing. There was only one way and that was up because it's pretty hard to abseil out of when you didn't have a place to put a peg in."

Cunningham recalled: "We had heard about Spartan Slab and went down to have a look, that was Bill Smith, Noon and myself. We thought the slabs were great and immediately picked off the more obvious lines and put up Agony. On the second pitch we had to use a few pegs which we borrowed from Hamish. Earlier he and I had done Porcupine Wall on the Cobbler so I had an idea what to do on Agony. After Agony, Noon and I went on to do Hammer. Noon was very good and got hooked on the place and went on to do a load of other fine routes. I got involved in a long drawn-out battle with the Long Wait, which was really an attempt to find a way up the big blank slab left of Spartan. I tried it first with Bill and then with Don Whillans. On all these we pushed a bit higher, but it was a very long and difficult route. Finally Robin Smith and I finished it with him leading all the early routes and me the new ones, after all I had done most of the work on it. When we tried Long Wait for the first time I didn't know Whillans too well and he really impressed me. He shot up what is now the crux pitch but got stuck about 100 feet up. So he just turned round and said: 'Watch the rope, I'm going to slide down'. I had no gloves on and I wasn't having that so I told him so. When he persisted I took the rope off and tied it round the belay peg and then he had second thoughts and promised to climb down with me belaying him."

After Carnivore and his session of one-upmanship with Whillans in August, 1958, Cunningham turned his attention back to the Buachaille's North Buttress and a line he had long coveted up the overhanging groove right of Bottleneck Chimney. Bluebell Grooves was to become arguably his hardest route, an opinion that his second on the August day in 1958 would endorse wholeheartedly. Frith Finlayson was making a climbing comeback at the time after devoting many years almost exclusively to his first love of skiing and found himself tied on the end of Cunningham's rope as he set off up the first undercut groove.

"At that time I think Johnny was climbing as well as at any time in his career," says Finlayson. "I still don't know to this day how I finished up on Bluebell Grooves but it was probably because there was no-one else around at the time. There was a lot of gardening going on up above me and Johnny was taking a long time so I had a good idea what I was in for. I was sat there holding the rope when a lone bluebell drifted down from above and landed on me. I think Johnny used a peg or two on the overhanging bit and I never got to finish the route. I got quite high but it was cold and getting dark and he had to lower me off. I remember hanging about 15ft out in space on the way down."

Bluebell Grooves, insists Jimmy Marshall, is a 'classic modern climb'.

"There was no puff-puff nylon in those days, I think Johnny was holding the runners on with his hand then moving up past them. People often ask me to compare Johnny with Robin Smith and Dougal Haston, who came along a bit later, but you have to remember that Cunningham and that gang didn't have any runner technology, no nuts, lightweight ropes anything like that. One would climb a new route, then the rest. Their attitude was that no-one could climb outside the Creagh Dhu and that was pretty well true at the time. Young boys came in and just climbed. A typical example was McLean when Johnny and the rest were working on The Nook at the Cobbler. 'Like a wee shot?' they would ask. McLean did extremely well and that's why he became the Great White Hope, a bridge between the Cunningham era and the modern one. There was no concept of rising through the grades like the rest of us. They also had the intelligence to go and do other advanced rock climbs throughout Britain, learn and come back to Arrochar and Glencoe and move on again. They upset the establishment, too, of course. It didn't help in the eyes of Murray and the rest with their continual undergrading of routes. I think Bill Murray was offended by their up-front approach, they had no compunctions about pegging and how that was perceived. There was Hamish on Engineer's Crack, penduluming in off Fracture Route with his loud war whoops. That upset a lot of people."

Cunningham's climbing partnership with Bill Smith began on Ben An in 1942 and finished in 1966 with their last first ascent together, Stumblebum right of E Buttress on Aonach Dubh. Over those 24 years they were undoubtedly the Creagh Dhu A Team, but there was always healthy competition around.

THE BOYS

The golden age of the Creagh Dhu Mountaineering Club can be said to have started with the meeting of Cunningham and Smith at Ben An during the Second World War, but there was more to the club of this era than just that partnership. Behind the club A Team was a formidable backup, all fine climbers in their own right. Many in fact would rank Pat Walsh, George Shields and John McLean the equal of Cunningham in technical ability while John Cullen, Tommy Paul, Mick Noon, Willie Rowney and Charlie Vigano provided the vital element of competition without which climbing advances of any age would simply not have occurred. A little later still there were the two Davids, Todd and Agnew, and flitting in between on a sort of freelance basis was the club's most famous non-member, Hamish MacInnes. The common factor to all was Cunningham who at one time or another climbed with every one of them. He knew them as The Boys and while the Boys shared a similar background and temperament, Jimmy Marshall noticed another something peculiar to the club.

"All of them with a couple of exceptions like Agnew who was built like a body-builder, had the same physique, thin, flat-chested but powerful. It's strange how this has recurred in the club. Cunningham was the typical example, the prototype Creagh Dhu build."

While he would never admit it, Marshall is a seminal figure in Scottish mountaineering circles and his first ascents in both summer and winter demonstrate not only high technical ability but a rare eye for a line. His writings, too, particularly of his winter epics on Ben Nevis with Robin Smith, have proved hugely influential. Uniquely too, he is a man who has managed to earn acceptance with the Creagh Dhu, their Edinburgh equivalent The Squirrels and the SMC without upsetting any; and over the years has become a shrewd observer of all of them.

He says: "My father was a baker and a hard worker and like a lot of socialists or communists believed the answer to all the world's ills was a good education, which is what my brother Ronnie and I got. The Creagh

Dhu and the Squirrels were similar in a lot of ways and Elly Moriarty and myself were really Creagh Dhu members, although this was not official. We knocked around a lot with them. We had our fighters. Elly was a fine boxer and my brother, Ronnie, was quite notorious in that department, too. I started off with a guy called Cole, who was like a Chinese coolie with these tremendous calf muscles, and he would walk the legs off us. Cole's sister was going with a boy in the Lomonds and we were at the Cobbler in the caves when the Creagh Dhu turned up. Cunningham was showing them all these problems and I realised then, there was the climbing we had been doing and then there was that. It was an eye-opener to put it mildly. That was reinforced when we went up to Ben An about 1949-50. They were all there with their baggy jeans and flat caps and stripped to the waist. There was a climb on the Last Eighty, a pull-up over an overhang where you had to come back into balance and they were all trying this but only Cunningham and George Shields could do it. We waited till they had gone and went and had a go and couldn't get near it, and realised this was real climbing. This was power and grace that we didn't have and we had a long way to go. They came to know us over the next few years and if we were staying in Glencoe, Willie Smith, especially, would give us the leftovers. We stayed in Jacksonville when it was a hole, and in fact it was my brother Ronnie who led the rebuilding of the second Jacksonville."

Marshall could have mentioned another factor endemic to the Creagh Dhu: they were, and still are, all master storytellers, highly-erudite patter merchants of the first order.

Tommy Paul was born in 1931 in Springburn on the north side of Glasgow and started climbing while still at school before beginning the ubiquitous engineering apprenticeship.

"I had been going out climbing and scrambling around since I was about 12, my brother used to go away so I just followed. I used to stand around in pubs with them and they could never understand why I didn't drink but that was it: I was still a schoolboy. At that time I was doing it on my own because there were a lot of people away in the war. Of course there were fewer people climbing then and you tended to know everyone who was doing it, there was a sort of grapevine. It was a fantastic period and a marvellous education. I met Johnny at LMS Rovers when I took up wrestling and he came up to me afterwards and asked me if I climbed and I said a wee bit. In those days you were supposed to find your way through all the old classics first. But Johnny changed all that. He was telling me about this great climber coming out of the army who had been out in Palestine, Bill Smith of course. I didn't even know where Palestine was at that time. Johnny was shy, confident and shy, if that doesn't sound too crazy. I found him slightly aloof and he probably wasn't easy to get to know. He was very choosy about who he climbed with but he could afford to be."

Paul was an early member of the Sandbagged by Cunningham Club with his initiation taking place high up on the Buachaille.

"Me, Johnny, Bill and Johnny's brother James started going out together and of course brothers didn't climb together, so I ended up with Jimmy a lot of the time. We went out to the Buachaille and they were trying some new route so they sent me on Bottleneck Chimney which I think was a severe on North Buttress. So I went up this and thought I'd found a nice crack at the top and finished up on Hangmans thinking it was a new route. It was a bit ridiculous sending me up there but I came down thinking I had done a new route and Johnny just said: 'Oh no, that's been done before'. Then they played another trick on me later on. They asked me what climb I wanted to do and I said I had always wanted to do Agag's Groove. This was late in the evening on a Saturday because we would just go straight up the hill from the bus. I had heard all about Hamish Hamilton and W H Murray and Agag's Groove and this was the one I really fancied. So they said OK but we'll have to get at it by going up Fracture Route so we went up there, did the high level traverse and then we came down and they said 'We'll descend this bit'. So we climbed down and there's a big group of folk on it coming up and we got to the bottom and there's about 12 people sat there including Kenny Copland who was having a word with Johnny and I learned after was in fact tearing a strip off him. So then Johnny said: 'Right, what do you want to do now?' And I said: 'Agag's Groove' and they all burst out laughing. I didn't see what the joke was and Bill says: 'You'll have to find another one'. And I said 'Why's that?' 'Because you've just descended Agag's Groove.'

"I never forgave them for that. But that was the way it was. On the Cobbler you were encouraged to climb routes then descend easier ones, it was supposed to prepare you for the big mountains. But this was the learning process, although they never actually taught you to climb. They wouldn't take you along unless you had climbed and there was no way they were going to stop what they were doing to try and teach you. If you wanted to be taught to climb you would go join the Lomonds. Anyway, in the Creagh Dhu it was near impossible to do standard routes because as soon as you did a standard route, Johnny and Bill had gone and done a new route and so there was a new standard to aim for."

To visiting outsiders, the very image of Creagh Dhu belligerence and intolerance was personified in the formidable figure of John McLean, the Great White Hope of the club, so nicknamed because he was to bridge the gap between the old gang, represented by Cunningham and the newcomers of the 60s and 70s. McLean, in fact, started his outdoor career with the Boy Scouts in Anniesland in the west end of Glasgow.

"I was born in Maryhill until we moved out to Anniesland at the age of 11. I was in the Scouts and used to go away on my own at 12 lighting a fire and things like that. Then my cousin's husband, George, offered to take me out and show me climbing and I thought that would be quite good. I left school at 15 because I hated it and left before I even took my exams, and eventually I had to go to night school to get City and Guilds for engineering. I met Cunningham and the Boys in the usual place up at Ben An and their attitude appealed to me from the start. At the tail-end of the Johnny era there didn't seem many good young climbers coming along, at least not suitable for the club, so I became the Great White Hope. I was supposed to be the club's future. I got on great with Johhny and we did some great climbing together but there was some major bantering sessions as well."

McLean tells many a good story against himself, most of them involving some perverse iniquity visited on him by Cunningham or others and invariably ending " ... the Bah-stards". The Great White Hope found himself in the Cunningham black books several times over the years, most notably in the incident of the barrage balloon.

"Johnny had this huge piece of balloon fabric which he was very proud of. The fabric was great and it could be used for lots of things, groundsheet, tent etc. Johnny and the rest were going away for a few weeks and he gave me a loan of his balloon which I had taken a great shine to. While he was away I decided I would have a bit for myself for a groundsheet but unfortunately when I cut a lump out I didn't bother with the sides or corner I just cut a bit out of the middle. When I handed it back to Johnny it's all wrapped up and the first time he goes to use it there's this six foot square missing out of the middle, it's absolutely hopeless for what he wanted to do with it. Johnny thought it was a low life trick and would always have a saying when someone pulled a stunt after that: 'That McLean, he's a right bastard but even he wouldn't pull a stunt like that!' One time we were out at Ben An and I cut my hand on a rock and on the way back down from the glades we ran into this tourist couple, so I smeared the blood all over my face and posed for a picture with Johnny for them. They must have thought we were real wild men; they were so worried they shared their tea with us."

The hopes the club had for McLean soon became something more substantial and some of his first ascents rank among the best in Scotland, most notably the Long Reach on the Etive Slabs in 1963 and Torro on Carn Dearg of Ben Nevis, in 1962, both seconded by Bill Smith. To McLean's delight, Cunningham later failed on Torro.

McLean tended to make an impression wherever he went and Jack Hool, then a 17-year-old novice and now president of the Barrow Mountaineering Club, remembers meeting the Great White Hope in Langdale in 1959.

"I was in the barn at the Old Dungeon Ghyll waiting for a mate who hadn't turned up. As it happened that didn't matter because it was chucking it down outside and there was no question of going climbing. I was just sat there brewing up when all of a sudden this fearsome-looking guy climbs up the ladder. He has this steel comb hair, a number 2 cut and piercing blue eyes and looks very formidable. He didn't say anything, just nodded and I asked him if he wanted a brew and he said Aye, no please or thank you. He asked me where I was going and I said probably East Raven because there was no wind and I thought it would be possible to do a route there. He then announced we were going up to Gimmer to do Kipling Groove and I wasn't going to argue so I offered him the makings, rolled a fag and we set off. All the way up I thought he would turn back or pick somewhere different but, no, he just carried on. We never saw another soul. He went up in PAs which I had never seen before and I had on these old Gimmer boots. He went up into the sentry box and I was following but at this time I had never been on gritstone and didn't know how to handjam. This voice just kept coming down through the mist and the rain: 'Handjam it you little bastard.' I said I couldn't and he said again: 'Handjam it you little bastard'. I was more terrified of him than the climb and got up eventually. McLean went up in fine style, I have to say. On the way down we got talking for the first time and he asked me what I did and I told him an apprentice fitter and his eyes lit up and he said: 'Well I'm a fitter, too!' Then we went down to Ambleside and we were in a pub with a load of these characters – I was broke and he bought me a drink – and a lot of people knew this guy and someone came up and said: 'That's the White Hope you're with'. He wanted me to go up to White Ghyll next day because there was a line there, called the Peapod I think, which he wanted to do free because Brown and Paul Ross had stood in a sling or something. I think it was the line that became Eliminot later.

"Later on some other guy turned up at the barn and he was a well-known hardman I knew and he took a shine to the spot I had in the sleeping area and this guy said: 'I want this place, shift your gear'. I was going to do just that when McLean said: 'He's with me' and this guy blanched, literally blanched, and backed off right away.

"Thirty years later I ran across John again at a club dinner at Ravenglass and he looked just the same to me, same blond crewcut and same piercing blue eyes. There were about 100 people there and we met up for a drink and he asked me if I wanted a brandy and pulled out a half-pint tumbler and he explained: 'It's the pub's drink, I've no idea where the barman has gone.' Later we were outside and we heard the sound of breaking glass and there's McLean 'destroying the evidence' as he put it. He smoked and drank like hell and it never seemed to affect him. He had always said to look him up if we were ever in Aviemore. So when we went up to have a go at Sticil Face in Loch Avon, I rang him up. For all his reputation I have always found John very generous and he said we could doss at his house, but we were to meet him for Happy Hour at the Red McGregor. Then there was a Chinese and more drink, then back to his house to drop the gear and more drink then back to the Red McGregor and even more drink. My mate had never seen anything like it. The weather was crap, even the chairlift was closed and we were lying there in our pits at McLean's house when we heard the alarm go and John is off to work at 7.30. He was very generous natured, they all were, but he could look really mean when he wanted to. Walsh was the same, I met him a few times and once had to dissuade him from pushing an armchair and a deer's head on the fire at our hut in the Coppermines valley. Fortunately, he took it quite well and told me he was having a party at his place in Windermere the week after and I could come in crampons and ice axe and wreck the place if I wanted!"

Many of the old Creagh Dhu could detect a hint of rivalry between Cunningham and Pat Walsh, the Clydebank docker's son whose climbing reputation has had to compete for most of his career with his skills at unarmed combat all over Britain.

"I think Johnny saw Pat as competition," says Willie Rowney. "Like Frith Finlayson, Pat came in and started doing very hard routes very quickly. People spoke of him as the up and coming top climber."

Perhaps Cunningham and Walsh were too similar in ability, but whether by intent or not, their new route output together was limited to Pendulum, a nasty little E2 next to Gallows on the Buachaille's North Buttress. Some of Walsh's own creations are immense. Club Crack, a vicious, unprotected E2 on the North Peak of the Cobbler became a test-piece for the Creagh Dhu and other visitors with more failures than successes, as Cunningham was among the first to admit: "Marshall failed on it, so did Robin Smith and Haston. It's a sort of rounded layback on an overhanging face and there's only one runner on it so you could well get chopped if you fall off. You have to be very, very strong, which of course Walsh was."

"I think MacInnes had tried to peg it," says Walsh. "When I first tried it I fell off on one of his old pitons. The next week I was back with a big bunch of the Boys watching. Some of them followed, most on a tight rope I should say."

Walsh's new routes were often credited to his short-sightedness but that is doing him less than justice. His quintet of hard routes on Slime Wall – Bloody Crack, Doom Arête, Revelation, Nightmare Traverse and the Girdle are testimony to a climber with an eye for a fierce line and the ability to force that line; while many climbers on Clogwyn du'r Arddu in North Wales must doff a cap from time to time in the Scot's direction when fighting their way up Walsh's Groove on White Slab Eliminate.

This was done in 1959 and popular mythology had it that Walsh and Charlie Vigano had done it in mistake for Sheaf, Walsh's myopia doing the rest.

"The business about the eyesight was a load of bollocks," he says. "On Nightmare Traverse they even said I had stepped on to a white patch on the wall. The line of Sheaf was a deliberate attempt. Charlie and I went over the overhang for the first time and I knew a lot of good climbers, including Whillans, had failed on it."

Unfortunately, Walsh's thick glasses, along with a slight build and mild manner, were to lead him into many a bar-room rammy and caused many to underestimate him to their cost. Walsh, in his own quiet way, can justify every incident. "Oh, I've been locked up a few times," he admits. "In Kendal, Windermere, places like that. The time in the Salutation in Ambleside, I was there for a quiet drink and the juke box was going full-blast and I asked them three times to turn it down. In the end I just smashed it. Out here in Skye there's a load of English people and of course they revert and try and learn the Gaelic and things like that; they've all got kilts on. So I was in the local pub one night and put a load of shotgun cartridges on the fire and told them: 'Let's hear you swear in Gaelic then'."

After Walsh's mother suffered a nervous breakdown, Walsh went to see his brother – who had emigrated to Australia years before – in Sydney and after a disagreement, Pat's brother ended up with a broken leg.

"Most of the punch-up stories revolved round Patsy, who was a docker and inherited his dad's job," says John Cullen. "He was an unusually strong guy but had this wee fat face with glasses, just a wee fatty, so some people probably underestimated him. But he was like steel. At

Arrochar once there was a rammy starting and to settle it, this other bunch said: 'We'll put our best guy against yours' and Johnny Cunningham looked round and pointed out Pat and told them; 'Well, there's our best guy' and of course the other gang are sat there looking smug. So Pat puts down his newspaper and takes off his glasses and goes outside with this other guy. After about 10 seconds there's the most awful screaming and the other guys are looking at us and smiling and nodding. Next minute Walsh came back in, picked up his glasses and carried on reading, although he turned to the other gang and said: 'I'd get some help for your mate if I were you.' What he'd done as soon as he got out was fling the guy on the floor put his feet on his chest, fingers in his nostrils and just levered away until something gave."

"We were in some pub in the Lakes, I think it was in Ambleside," says John McLean. "We had this guy Pops with us and he was on the guitar and singing away when some guy kept interrupting. Pat was patience itself. He said things like; 'Well, why not suggest a song we can join in with', things like this but the guy wouldn't have it. He went on and on until finally and with no warning at all Pat just flew across the table, straight over the ashtrays and pint pots at this guy."

Walsh says: "I started climbing on my own at 14 when I came across Chris Lyon and the Creagh Dhu. Chris was like a father figure to me and later got me a job in John Browns. It was Chris really who kept the club going, although it's finished now. When I heard he had died, I told my wife to pull over at the nearest pub. I had a lot of respect for Johnny, too, although I thought I had fallen out with him once. A burd had turned up at the Kingshouse looking for him and I said: 'Oh, you mean the veritable Adonis?' which he was of course but I thought he had taken exception to that. Much later I was in the Gorms and Johnny must have heard I was on the hill because he came skiing down and put his arms round me and said: 'Pat, it's so good to see you'. I was so pleased at that because I regarded Johnny as a friend and he was the man who really pushed the standards of Scottish climbing up. I think it was that same trip I was there with Ian Allen and we went for a drink with Frith in Aviemore. It got a bit outrageous. Ian was extremely well-endowed and we were buying Frith these cocktails and Ian was dipping his thing in them and Frith was happily drinking away."

Walsh lives now on Isle Oronsay in Skye with a view of the Sound of Sleat and the hills of Knoydart. He bought and converted three crofts there and although he has no children, this is one of the few regrets of a colourful life and climbing career.

George Shields, once renowned as the Climbing Cobbler of Aviemore, was born in Dunfermline but insist quite vehemently that he was conceived in Glasgow.

"All my folks were born in Glasgow. My father was one of the Red Clydesiders and he worked in John Browns and was very much involved in the rent strike. Eventually he was blacklisted and had to move out to find work so he went to Fife which is where I came in. Fifers were always wary of Glasgow people and I always felt an outsider there which is why I started getting away at weekends. My father took me out when I was about 10, going away to the hostels in the Trossachs and I started climbing when I was 13, then left school at 14. The first time I met the Creagh Dhu was at Ben An and I would be about 15 or 16 at the time. They were on the Last Eighty and had all finished except for one guy who was stuck and shouting 'Help, Help'. The Creagh Dhu – I knew it was the Creagh Dhu because they had these Lawrie boots on and they were the crème de la crème of boots at the time – were lying on their bellies looking down at him and shouting 'JUMP' and I thought these are the kind of guys I like. It was one of the funniest things I have ever seen. I met John Cullen before I met John Cunningham and I remember him talking about this phenomenal climber – it was the first time I had ever heard the word used so much. I was at Jimmy Jackson's and I said to this guy: 'Have you ever heard of this guy called Cunningham?' Of course it was Cunningham I was speaking to and he said: 'Aye, I've heard of that bastard' and led me on a wee bit, I was just a wee kid at the time. So I started knocking around with them climbing and occasionally vandalising things."

As well as a formidable climber, Shields became one of the best-known and most proficient ski instructors in Scotland and one of the leading lights of Frith Finlayson's Cairngorms-based school, although the two are far from bosom buddies now.

Shields says: "Frith wrote a book about his skiing experiences and I would say my name is conspicuous by its absence. He became a very bitter man when he was thrown out of BASI and blamed a lot of people. I had had one go at skiing in 1947 when my brother, who was in the army, got hold of these German paratrooper skis and I carried them up this hill near home, skied down and then just fell over on my side. I had such a bloody struggle getting back to my feet. I swore I would never try skiing again and never did until I was about 28 when I decided I would do it properly.

"I also tried canoeing thanks to Johnny. It was dead calm and I'm not frightened of water – Johnny was, you could see that. I went right over and got out of it easily. He never told me how to get out, that was what he was like. He liked setting traps and he would tell you something then leave out the most important element of whatever you were doing."

Like Shields, Willie Rowney discovered early on in his Creagh Dhu career that the learning curve could be steep. Born in Clydebank, his family was left homeless in the Blitz and climbing offered a healthy alternative to the grey depression of postwar Glasgow. On his early visits to Ben An he found himself taken under the wing of Cunningham and Bill Smith, and his real apprenticeship began.

"Johnny had been wrestling at Cowal Games when I first came across him and he'd caught the boat across from Dunoon then the bus to Drymen and from there walked all the way to Ben An. I remember we were all sat there awaiting his arrival because this was absolutely the big name at the time. He really had a presence, he was a fine-looking man and as a rock climber his reputation went before him. After the usual spell of hanging around with the lads, I moved into the combine with Bill and Johnny. I was their blackboy, the camp helper for the old hands. Bill was very straight. Coming down Glen Lyon one very hot day we stopped by a burn and I started gulping this water down. Bill sat there watching me for a bit then said: 'You'll be sick drinking like that'. And I thought what's he talking about? Then we carried on down and of course I was promptly sick at the bottom. In the club at the time there was still the old crowd like Chris Lyon and Jimmy Jackson and Jack Thomson. Johnny was the young upstart. The Lomonds used to be very critical of him, called him Johnny

Flybacon, so he must have been quite outrageous when he was very young.

"A lot of people from down south had the idea that the Creagh Dhu were drunk every weekend and there was a fight every weekend. I never actually witnessed a fight and in fact I'm ashamed to say it, but the only time I ever saw a punch thrown – and I would say that in close to three years I only missed maybe six weekends – it was me that threw it. It was just one chap behaving very badly and I just let fly, but he and I shook hands later and became great friends. But you kept hearing stories about this and that and it was always someone in the club doing the telling, so, yes it was greatly exaggerated. We did get barred out of the New Dungeon Ghyll down in Langdale once after a drunken evening when Pat Walsh commandeered the telephone and some woman phoned up, I think it was a wrong number, and he had this conversation that went on for hours, ridiculous.

"Cunningham, Smith and I, the three of us, knocked around together a lot and it was Johnny who invented the method of dividing something so everyone got half. Bill had a terrible sweet tooth, so with things like a chocolate Swiss roll Cunningham would say: 'I know, everyone gets half'. So he would take half himself then he cut the other half in two and that became the method of dividing the goodies from then on. I used to have great arguments with Johnny once I got really pally with him. I wouldn't let him get away with anything and Bill would usually end up as adjudicator. We had this ridiculous argument once when he swore that the South Peak of the Cobbler should have been the North Peak because it faced north and Bill just turned to me and said: 'You're right' and then to Johnny: 'You're wrong' so of course Johnny would just laugh and grab me and put me in a wrestling hold.

"He didn't suffer fools gladly though and could be a bit ruthless at times. We were on our way up to Gladiators on the Cobbler and as we were soloing up the Jughandle to the terrace there were two other blokes climbing on a route to the side. The leader was near the top of his climb but struggling and Johnny in typical fashion said: 'If you just get your leg up on that ledge you can rest a bit' which was good advice but the bloke just looked at him and more or less implied it was nothing to do with Johnny. So Johnny just left them to it. Anyway we got up and were changing our footwear and Johnny went across to look down again because these guys hadn't appeared and just at that moment the leader fell off and Johnny said something like 'Oh, dearie me'. I ran round and the guy had hit the deck; the second was tied on really badly and there was some slack in the belay and when the strain came on we reckoned he had just let go. The leader landed on some grass which saved him a really serious injury but he had still broken his leg and knocked all his teeth out with his knee. I wouldn't say I had to persuade Johnny to help but he more or less said 'Bugger off', then gave the second man a telling off in no uncertain terms. We organised a rescue party and you know when somebody is hurt they always pick on someone as their friend and I became this bloke's friend. He was asking how his teeth were and of course I said 'Well you've damaged them a wee bit' things like that. He was a great tall bloke and when the stretcher arrived his head hung over one end and his feet hung over the other. Then someone discovered a student nurse on the hill and we persuaded her to have a look. The problem was she was Italian and while Johnny is making a splint with a piton hammer and binding him up she is wiggling the bloke's toes and saying: 'Do your fingers hurt?' It was very amusing, not for the poor guy, but for the rest of us it was a scream. Johnny was having quite a good time."

Mick Noon was born in Denmark Street, Possilpark, one of the humblest parts of Glasgow even today. In 1932 at the height of the depression, like so many before and since, Noon found that the wilds of Scotland and the Creagh Dhu offered a welcome escape. He was to become a regular climbing partner of Cunningham's when Bill Smith's interest in climbing tailed off into skiing.

"I would say it would be a poor childhood. It was a normal working household. As a kid I would go to the afternoon matinée, that used to be pretty cheap, to see Tom Mix or somebody like that at cinemas such as the Magnet, Phoenix, Mecca or the Astoria, all of which have gone now or turned into bingo halls. I was seven when the war began and my father, who was in Royal Engineers, sent us to my mother's relatives in Ireland for a couple of years, but my father got sick and all us kids came home. I remember all the raids, we had to go down the shelter. We lived right

across the street from an ammunitions factory, of course we didn't know
that ... but there were some bombs fell all around. We used to go up the
street when there was a great big hole with a live bomb and of course
they'd taken the detonator off by the time anybody got near it and it didn't
go off, lucky for us ... it was a great big one. I remember they were mainly
after the Clyde and the factories there, but they hit all the tenements at the
side. I lost my father in 1943. I was only eleven and there were four of us
and I was the oldest, with my mother left a widow. She had to go out
working in the morning to the office filing stockcards and I'd have the
fire lit for her coming back in to get the kids ready for school. She made
us join the Boy Scouts, something to do on the weekends and you would
go up there at night and then up to the Campsies at the weekend where we
would climb on these little rocks by Jenny's Lum. A guy called George
White introduced me to another guy, Jimmy McClusky, who came out
one weekend, and that's how he got started with the Weekenders. It was
then I met Charlie Vigano and all the other guys. There was this other
group called the Cowboys, always going up to Arrochar, just for a good
time, just to get out of the city and they'd go up the pub and get drunk
while we'd go up the hill and camp. We couldn't afford to drink. There
was one big guy, they called him the Dummy, he always wore an Air-
borne jumping jacket and he'd a big mop of red hair. It seemed he was
quite a fighter, but he was in an entirely different group from our group
and I think he steered clear of Johnny and the rest because they wouldn't
put up with his carry-on. They were just a bunch of young guys out there
and there's nobody going to push them around. I think they were pretty
fair, any time they did get in a fight, it was valid. Some of it's exaggerated, I would think. But it's the usual thing, once they get a couple of
pints in them and an argument comes up, it comes to fisticuffs if things
don't work out right.

   "So that was where I first met Johnny up at Arrochar. They were
drumming up, him and Bill Smith and Tommy Paul. We'd heard about
Cunningham but I'd never seen him before, I'd just heard what a fantastic
climber he was and that he was putting up all these big routes up Glencoe
and stuff like this. Someone said: 'That's Cunningham there' so Charlie
Vigano and Davey Young and myself and McClusky all overawed, fol-

lowed them up the Cobbler and I remember we had to run behind them because they were steaming ahead to get the best doss at the Boulder. Him and Smith were always doing all these problems and we couldn't even get off the ground. On the Cobbler they'd be on hard routes and we'd be on the easy routes. We had a lot to learn and they were quite willing to teach us, there was nothing big-time about them. For all that, he was one of the boys really, and he would show you how to do something on the routes. He was an expert on the Corner ... it took me a few years to get doing that one. The thing is, he would do it in the rain and everything and it was slippy and he was in boots.

"Of course we started off with the clinkers. I had an old sleeping bag from the Ex-Army store and it cost 2s 6d and when it got wet, boy, did it get wet ... Johnny always believed in good gear. He looked at it that if you were doing something for a long time you might as well get the best stuff.

"Some of the routes that Johnny put up were really good because in those days we used hemp ropes – it was before the nylon came in – but he was doing these long ascents and there were no runners. Lucky for him he never fell off. Guerdon Grooves, if he had come off that he'd have been a goner, there was a long run-out on that. Cunningham and Smith, they were away above everybody else ... they were the A Team. They would do route for route. Johnny would lead one, Bill would lead the other, through leading all the time. Smith came home one time on leave, from the Paratroopers, and he did all the routes on Rannoch Wall, just to see how fit he was. Chris Lyon was a good climber, but it was Johnny and Smith who brought the standards up. I was invited to join the Creagh Dhu after a trip to Arran with Sunshine (Tommy Lawrie) and there was a whole little group of them there. We did a few routes, some very severes and some of them we had to use combined tactics like on the Direct Route on the South Ridge, that's how green we were. When we came back after that weekend I went over to the Coe and did Red Slab and that was when Johnny invited me to join the club, mainly because I was always hanging around to get in. So Cunningham was the one that sponsored me and invited me to be in, so I was quite happy about that. The feeling was 'I'll try not to let you down Johnny'. Johnny did put a few people off climbing for good, though. They would always go for things like Ravens when it was raining. Johnny wouldn't wait for summer like a lot of people. He would say 'Let's go you guys' and he and Bill would take a whole load of us up Ravens. The only two who could do it were Johnny and Bill, the rest of us would fall off. There were some guys who never came back after that, that was the end of them. I think the limited membership policy was a good idea. The idea was that it was a rock-climbing club, not a hiking club. They just wanted rock-climbers. It's true, there were some non-climbers but how they got in is another story. If people couldn't get in it was maybe because they weren't liked. If somebody in the club said no, that was it. You had to have almost 100% to accept them into the club. It was the done thing to start as a blackboy, the youngest one was always getting the water and stuff like that. I put it down to laziness. They still have blackboys today, never mind then. We'd usually go out on the Club Bus but later on the bikes came in and I had a bike with a sidecar and we would have these epic trips all the way up to Fort William, there was no bridge at Ballachulish in those days.

"One day I broke the chain, on the way up to Kinlochleven and I went back and found all the parts for it, even the lock-link. I had to store it at the Kingshouse and came back the next week. It was in the coal shed, so naturally we filled up the thing with coal, sat on the top, and drove out the bike –   that's terrible isn't it? I gave them a couple of shillings or something for stowing the bike but we helped ourselves to some coal for the doss and we were all pot black from the coal. When Bill got interested in skiing that was when Johnny and me got together for the winter climb-ing, gullies and things like that. And of course we always went to the Lake District at Easter and down to Wales. I did Cemetery Gates, about the fourth ascent and I think about the sixth ascent of Cenotaph Corner. I found it OK and didn't seem to have any difficult problems on it.

"I left Scotland in May, 1959, and went to Canada for five years then on to the States in 1964. I worked in Canada as a welder, then in the States for MGM for two years painting film sets, haunted houses, things like that. After that I got a job with American Airlines and worked as a maintenance engineer for 21 years at LA airport: I learned that trade by going to night school. My eldest son was born in Glasgow, my daughter in Canada and the youngest son in California so it's a pretty cosmopolitan family. I remember reading the Chouinard book on ice-climbing over here and thought I was reading John Cunningham. He was the first to think about front-pointing that way with crampons, but then he was definitely always an adventurer trying out new things. If he thought it was going to make things easier he would go out and buy it. He wasn't afraid to spend money on it if he thought it would work. The idea was to do harder climbs, not do hard climbs easier. You had to climb hard to push your standard up. In all the time I knew him, I never saw Johnny off form."

John Cullen earned the nickname of Shalako from Cunningham because of his laid-back nature, Shalako being a character in one of Cunningham's favourite Louis L'Amour westerns where 'in the desert only the eyes moved, Shalako'. On a trip to the Alps with Cunningham and Todd in the 60s, Cullen, the only driver in the party, was still waiting for his passport to arrive on the day of departure. 'Shalako' must have surprised Cunningham in later life, as Cullen finished up as a noted civil engineer and designed the Glasgow sections of the M8.

"I was born in a tenement in Maryhill, but unlike most finished up behind a desk and in civil engineering. I was a founder member of the Glencoe Mountaineering Club and in about 1949/50 started going away with Johnny and Bill Smith although I actually started climbing at the age of three on the walls near the canal where we lived, so I always wanted to climb. I had read every book on climbing when I was young. I can remember when I was about seven or eight my father taking me past Glencoe and looking at the face of the Buachaille, absolutely marvellous, so I just started at the first opportunity. In 1948 some of the old Creagh Dhu vanished off the scene in an amazingly short time, within a year basically. The old team was just gone, with only Chris Lyon left in the background. Johnny was a better climber than Bill. I am in a position to know because I've seen them climbing and seen them bouldering and without a doubt he was an outstandingly good climber. He started when he was 14 and was still climbing when he was killed so that will be 38 years climbing at a high standard and all that time well within his capability. I think he only had one fall when he burst his nose but as far as I know he never had an injury after that. There was a series of six programmes on TV about Scottish climbing (The Edge) and I'm really amazed he wasn't in there because he really created modern Scottish climbing and regardless of how you compare him with later people, he represented a quantum leap at the time. Like a lot of others I met him at The Cobbler. We worked Saturday mornings so we would go up at lunchtime and either sleep under the boulder or camp. I saw Johnny doing the boulder problems and he was already a legend then although still quite young. My regular partner was Charlie Vigano and I think we looked on ourselves as independents in our own right although nothing near their class. There were some other good climbers. We were down in Manchester for Charlie's wedding, I was supposed to be best man but when we got there Charlie announced the wedding was off – he was sleeping in the bed and his bride-to-be was sleeping on the floor – so we went climbing on a local crag instead and Pat Walsh was soloing up these climbs in wellies and with a big heavy coat on. Very impressive.

"The wild image? Well all I can say is that in the case of the regular club dance we were never invited back to the same place twice in our heyday. One special occasion was when Johnny was going off to New Zealand and there was a notorious booze-up at Arrochar. What was remarkable was that quite a proportion of the lads were in their teens and hardly drank. Bill Rowney and none of that crowd were routine drinkers. We were camping up in the Glades and no one had the slightest intention of having a wild night. I think there was a bunch there we knew as the Trossachs Lads and they were there drinking in the bar as usual. It was all in good spirits, no violence or nasty business. I recall Johnny standing on a table to deliver a speech and his farewell words were something like 'Keep the heat at all times, keep the heat.' People started throwing glasses and mugs of beer, all in good humour, and Hamish MacInnes took the dartboard and rolled it down the road and a window got broken. But it all ended as soon as it started and folk drifted back to the campsite, although one or two were crawling up the path."

Davie Todd, who emigrated to Canada in October, 1976, regards the apprenticeship from shipyard worker to outdoorsman as similar to a war. There were generals, officers and privates in the shipyards; in the hills it was different.

Todd, who thinks and writes as well as he once climbed, says: "I wasn't a regular soldier in the yards but a conscript aged 15 and the war had been going on so long the glory had been going out of it and if you weren't careful it could kill you. You still had to be brave or exceptional to say No to it. By the time I got to 19 and met Cunningham he was 31 and in mind, if not body for a while, I left the war to become a disciple."

Todd's story of his first meeting with his mentor has a familiar ring.

"It was the spring of 1959 and with a couple of other friends I was out at Ben An at the foot of Birch Wall, which was to be my first severe. We had a rope and two slings between us. I was stepping off the belay ledge and approaching the crux bulge when the soles of a pair of PAs appeared followed by a climber drifting down the route unroped.

"Trying to look unimpressed with this interpretation of Swan Lake on rock I asked: 'How hard is that route, Jimmy?' "I don't know, Jimmy. I've only ever climbed down it,' came the reply."

Shortly after, Todd was to meet his tormentor again and a lifelong friendship began. "I'd just recovered from a massive fall the length of Crowberry Gully which upset my father to put it mildly, as he punched me unconscious. It would be March with the winter just breaking up. It was a miserable weekend but the tolerance of conditions like this were the trademark of the west coast climber. We used the caves at Arrochar and slipped and slithered around the rocks there in an effort to get fit, or perhaps stay fit. The caves were damp and soggy but compared with working in the bowels of a cold, rusty, noisy, filthy embryonic ship on some Clydeside slips, not too bad.

"Cunningham was there with this super-arrogant and confident and thirsty and nasty character McLean, a big snarly bastard in an oilskin jacket. There's also a Canadian guy and McLean's new blackboy, who it turns out is Davey Agnew.

"Johnny shouts to us: 'Where are you guys going?' and we say we're heading for the hostel in Arrochar and Johnny says: 'We're going to the caves, would you like to come?' And really of course, he's setting you up, he's going to have some fun but we're young and impressionable and, Oh, we'd love to come. So they took us to the caves, and they're showing us all these climbs in the caves. Johnny has his long poacher's coat on and PAs, and he's wiping the hidden holds and moving up where we can't see for this coat.

"Then he gets to the top and shouts 'Up you come' and we're on the rock and Johnny is continually saying things like 'That's incredible, amazing, I have NEVER seen anyone move like that', but he's just leading you on to the crux.

" 'Now all you have to do is S-T-R-E-T-C-H across to the left and you've cracked it'. And as soon as you stretch over, of course, you're off. It's only a 15-foot slab but there's a big puddle at the bottom and the mud is all over your boots and socks and he's up there saying: 'That was so close, now come on, just one more go. ... ' That's when I knew it was going to be a long apprenticeship.

"We had a day in the caves and at night they took us down to the Ross Hotel where all these morons hung out, guys who had come out from Glasgow for the weekend, wine drinkers, Bergen thieves. When we went in they were cooking over the fire – bacon, eggs and a big pot of cheap wine bubbling away. When we came in they'd all snarl at us but then they recognised Cunningham and McLean and they had probably run across Patsy Walsh in the past which was great for us as we were wee kids and of course they would have eaten us alive on our own. They're talking cowboy, we called them the Cowboys, and they're saying things like 'OK, man, when does the seven o'clock stage get in from Glasgow?' They're apparently waiting for a guy called Garth and it's Garth this and Garth that and Garth and his *knives*.

"We're playing darts and one of them pipes up and says 'We want to play darts' and Johnny turns round and says 'Fine, just put your names on the board and you can play next.' 'We don't usually work like that,' they say. 'We usually play when we want to.' So Johnny says 'No, just put your name up on the board like everyone else and then you can play'. 'It won't be like this when Garth gets here, just wait till Garth arrives.'

"The seven o'clock stage gets in and five after seven the doors fly open and Garth walks in. He's like a comic strip, the skinniest guy you've ever seen, dressed in army fatigues and he opens his jacket and he's got throwing knives all in a line. Then he says 'And look at this beauty' and he pulls out a Bowie knife and, thud, throws it into the table almost splitting it in half, just quivering there. All his pals are mightily impressed with this, but Cunningham pulls the knife out of the table, cleans his nails with it and tells Garth: 'Yes, very useful that'.

"Then Garth decides he wants a game of darts but Johnny just tells him: 'Name on the board, guys'. Garth is totally pissed off by now and while Johnny is up collecting his darts he flings this throwing knife right into the board by his head. Johnny pulls it out drops it on the floor and says: 'Told you, name on the board'.

"The problem with the Cobbler was that I was a practising Roman Catholic and had to get from the high doss there to church in Arrochar on a Sunday morning or I was going to hell. So I would run down and run back up. I always enjoyed solo climbing after I had been to Mass because I knew if I died I would go to heaven. Anyway, I would be on my way down and crossing this field and these Cowboys would be lying there still drunk from the night before and getting stuck into the cheap wine again. They would send this Alsatian dog after me and this dog would chase me and bite me. So when I finally gave up being a Catholic it was great.

"Johnny pushed things on the rock and he pushed things socially. Hamish had these new karabiners and of course if you have new krabs you always mark them, so Hamish's mark is one notch filed on the gate. After a weekend's climbing, gear tends to get mixed up and next week Bill Smith appears with a similar new krab and Hamish says: 'That looks like mine' and Bill says: 'No, it's got my mark on ... two notches on the gate.'

"Another weekend and another gear mix-up and of course Johnny appears for the next weekend with a very familiar-looking krab ... but with three notches on the gate. He was one step ahead all the time.

"The only time I really saw him bettered was when he came to wrestle the new boy, Davey Agnew, who is probably 5ft 6ins tall but if you laid him on his side he'd be about 5ft 8ins. I think it was after he'd come back from Antarctica and we were all at Jacksonville for the homecoming party. Now Johnny had invented this new wrestling hold, or throw, and he'd hurt Bill Smith with it and he'd hurt Tommy Paul with it and there's the new boy Agnew, so Johnny is asking him to show him some wrestling holds but of course is thinking all the time of putting this hold on Agnew. They are outside Jacksonville and moving with incredible speed, I have never seen anything like it and Johnny puts this hold on Agnew and Agnew just breaks it – twice just straightens and breaks it; Johnny tries again and Agnew just shrugs him off, so Johnny pats him on the backside like a horse and tells him 'OK. You're pretty good'. He just couldn't believe Agnew's strength, and this a guy who was so ill as a kid they had told him to go and do some physical exercise to build himself up.

"The American climber Royal Robbins told this story about Agnew in the Vagabond Club in Leysin when Davey gets up to go to the toilet and when he comes back there is this American guy with Davey's bird and, what's worse, Davey's drink. Davy says not 'That's my bird' but 'That's my beer' and the guy told him to get lost, to F... off. Davy just reached quickly forward and grabbed this guy by the hand holding the pint and broke two of his fingers."

Todd had two seasons in the Alps with Cunningham, in 1963 and four years later in 1967. In 1963, on the north face of the Civetta, Todd was much taken with Cunningham's footwear which was square-toed ski boots issued by the British Antarctic Survey.

"One of the square boots jammed immovably in a crack and hanging from a handjam he had to loosen the lace, remove his foot and retrieve the boot without dropping it. That night in camp he took a ruddy great knife to the offending boots and rounded off the toes. Maybe if he hadn't been a carpenter, like another JC, he could have been a cobbler."

But the main target of that summer was the North Face of the Eiger, a route long coveted by Cunningham. Like many before them there were long days waiting out the weather in their tent at Alpiglen in the midst of the usual Eiger circus.

"Whillans and Patey were there and a bunch of Americans, led by John Harlin and including Stuart Fulton, doing a recce of the Direct Route," says Todd. "Harlin was amazing, everywhere he went there were camera crews and journalists following and he knew exactly the profile to present to the cameras. There he would be with his eyes narrowed and looking into the distance while they clicked away. Everyone had a title: Harlin was the leader, the Finest Mixed Climber in Europe, Stuart Fulton was the Greatest Rock Climber in Europe and Gary Hemming was the Greatest Aid Climber in the World. Harlin, this big, blond guy with the film star looks was looking to put together a team to have a go at the Direct Route and of course cottoned on to Johnny straight away.

'John, we are going for the Direct, we would love it if you came along and joined our team.'

'No, I don't think so,' says Johnny, 'I'm happy just going up the Ordinary Route.'

'John, you just don't seem to understand, this is your chance to make a NAME for yourself.'

'Well, thanks very much, but I think I'll just stick with Davie here. We're off to the Dollies soon anyway.'

'Davie? – and with this Harlin looks me up and down like something that has just crawled out of somewhere – 'the Dolomites? John, don't you understand that if you die in the Dolomites no-one will know a thing; die here and you will be famous!'

'Well, thanks again, but I don't have any intention of dying anywhere.'

"Anyway, later that night we'd been out to the Vagabond Club for a few drinks and they were all there and obviously we weren't their flavour of the month any more. We'd been back in the tent and in our pits for about an hour when we heard this whispering outside and next minute they were shaking the guylines. Johnny very quietly asked them to go away, but they carried on, getting louder and louder about it until Johnny says: 'Right, once more and we are putting our boots on and coming out there' which has little effect so then Johnny, who incidentally is 36-37 at the time, starts saying to me: 'Right, you take Fulton, Davie, and I'll take the other three' which of course greatly alarmed me as Fulton was a real hardman.

"Johnny says: 'Right, the boots are on now' and throws open the tent door ... and they all ran like hell off into the night!"

In 1967 the pair climbed the North Face of the Piz Badile in a record, at the time, five and three quarter hours, just beating a blizzard to the summit and with a trying 'buddy bonding' descent of the North Ridge in a blizzard. Six Polish climbers were left stuck on the face. There was also a second (first free) ascent of the NE Face of the Catinaccio d'Antermoia in the Dolomites in three hours.

For all these adventures, Cunningham's Alpine experience was curiously unsatisfying. Jimmy Marshall for one was astonished, and still is, by his small breadth of success and lack of ambition there, although circumstances usually conspired against him. But then again, Cunningham never had much luck on big mountains – starting with the biggest of them all.

TWO AND ONE SHEEP TO EVEREST

Cunningham was bored. It was a typical west coast summer of 1952 and had rained for 12 consecutive weekends. The Creagh Dhu had spent most of the time dossing, sheltering from the rain and climbing on the greasy walls of the caves at Glen Lyon at Arrochar, the only breaks in the routine being "the weekly difference of opinion with the forestry officials as to whether or not we should be there" according to Cunningham.

"Once the baiting was finished and they disappeared we would spend the rest of the days climbing the dripping walls round the caves, we being usually Bill Smith, Mick Noon, Long John Cullen, Charlie Vigano, Patsy Walsh, Bill Rowney, Hugh Currie and Jimmy Jackson. The climbing was hard and the competition fierce but it was a depressing time and eventually, on a sort of whim, Pete McGonigle and I decided we would emigrate to New Zealand. The weather had to be better out there."

Emigration was one of the unfortunate by-products of the depression years in Glasgow and Cunningham and McGonigle were simply following a well-worn path. Other Weekenders like Bob Hamilton, John Kay, Roddy (Blondie) Cameron, Walter Hutton and Pat O'Donnell had already taken advantage of assisted passages and were encamped in Christchurch. Early in May, 1952, Cunningham and McGonigle stood on the deck of the Captain Cook as it sailed slowly down the Clyde, passing John Browns shipyard where Cunningham could see all his old mates on the stern of the vessel he had been working on a week earlier. He did not feel any regrets. Thirty five days later the Cook docked in Wellington where the two Glaswegians parted company, McGonigle heading off to Christchurch in the South Island while Cunningham went to a public works camp in Porirua near Wellington. He stuck it for six weeks, working as a house builder, before getting fed up and moving down to Christchurch.

"I was keen to join the rest of the Creagh Dhu who consisted of guys who had moved there en masse 12 months previously. I arrived in the middle of the ski season and the lads were all addicts by the time I got there. They had flats in the centre of Christchurch and were cooking for themselves. They had to forage for food a lot, but we knew all the tricks from back home. When looking for something new to eat we would go along the side of the River Avon at midnight and try to catch any ducks sleeping by the side of the river. I was never one of the lucky ones and usually ended up buying mine.

"The area we skied was called Craigieburn and it was a good three-mile trek to get to the ski village from the main road. Every time we went to Craigieburn there was a tremendous race uphill to get the best beds (the ones nearest the stove) . One time we were tearing uphill as fast as we could when we suddenly realised there was a stranger in our midst, a New Zealander probably thinking this was a regular pace to travel. Five minutes from the hut he began to weaken and gasped: 'How much further?'

"I said: 'Don't worry, we'll be going like this most of the night' and he just collapsed by the side of the path. But the wind-up rebounded because not only did we have to carry him up the hill to the hut, we also had to give him one of the best beds by the stove while he recovered, and even made his dinner for him. January 1953, the New Zealand summer, was a long holiday and we all packed in our jobs, piled aboard the club's Willis Knight sleeve valve truck and headed for the hills. It was supposed to be a sort of touring/climbing holiday but in true Creagh Dhu fashion we didn't have much of a plan. We trekked up the Waimakarire River and marvelled at the huge packs the New Zealanders had and they in turn laughed at our short ice axes – theirs came up to shoulder height. On Mount Harper, instead of climbing the normal route, six of us found a new route up a rock ridge, avoiding the snow trudge up a long couloir. Then we drove round to the Matukituki Valley for an attempt on Mount Aspiring but the weather was desperate and we descended to the flesh-pots of Wanaku and Queenstown and camped at Lake Wakatipu beneath the Remarkable Mountains. We just wandered round in a lackadaisical fashion going nowhere in particular but eventually came to a halt at the Hermitage below Mount Cook. There was a bit of a schism in the group by now with some of them starting to lose their enthusiasm and there was a bit of a row until four of us set out to try Cook. Snow conditions were unbelievably grim and we abandoned the attempt after ploughing through waist-deep snow. So we just sunbathed and fed our faces for the rest of the summer. The Creagh Dhu were always pretty sociable going to lots of dances and booze-ups and the like. They were fiercely competitive even about women and would always try and get off with the local birds at the dance hall. They also had competitions to see who could get off with the ugliest bird with a round of drinks as the prize. They used to trap some ghastly specimens, terrible uglies. We would all shield our eyes as the conquering hero went past and say: 'You are definitely the winner.' This led to trouble in Christchurch when we were set upon by a bunch of local hoods who thought they were going to get things their own way. The next minute one had gone through a shop window and one into the river. The police came and an ambulance to cart away the casualties. We were all arrested and spent a night in jail until things had cooled down."

"There wasn't a lot of climbing done," says John Kay who was in New Zealand with his wife, Helen. "Ped McGonigle was quite adept at shoplifting and he regularly nicked stuff from Oscar Koberger's shop at Arthur's Pass, a pricey climbing shop. The ski boots were about £20 a pair even in those days, so you could imagine his mark-up. The Kiwis didn't like the prices he charged and it became a bit of a thing to nick stuff from there. Ped arrived back once with a rope and a sweater. But I always wondered why Johnny and the others didn't take New Zealand by storm. The place was full of unclimbed mountains and there were some very good climbers around like George Lowe, the Everest packhorse, but they just never got into it. They didn't go out much at night, either, and I had the impression they were saving for something."

The perceptive Kay was right. Arriving back in Christchurch from the holidays with a job to find and digs to locate Cunningham had found a telegram waiting.

"It was from Hamish MacInnes asking if I wanted to join an expedition to climb Everest in June, 1953. I envisaged Hamish myself, a bunch of sahibs and an army of Sherpas knocking off Everest and immediately cabled back to accept. Hamish arrived in March, 1953 and I met him at the railway station. He was easy to spot: rucksack on his back, a large box under each arm and a suitcase in each hand. I took him back to the digs but unfortunately my landlady took an instant dislike to him and promptly threw us both out. Hamish got digs elsewhere and I moved in with Pat O'Donnell. Still, there was the expedition to look forward to and I couldn't wait to hear the details from Hamish. It was then that he told me the expedition consisted of me ... and him."

There had been small expeditions to the Himalaya before. Alfred Mummery, the great English climber, had optimistically attempted Nanga Parbat, the tenth highest mountain in the world as far back as 1895, incredibly reaching a height of close to 7000m on the Diamir Face. His 20th century counterparts like Eric Shipton and Bill Tilman were adherents of the principle of lightweight attempts unemcumbered by armies of climbers, porters and Sherpas and the logistical problems they presented. In the case of Everest, however, the simple fact that it was very large, very high, unclimbed and that there were nationalist kudos attached to being first to the top had produced a battering ram mentality. Like the North and South Poles it had become an international status symbol with Britain, presumably by dint of time and effort and lives expended on it, assumed to have first claim; in the same way that the French coveted Annapurna, the Germans Nanga Parbat and the Italians K2. The announcement of Hunt's successful attempt on Everest in 1953 had been made, fortuitously, to coincide with the Coronation and although it was a New Zealander and a Nepalese Sherpa who reached the top, this did not stop an orgy of flag-waving back home. The *News Chronicle* carried the news on June 2, three days after Edmund Hillary and Tenzing Norgay planted the flags on the summit, and the opening paragraph of the main story read 'Glorious Coronation Day news! Everest – Everest the Unconquerable – has been conquered. And conquered by men of British blood and breed.'

The Hunt expedition was a microcosm of British climbing of the 30s having a distinct middle-class air about it with his crew drawn from a distinguished spectrum of professional soldiers, doctors, physicists and ex-presidents of the Cambridge and Oxford Mountaineering Clubs. The Creagh Dhu expedition, for all its haphazard nature, was the first foray by the working classes into this privileged playground and one other thing was certain: there was no Saltire on the equipment list.

The early British expeditions on the north side had been from Tibet via

the Rongbuk glacier and had reached a high point with the disappearance
of Mallory and Irvine on the North Ridge. When Nepal finally opened its
frontiers to foreigners in 1949 and the manifestly easier and more accessible south side of the mountain was available to all, little changed in the
size of assaults and the first three expeditions were as follows:

1951: The British Everest Reconnaissance Expedition.

1952: The Swiss Everest Expedition.

1953: The British and Commonwealth Everest expedition.

The fourth, much to the chagrin of a Nepalese populace engorged
by the largesse of the preceding sahibs, was the Creagh Dhu Mountaineering Club Everest Expedition and, it is safe to say, the most cavalier,
most disorganised, least successful and arguably the most fulfilling of
these four was the latter.

When MacInnes explained his Everest master plan in Christchurch
Cunningham was more than a little concerned. His cavalier friend from
Greenock had been to see a lecture in Edinburgh's Usher Hall in late 1952
given by André Roche, a member of the Swiss Everest team, and Roche
had mentioned that at the end of their unsuccessful attempt (which nevertheless reached the South Col for the first time) the Swiss had not only
left their tents in place but a massive supply of food, equipment and oxygen. Some discreet prodding of Roche in the bar later confirmed this.
MacInnes's plan was simple: a lightweight team of Scots would travel to
Nepal, storm the Khumbu Icefall and use the purloined gear to reach the
summit of Everest for the first time. That Sir John Hunt and a party of 10
climbers, 34 Sherpas and 300 porters were already in Kathmandu by that
March seemed not to matter: "Hamish just assumed they would fail," said
Cunningham. There was also the matter of a permit to enter Nepal, the
wherewithal for food, personal equipment and travelling expenses and
last, but no means least, big mountain experience.

Cunningham said: "I tried to explain to Hamish that I hadn't done
any climbing of consequence in the high mountains but his reasoning
went on the lines: 'Well, you've done Ben Nevis and a couple of peaks
like Mount Hamilton in New Zealand, so the next logical step is Everest'.
We did apply for permission but of course didn't get it so we thought
we'd apply to the Himalayan Club and got sponsored by Shipton and

Tilman who of course thought our approach was great."

The Creagh Dhu expedition, in fact, should have consisted of four members and the two who missed out were Bill Smith and Tommy Paul.

Paul says: "We'd suffered through 26 weekends of rain in a row and decided we would go and join Johnny in New Zealand. We took a lot of gear out because at the time Hamish was talking about going into Everest base camp and he wanted us to meet him there. It was all incredibly vague, as things usually were with Hamish. So vague it was untrue. Hamish had money and took a ship out and I don't know what he told Johnny but he ended up with just the two tickets and they went out to India prematurely. He probably told Johnny we were meeting them there. Four would have been a lot stronger than two and we had all that extra equipment."

Smith, too, has little doubt where to point the finger of blame: "Johnny had been out in New Zealand for about a year when I wrote to tell him that Tommy and I were going out there. What we had hoped to do was go out and get some work and then go to the Himalaya to do some climbing there. But in the meantime Hamish had gone out and met up with Johnny and told him we weren't coming out despite the fact that Johnny had a letter from us. Hamish had money, we had to go through the emigration system with an assisted passage and that took a long time. By the time Tommy and I arrived in New Zealand they were away to the Himalaya. By the time they got back Johnny had had enough of the Himalaya, especially with Hamish. It was a pity he jumped the gun when I think about it because you are far better with four in the Himalaya because if you get sick with just two you are left on your own. You can organise for four better than two."

MacInnes, however, had left Smith and Paul something to remember him by. Paul says: "When we eventually went out we took Hamish's old man's car, he just had the bloody thing shipped out. The big end had gone and Hamish had said he was going to get it fixed but of course he was away climbing Everest and we had to get it off the dock. We cursed him, Bill and I, and then of course it broke down on the way south. When he came back Hamish sold it for a boat and we were left without transport again!"

MacInnes and Cunningham, meanwhile, fine-honed their preparations in the same mode of disorganised chaos.

Cunningham said: "We intended to try the route post monsoon to avoid other expeditions, including Hunt's and we had a copy of the Daily Express which showed the Swiss route and the camps marked. Bill Murray, who had been out with the British 1951 reconnaissance, had also loaned us a map of Nepal which we had photocopied and this measured 12" x 9" and covered an area of 400 x 300 miles. The Swiss had done all the hard work, now we were going to acclimatise, reach the South Col and then strap on their abandoned oxygen and head for the summit. In the unlikely event of Everest being climbed by Hunt and the Brits who were already en route to India, the secondary target for me and Hamish was Pumori (23,129ft) behind Everest base camp."

The pair did train assiduously in New Zealand, climbing and walking with massive loads "until we were almost bow-legged".

"Even with the Himalaya Club supposedly behind us, we still couldn't get permission so just thought to hell with it and take each day as it comes and see what happens," said Cunningham. "There was a slight hiccup when Hamish drove his Norton bike over a cliff edge and forgot to let go of the handlebars. The bike was a write-off and Hamish landed in hospital but the insurance money came in very useful for things like boat fares and other incidentals."

The sea route was to take MacInnes and Cunningham from Auckland on the SS Monowai, first to Sydney and then Bombay and although they found the fares, there was a distinct reticence among potential sponsors to back the two Scots.

Cunningham said: "While in New Zealand we approached several food suppliers but the only one to respond was Nestlé who sent a rep round to the digs with a case full of different chocolate, dehydrated veg and soups. We ate most of the chocolate on the way across to India, unfortunately."

The two then worked out their loads. Apart from their weekend gear they carried 100 bars of chocolate (free, courtesy of Nestles), 14 pounds of sugar (10s 6d), 10 lb of butter (17s 6d), 12 packets of soup (free), one large tin of Pawcrisp and assorted vegetables. The rest of the food was going to come off the fat of the Indian and Nepalese land and for this they had discreetly disassembled and packed a ·22 rifle, along with 500 rounds of ammunition. In case of accident or illness there was a first-aid kit consisting of two tubes of penicillin, one bottle of iodine, one large box of elastoplast, two one-inch bandages and two two-inch bandages, one pair of scissors, one bottle of calamine lotion, one bottle of Aspros, a bottle of benzedrine tablets, the sum total of which came to 25s. For lighting and cooking they also packed 12 candles, one high altitude stove and one gallon of paraffin.

"I had my basic weekend gear and Hamish also had an all-in-one ventile suit which was bright red and caused a bit of consternation on the walk-in, particularly to the cattle in the villages," said Cunningham.

There was one final hitch before departure when the two adventurers prepared to embark at Christchurch.

"Most of the boys came down to see us off and the rucksacks weighed about 140 lbs each. Little Pat O'Donnell (ex-Lomond MC) couldn't believe the size of our packs and said: 'That's incredible you must be carrying the kitchen sink even, what size tent is it ?' Hamish looked at me, I looked at Hamish ... we had forgotten the tent. Fortunately Pat had one in his digs and ran back there to bring us a small American Yak tent measuring six feet long by four feet wide, it was quite light and it didn't have a sewn-in groundsheet or a flysheet but it was definitely better than nothing. On the way to Sydney, Hamish and I were in a cabin just above the waterline sharing with a Mr Bishop from Wellington. Mac, being a fresh-air fiend wanted the porthole open but it was jammed shut so he went off to the engine room and returned with a huge spanner to unjar it. We locked the door and settled down for the night but a squall blew up on the way across the Tasman Sea. We slept through it only to be wakened by a banging on the door. The cabin was flooded and Mr Bishop's cases were floating in the middle. While Bish cowered at the back trying to avoid the water slopping through, we tried to placate the crew who were upset by the amount of water pouring down the companionways.

"Our base camp in Sydney was an uncle of Hamish's on the outskirts of the city and we took the chance to enjoy a bit of night life in the city before we boarded the SS Stratheden which in three weeks called in at Melbourne, Adelaide and Perth before docking in Bombay."

On board the travellers passed the time playing deck tennis and occasional nocturnal jogging in an effort to remain fit. There was also an Anglo-Indian girl who taught them the rudimentaries of Urdu, the fact that no-one spoke Urdu in Nepal failing to detract from her charms.

After living in the lap of luxury for three weeks it was two very reluctant mountaineers who walked down the gangway into the hubbub of India's second largest city. As newly-enrolled members of the Himalaya Club they were entitled to the services of a representative and an incredulous Mr A.R. Leyden met the pair by the dockside.

"He was accompanied by half a dozen porters to take what he thought would be vast loads and he was quite horrified when Hamish and I shouldered our sacks and walked down into the customs shed. Mr Leyden knew his stuff, however, and with a lot of shouting and waving and threats, which seemed to them the right way to do things, he got us through customs which was fortunate because we didn't want people rooting through the gear and finding the rifle. Mr Leyden also treated us to dinner at the Taj Mahal Hotel before seeing us off from Bombay Central. He was a bit puzzled as we had told him we were going to the Hindu Kush and we then proceeded to buy tickets on the Calcutta Mail, third class to Patna, by the side of the Ganges. We were in fact travelling east, instead of north, but I think by then it had begun to sink in with him that we weren't the usual Himalayan expedition.

"We found third class a bit tedious and heavy going so we upgraded ourselves to first where they had luxuries like showers and soap. When the collector came along we just talked in broad Scots and after trying for a few minutes he would just give up and we would lock the door, spread ourselves out on the seats and sleep for most of the rest of the journey."

The sights and sounds of the subcontinent were proving an eye-opener. At Patna, the combination of the 135 lb loads and the heat proved overpowering and they decided to splash out on a horse-drawn gharry to take them to the local mission hospital with the populace turning out in force to watch the sahibs from the West of Scotland perambulate slowly down the main street. On the steamer up the Ganges, Cunningham looked on in amazement as the funeral pyres drifted slowly downriver and at Raxaul as they disembarked at Sonpur Ghat, a portly policeman stood

Buachaille Etive Mor and Jacksonville

Cunningham on the first ascent of Bluebell Grooves, Buachaille Etive Mor, East Face of the North Buttress, Lower Tier

Photo: Cunningham coll.

Above left: Cunningham with a blooded John McLean after the Ben An incident

Above right: Bill Smith

Below: Cunningham on the first ascent of Carnivore, Creag a'Bhancair, Buachaille Etive Mor

Photos: Cunningham coll.

Above: Mick Noon abseiling from the second pitch of Point Five Gully, Ben Nevis. (Insert Mick Noon after the retreat)

Below: Cunningham and Iain Finlayson – future Olympic skier – on Meall a' Bhuiridh.

Photos: Cunningham coll.

Above: The original ski-doss under Meall a'Bhuiridh

Below: Someone forgot the key to the CIC Hut. Cunningham, Bill Smith and Tommy Paul making an entry.

Photos: Cunningham coll.

Left: Bill Smith on the first ascent of The Gut, East Face of Aonach Dubh.
Photo: John Cunningham

Below: Patsy Walsh on the second pitch and during the second ascent (July 1956) of Bastinado, Cioch Buttress of Sron na Ciche, Skye.
Photo: John Cunningham

Above: John McLean and George Shields at a Trois Vallées ski resort

Photo: Tommy Paul

Below left: John and Helen Kay
Below right: Fred Harper

Photos: Jeff Connor

Above: Bill Smith

Photo: Tommy Paul

Below left: Mick Noon in 1999
Below right: Tommy Paul in 1999

Photos: Jeff Connor

Above: Davie Todd at home in 1998

Above: John Cullen in 1998   *Photos: Jeff Connor*

Below: Willie Rowney   *Photo: Tommy Paul*

Below: Bill March *en route* to The Maiden, Cape Wrath   *Photo: John Cunningham*

Above: Cunningham during the ascent of Pingero with Pumori in the background.

Below left: Cunningham descending Pingero

Below right: Load carrying – porter and Cunningham   *Photos: Hamish MacInnes*

Between Camps 1 and 2 on Disteghil Sar in 1956. Inserts: left, Dennis Davis; right, Keith Warburton extracting a tooth.

Photos: Cunningham coll.

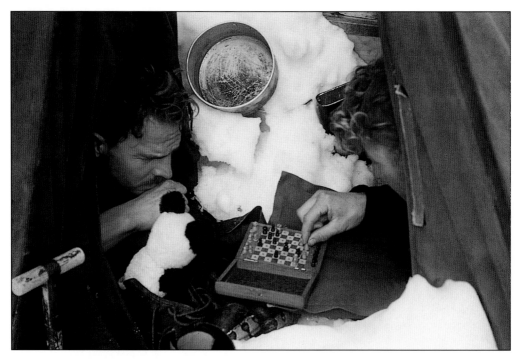

Above: Cunningham (right) giving Tony Bomford a hard time at chess, while the expedition mascot looks on.   *Photo: Tom Price*

Below: The Shackleton Cross, in left foreground, at the entrance to King Edward Cove with Mount Paget in the background.   *Photo: Cunningham coll.*

Mount Andrew Jackson, 11,700 ft, the highest peak on the Antarctic Peninsula. First ascended by John Cunningham, Jimmy Gardiner, Bill Smith and Davie Todd – all Creagh Dhu members – by its NE ridge (curving up from bottom right to top centre), in November 1964.　　　　　*Photo: Davie Todd*

Above: On Mount Andrew Jackson

Photo: Davie Todd

Below left: Entering the summit 'mushroom' on Mount Andrew Jackson.

Photo: Davie Todd

Below right: Cunningham on the McClary Glacier

Photo: Iain McMorrin

Above left: Cunningham on the first ascent of The Chancer, January 1970, and right, on the first ascent of Devil's Delight, February 1973 – both on Hell's Lum Crag. *Photos: Bill March*
Below left: Hamish MacInnes and Cunningham on the avalanche debris from No 2 Gully, Ben Nevis that nearly caught Yvon Chouinard, and right, Cunningham and bike with Chouinard on the Ballachulish Ferry.
Photos: Yvon Chouinard and Ian Nicholson resp.

Above left: Cunningham front-pointing on the Bossons Glacier, and right, on the Orion Face, Ben Nevis

Below: J R Marshall on Whortleberry Wall, Rannoch Wall, Buachaille Etive Mor, first ascended by Cunningham and Bill Smith in September 1956. *Photos: Cunningham coll.*

directing non-existent traffic in the middle of the road, relieved to justify his existence by waving the Scots through. Accommodation for the night was at the luxurious-sounding International Airways Hotel which, in fact, was an insanitary hovel with an open sewer at the rear. They spent a sleepless night throwing potatoes at rats and warding off a succession of burglars who tried to force their way in.

"Next morning it was a train to the village of Amliganje and then a ramshackle bus to Bimphedi. From there the route was a 20-mile hike over mountain passes to Kathmandu. So far so good, we were by then well into Nepal and there had been no sight of police or customs so it was a bit of a surprise when we got to the top of another pass to find a frontier post manned by a very well-educated Nepalese bloke who spoke better English than we did. He asked for permits, we showed him our passports but he wasn't going to be put off. Eventually I showed him an air mail letter I had received from my mother with an official-looking crest on the front and that seemed to satisfy him. A day's walk would take us to Kathmandu and the locals were amazed at the sight of the sahibs carrying huge packs like low-caste collies. After two days of stumbling we arrived in Patan on the outskirts of Kathmandu where we picked up the road again. There was another bus there and all the baggage was to go on top. One bloke was on the roof and Hamish handed up his sack and the guy came crashing to the ground causing no end of amusement to the locals. It was night by this time and we did not know where to go in Kathmandu. We found a taxi, a big open Lagonda and were trying to get through the town as quietly as possible without being seen but of course the taxi ran out of petrol right in the middle of town. Hamish went looking for another taxi and came back with a guy in a battered jeep. We told him we wanted to quietly slip away to a hotel and the first thing he did was drive up to a policeman to ask the way."

After a night in the Royal Hotel, the pair examined their finances and decided that they could afford a Sherpa to help with their massive loads up to Namche Bazar, the 200 miles there taking in the deep gorge of the Dudh Kosi, over mountain passes and with a final long climb up to the chief village of the Khumbu. Unfortunately, Ningma the Sherpa decided it was beneath him to carry for such low-caste sahibs but did agree to do the cooking.

Cunningham said: "The packs were desperate and if you fell over you just lay there in the mud unable to move until the other one helped you to your feet. The walk-in to Namche Bazar were fairly uneventful except we did get fitter and more devious when we met officials. I also got more devious with Hamish. We were carrying so much ironmongery so every night I disposed of the odd ice or rock peg, just the right amount each time so Hamish wouldn't notice. Then, every day when we made our packs up and I would try and finish with the slightly lighter pack. Finally, Hamish twigged that the loads were subtly different so I had to get more cunning. When it came time to depart I would move for the heavy one pretending I wanted that and Hamish would dive in and beat me to it and carry on quite happily for the day.

"Every so often we would come across the occasional frontier post and I made sure I was walking half a mile ahead of Hamish. I would bluff my way past and tell him that the 'big sahib' behind had the permits, so Hamish was landed in it. At one village we stopped for four days, bought a sheep and much to Ningma's surprise, shot it and ate it. At another stop we slaked our thirst from a nasty-looking pool and then started to wonder where all the villagers were. Ningma then informed us they had been wiped out by a cholera epidemic which caused us an anxious few weeks after that."

At Namche and after three weeks of walking, came the first major crisis of the expedition. As Hunt had found out before, the village had a small wireless station manned by a Mr Tiwari and his colleague from the Indian police and they were eager to demonstrate its worth.

"The CDMC was the fourth expedition to come this way and I think they were quite excited to see us, although we must have made a bit of a contrast to the previous three. The police told us alarmingly they had a radio but then we breathed a sigh of relief when they told us it wasn't working. I was horrified when Hamish offered to fix it as he was very good with the electrics, but Hamish was no fool – in fact he made such a good job of it that it still wasn't working when we came back through months later."

It was at Namche that they said goodbye to Ningma who, after

being paid off, took pity on his two impecunious employers and presented
them with a cup and some cutlery (Hunt's expedition had their own per-
sonalised mugs).

Namche provided a relaxing three days until the day before departure.

"There was some sort of Highland Games meeting going on and
being honoured guests they invited us to take part, when we proceeded to
clean up. Hamish won throwing the heavy stone, then throwing the light
stone, then the 100 yards dash, then the high jump. I won the pole vault at
5ft 6ins using a small tree as a pole. Then I noticed a kind of square
surrounded by a huge crowd and when Hamish arrived at my side I asked
him what was going on and he said 'It's a wrestling match and I'm your
second'. The opposition turned out to be the largest of the policemen,
about six feet in height and frothing at the mouth. He was being held back
by his mates and when they let him go he charged straight at me. I side-
stepped and got him in a hold and was declared the winner, which he took
really badly and left the sports ground in a massive sulk, refusing to speak
to anyone."

The pair were now on the last lap to Everest base camp and an easy
day's walk took them to Thyangboche which at 12,000ft must be one of
the most spectacular places on earth. The vast wall of the Everest group
bars the head of the valley and in the middle distance the Matterhorn-like
fang of Ama Dablam rises to 22,700ft, a peak to which Cunningham was
to return five years later. Camp was a grassy alp surrounded by this amazing vista in a derelict area by the Thyangboche monastery where they
discovered another problem.

"All the way across Nepal we had been cooking over wood fires to
save our paraffin supplies but here we found that the priests had gathered
all the spare wood around so we helped ourselves to a few wooden slats
off the roof of the monastery. We then moved up to an amazing camp site
below the shapely peak of Taweche, left our gear there and headed back
down to a village to buy some food. We bought 1cwt of spuds, a large tin
of cooking grease and a sheep, which was still alive."

The sheep turned out to be one of the more perceptive of its species.

"I was in charge of the potatoes, Hamish was in charge of the cooking grease and the sheep and that was the demarcation line on this trip. But about a mile from camp the sheep must have got wind of what lay ahead and got a bit reluctant. Hamish finished up half-dragging it and half-carrying it the rest of the way. Then came the problem of killing it. The monsoon rains had ruined the gun and ammo and the only knife we had (Ningma's parting gift) was blunt so we couldn't cut its throat. Bashing its head in was out of the question as we wanted to eat the brains. Anyway, it wasn't my problem, it was Hamish's, I was in charge of the potatoes and they were ready for eating.

"Hamish announced he would strangle it which I thought seemed logical and I brewed up and sat back to watch the battle with interest. He certainly wasn't getting his own way at first and the sheep was giving as good as it got but eventually he got his garotte round its neck and the food was ready."

The Creagh Dhu expedition had by now long given up its primary target. Everest had been climbed and "we didn't want to do the second ascent up the ordinary route" so attention turned to Pumori, the pencil-like peak of 23,550ft behind Everest Base Camp.

"By now our loads were even heavier as the sacks were prepared for the attempt on Pumori. By the way of food for the attempt we had 40 bars of chocolate, 15 lbs of sugar, 2 lbs of butter, 2 dozen eggs, one small sack of flour, one small sack of rice, one hindleg of mutton, 40 lbs of potatoes, two tins of marmalade, one tin of cheese and one tin of goose liver pâté, and by now with all this weight we were using the method we had got off the Sherpas, which was with a band round the head. Our survey of Pumori showed a number of likely-looking ridges with the one in the middle, which we christened Central Ridge the likeliest. We could see the rock ridge went up to about 2,000 feet and then there looked to be a decent couloir to the summit ridge. We had decided we would need two more camps, a bit of a problem with only one tent but then if there was snow we could always dig a cave. We relayed the food and gear up for the attempt and the way up from the base camp lay up an easy-angled slabby ridge to a ledge for the camp but we were held up by poor weather and whiled away the time reading poetry the only two books for the expedition being *The Golden Book of Verse*, the other the *Compete Works of Robbie Burns*.

"After an endless period of hanging around and having got through the Burns book twice and knowing *Gray's Elegy* backwards the weather cleared and we were on our way again. The plan was to move the tent up, descend for some loads, go back up to tent, edge the tent a couple of thousand feet higher, descend for more loads and so forth until, hopefully, we got to a top camp and could have a go for the top. We made a recce up a ridge and were resting on a snow slope when the weather came in again and an avalanche whishing past nearby decided us to descend but on arriving at the camp found it was no more. The rocks around it had moved and the tent was a write-off meaning a descent to lower altitudes.

"Our loads were much reduced by now but the mutton had begun to take on an unhealthy glow at night necessitating a switch to an all-potato diet. We descended to Gorak Shep and slept under a rock with remains of tent wrapped round us before going on down to a small Sherpa settlement below Taweche called Palongkarpo where we built a crude shelter against a wall there."

Without a tent and running swiftly out of food the expedition was in danger of descending into total chaos but the indefatigable Scots hadn't finished yet.

"Quite close to Taweche there was a small rock pinnacle of 19,500 feet called Pingero, The Finger, and we decided to go for this. There were three possible routes, the left-hand ridge which looked like Crowberry Ridge on the Buachaille, the second a gully running up the main face and the third the right-hand ridge which looked fairly easy apart from the last thousand feet which steepened considerably. We decided on the last. This really was a lightweight attempt as of course we had no tent. Food was two turnips which we had liberated from a local vegetable plot, four bars of chocolate and a small tin of meat paste. But the ascent went fairly uneventfully although we reached the summit just before 5.15 pm in almost total darkness and there was a bit of a near miss when a loose rock almost took Hamish away. We arrived back at camp at 3 am after a descent without torches, but at least we had got up something."

After another abortive attempt on a rock peak they had spotted above the village of Ghat that was halted by trackless and unexplored jungle above a vegetated, Clachaig Gully-type gorge it was obvious to both that the expedition was over and by unanimous vote they decided to return to Bombay.

"Without a tent any exploration was pretty much out of the question but we still had the problem of a return through Nepal and probable arrest as illegal immigrants so we decided to walk out to India and the railhead at Jaynagar. At Namche Bazar our two Indian policemen friends greeted us like long-lost brothers and showed us the great job Hamish had done on their radio: it was still defunct. Hamish also swapped his sleeping bag for some corn on the cob which was a nice supplement to the endless diet of spuds. On the way back we had some desperate river crossings across the Dudh Kosi and the Sun Kosi (once in a bosun's chair and another time by rustic canoe) because all the bridges had been swept away by monsoon floods. Finally, we came out of the jungle and saw the plain of India in front of us.

"At Jaynagar we decided to stay in the station's first-class waiting room where I found a tin tub and was enjoying a bath when a crowd of blokes burst in, shouting blue murder and looking very menacing. They identified themselves as the Indian CID – armed with umbrellas – and they started going through my clothes. They thought we were communists coming over from Tibet.

"They took us into custody but after an hour of questioning it was obvious we were not the infiltrators they had been expecting. There were smiles all round and they invited us to the cinema. Midway through the film one of the police leaned over to Hamish and asked him what he fancied to eat. Hamish said 'bacon and eggs' and the next thing the lights went up, a table was brought in and within 10 minutes we were tucking in to eggs and bacon, toast and tea watched by the cinema audience.

"Out in the streets there was a row of tables and another meal of curry followed by sticky sweetmeats with a large population of the town gathered there to watch, applauding us as we returned to the waiting room. For some reason they looked on white men eating as first-class entertainment, even better than the cinema."

The impromptu feast, in fact, proved fortuitous as the two were nearly broke.

"Checking the finances next day we found we had enough for two third class tickets to Bombay but nothing left for food so we decided to dodge the ticket collector for a day and a half, then buy cheaper tickets but at least we were able to eat from time to time. When we met Mr Leyden in Bombay we tapped him for 100 rupees, stayed in the Sally Army hotel on the waterfront for three weeks then started worrying about getting a passage back to New Zealand for me and Australia for Hamish."

The fact that they got home at all, in fact, owed everything to the largesse of John and Helen Kay over in Christchurch.

"We had been away for a few days and we got back to find a neighbour telling us the police had called in our absence," says Helen "They were looking for bail for John and Hamish who had run out of money and were in the Sally Army hostel in Bombay on their uppers. They wanted us to fork out bail guarantee of £70 each to stand the loss of the fare and get them back to New Zealand."

In the light of the trials and tribulations of the expedition, it seems amazing that the two Scots managed to remain friends. According to MacInnes "we never had a cross word" but John Kay now insists: "That was the holiday when MacInnes had the leeches on his back and John told us he never stopped whingeing, it was like Humphrey Bogart in the 'African Queen'. 'I was burning them off his back with great relish,' John told us. Later John was quite scathing about Hamish on that trip. They had a long trek back and Hamish was beginning to whine about various things and I think they had a bit of a rammy."

Cunningham, after another long sea trip that tested his vulnerability to sea sickness to the limit, returned to Christchurch where "I met up with the rest of the boys and after working for three weeks went off for a holiday ... climbing in the Southern Alps."

John returned twice more to the Himalaya on a more organised basis and on both occasions with parties under the leadership of Alf Gregory, a small, tough wiry man who in 1953 and at the age of 39 had been the second oldest in Hunt's successful Everest climbing party.

Disteghil Sar (25,250ft) in the Karakoram was the target in the May, June and July of 1956 and the party was to consist of Gregory, Cunningham, Keith Warburton, Dennis Davis, Piero Ghiglione and Dave Briggs. Warburton, the doctor, had been involved with Cunningham in a major epic on a trip to South Georgia the year previously and there is little doubt that the Scot's invitation to the Karakoram owed much to his performance there.

Dave Briggs was from Manchester and Dennis Davis, in addition to being a well-known member of the Wayfarer' and Rucksack Clubs, was a formidable alpinist who had been a member of a famously fractious expedition to Nuptse during which he had reached the summit of the Everest satellite, closely followed by a young Chris Bonington. Ghiglione, who was in his 70s, was a moneyed Italian explorer who was also the expedition's main sponsor. He had offered a Rolex watch, in fact, for any man who reached the summit.

Blackburn-born Gregory, who in 1998 was 85 and living in Australia where he had recently made one of the biggest desert crossings in Toyota LandCruisers ("I am slowing down a little and have had a couple of operations on my ankles but you have to lower your sights gradually") had in fact already considered Cunningham an ideal candidate and Warburton's recommendation simply confirmed what he already knew.

"I was living in Blackpool after the Everest trip and I had seen John around on some of his fairly frequent trips down to the Lakes. We were looking for a small team and John's name cropped up and I recalled I had climbed with him in Langdale on one of the Creagh Dhu trips there. It was a frightful day and we were going to Bowfell Buttress, with me expecting that we would climb a V Diff or something like that. John, however, decided we would do a VS even though it was pouring with rain. Of course he just waltzed up this thing brilliantly and was obviously a man who did not like wasting his weekends. He was also charming company, but then I knew the Scots sense of humour because I served in the Black Watch during the war."

Cunningham, who had been broke on his return from South Georgia, had managed to find jobbing work at Browns on his return and Gregory adds: "John had to find some money for both my trips although there was invaluable help from Piero. I spoke Italian and French and had done lectures abroad on Everest and met Piero in Europe. He was quite elderly in our terms but had a certain charm. He had also done a great deal of exploring all over the world, put a lot of money in and got us backing. We called it an Anglo-Italian expedition which it wasn't of course but it helped with sponsorship and we got some backing from the Mount Everest Foundation."

Davis was late arriving as he had been on an unsuccessful attempt on Annapurna II with Charles Evans, the deputy leader of the successful Everest expedition of 1953. Annapurna II, in fact, was climbed subsequently by an army expedition containing Bonington and Davis muses now: "I often wonder how mountaineering history may have been rewritten if we had been first to the top."

From London originally, Davis was well-known for an inability to suffer fools gladly as he had shown on Nuptse where friction within the party had almost led to high-altitude fisticuffs. Intolerant of others' laziness, on the face of it he would have formed a formidable team with Cunningham although, as it turned out, the pair were never to climb together. Davis, who now lives in Leek, Staffordshire, and pours all his still formidable energy into the game of golf, says: "I was suffering with throat problems although coming straight from Annapurna II, I was well acclimatised when I went over to Disteghil Sar. I had never met John before but I was an isolated climber out of the mainstream. In Lahore I found a letter from John waiting describing the route in along with a hand-drawn map of the route out to Hispar and the Khunyang Glacier where Base Camp was to be. He had also very kindly left 700 rupees. I was in a very bad way with my throat and I was having to be carried and the porters, it turned out were from a penal settlement, One day I caught one of them going through my rucksack and in every respect they were useless.

"When I got to Base Camp after 10 days I was very ill but Keith Warburton just gave me some Tyrozets. The pattern of weather soon settled in: seven bad days followed by three fine days. On July 1, I woke to tea and porridge at 5.30 am and the usual sight of Piero shaving. He and John shaved every day, in Piero's case reasoning that 'if I shave I don't look so old'. John presumably thought the same. Piero was quite a character and he even carried a small load to 20,000 ft. When the expedition came to a premature end all he could think of was his bad luck in missing the end of the summer skiing back home in Europe."

The Disteghil Sar expedition, like all three of Cunningham's Himalayan trips, was dogged by bad luck on and off the mountain.

Gregory recalls: "Base Camp was at 15,000 feet at the foot of the south face and after several recces we found a route which led to a col west of the summit. But the weather was appalling and there were what seemed continual avalanches. The route on the face was fairly well protected but off it, it was continually swept by them. Even so one camp was destroyed by avalanches, fortunately when no one was in it."

Davis recalls one close shave: "At Camp 1 we were looking up at the summit and suddenly saw this little puff of smoke which got larger and larger until we realised it was heading straight for us. We started looking for shelter, the tents were no good of course, but as it happened a big ridge separated us from it and the avalanche went down one side leaving what seemed like a snowstorm of particles for 15 minutes."

Nor were the problems confined to the weather. Both Davis and Cunningham had testy confrontations with the porters and Davis says: "The porters were useless, all Nagars who thought nothing of pinching equipment. None of them liked going far, even the sirdar who just wanted to collapse in the snow all the time. One time he was on my rope and I lost patience and just started dragging him. I had been spoiled by people like Dawa Tenzing on previous expeditions. After a time it became obvious the weather was not going to change so we started packing up to go. But at the time we were within striking distance of the left-hand ridge and it looked straightforward from there. John was ill at one time with chest problems and he had to go back down."

Gregory confirms: "We made four camps on the mountain and reached just under 22,000 feet. Finally we had to turn back when it became apparent that the weather was continuing to be so bad and the dangerous snow conditions would not improve this year. We had only eight good days in two months."

There were a couple of memorable incidents on the way home.

"We had a short stay in the British embassy in Kathmandu and we all got legless on 151% proof navy rum. They were pouring beakerfulls of the stuff down us." says Davis. "On the boat back from Bombay to Liverpool there was one incident that sticks in my mind when John was bending down for something and one of the stewards made some remark. John said to him very quietly and very menacingly: 'I wouldn't advise you to try anything.'

"I went back a couple of years ago, to Labuche Peak East, and was able to look straight across at Nuptse which brought back a lot of memories, most of them pleasant I should say. I also met Dawa Tensing's daughter which was very nice."

Cunningham's third and final trip to the Himalaya was in 1958 to Ama Dablam, the incredibly shapely peak five miles south of Everest which had been on climbers' wish list – including Cunningham's – since 1950 when Bill Tilman and the American Charles Houston first entered the area. Gregory, who had teamed up with Cunningham most of the time on Disteghil Sar, says: "John seemed to do well at altitude and had the right attitude for Himalayan trips. In the tent he talked a little about the trip with Hamish and I was intrigued because it sounded like a great adventure and quite comical, some of the things that happened to them. Anyway, I invited him back along with the indefatigable Piero to have a go at Ama Dablam but again we had little good fortune."

Ama Dablam's southern ridges stretching into the Mingbo valley, in fact, were formidable propositions and a hanging glacier at 21,5000 feet protects the south-west face. Cunningham got to 20,000 feet on the south ridge until stopped by a huge overhang at the foot of a yellow tower and the mountain was not climbed until 1960 by a party led by Mike Ward.

Ed Bishop, Gumen Dorje and Pemba Tensing had reason to be grateful for Cunningham's early pioneering, however, and Bishop reported: "We found a number of fixed ropes on the way and there was some really amazing climbing. The ridge above Camp 1 was truly Alpine in character, serrated and fantastically exposed. At one point below the tower the ridge became knife-edged and we had to go à cheval. A fixed rope, left by Cunningham, was found and, as it appeared safe, used."

Hamish MacInnes returned to Everest three times and was deputy leader of Bonington's successful South-West face expedition in 1975, a titanic project backed by Barclays Bank to the tune of £100,000 and with Bonington employing a computer programme to plan the logistics. A greater contrast between Bonington's military stratagems and the naive wanderings of MacInnes and Cunningham would be difficult to find, but for all the high-powered efficiency of Bonington's trips the expedition still lost a climber, Mick Burke, and a porter, while the Scots returned physically unscathed. MacInnes reflects: "Having been back to Everest I don't think John and I would have made it although dafter things have happened in the mountains. Technically we were well capable of it and at that time we were very fit. The Khumbu Icefall would have presented the biggest problems and I think probably we would have run out of steam somewhere there. John Hunt told me later that they had used all the food and gear of the Swiss anyway although the original concept was a good one. Now of course parties of that size are par for the course. Last year I had a communication from André Roche, the guy who had started it all saying: 'Sorry to hear you never made it!' And that was 45 years ago."

Chris Lyon saw the Everest expedition as of more meaningful social significance.

"John's contribution was not his great number of first ascents but that he was first Scot to crack the class barrier and get on high expeditions. During the war years it was almost impossible to mount an expedition to the Cuillin, let alone Kathmandu. Prewar each member of a Himalayan expedition was expected to ante up his share of the trip's expenses and also qualify that he could rough it with the chappies. The yardstick of a sportsman was playing silly mid-off for Surrey Cricket Club or a rowing Blue at Oxford. Not that these prewar expeditions did any harm but they did not conquer many great peaks, either."

More important to Cunningham than acceptance in mainstream mountaineering was his acceptance by his peers in the Creagh Dhu, whose high standards in this respect were well known.

When Lyon decided to step down as president, Cunningham was the unanimous choice as replacement and while not possessing his predecessor's gift with the spoken or written word, his deeds had given him the universal respect of the club. Lyon had in fact become disenchanted with what he saw as a commercial intrusion into climbing (Cunningham and MacInnes after their return from the Himalaya in 1953 had some explaining to do about a series of lurid newspaper accounts of the trip in the *Daily Record*) and Lyon said:

"Lesser men than John realised that if they were to follow his example and get on the big expeditions they had to get their faces known to the selectors. The new mass media of TV had brought the rock face to the armchairs of millions of viewers. It got to the stage where these young mountaineers were more concerned with camera angles than rock face angles. Worst still, if one of their number was selected to join an expedition ahead of them they carried on like pampered prima donnas. As the president of the Creagh Dhu who with the passage of time had lost the lithe resilience of youth I was no longer able to climb alongside them and appeal to reason Leading from the front was the only method I knew. When this became no longer possible a decision had to be taken."

Lyon stood down, ending 15 years as president, but his final club dinner was a memorable one and illustrates the problems any formal leader would have in the anachronistic club.

"I didn't want to go but I was persuaded by my wife Maggie," said Lyon. "It was in fact wonderful to be back yarning with the boys and swapping yarns of the glories of yesteryear. Then the new president, John Cunningham, rose to make a speech. Now in the past the Creagh Dhu considered speeches a waste of good drinking time and I had only once heard Johnny make a speech before and that had gone into Creagh Dhu legend. He was departing on one of his expeditions, so the Boys decided this was grand excuse for a farewell party. The venue was the wooden shack annexe of the posh Trossachs Hotel. The club, 30 handed, had got roaring fou and some of the young bloods decided Johnny had to give a farewell speech and carried him shoulder high through the milling throng, smashing a picture frame and a light bulb in the process. Johnny landed in the centre of a large circular table and was told to get on with it. By this time the barman had had enough and was on the phone to the police at Callander to break up the party. Overhearing the conversation I urged some of the stalwarts to get the boys out because the place was far too crowded to invite any gatecrashers. 'Let them all come', they growled.

"Johnny was going great guns and finished his oration. The Boys cheered, Johnny bowed, stepped back and the table upended, Johnny and 40 whisky glasses exiting through the rear window. The table rolled over and split in two. The phone rang and the bartender answered: the police car had skidded in snow at Kilmahog and the two cars behind had run into it. The barman poured himself a stiff dram and said: 'If you can't beat them ... ' Then Johnny's head popped through the gaping window opening and said: 'Sorry, barman it was a wee accident, I'll fix it tomorrow.'

'That's OK son, that's the only farewell speech that literally brought the house down and at the same time smashed up the whole of the Callender Flying Squad.'

"Now years later I listened with great expectation for Johnny's follow-up. He began stumbling through a prepared speech singing high the praises of the outgoing president. This I found to be uncomfortably embarrassing. The Creagh Dhu were never people to display sentimental emotion. By the nature of our chosen sport, where a climber could be jesting with his mates on a vertical rock wall one minute and the next be gazing at a rag bag of mangled bones and snoaters, it wasn't good for the nerves of the survivors to be outwardly emotional. The invitation card to any Creagh Dhu function never stated dress formal. It mattered not whether a member arrived in black tie and tails hired for the occasion from the West End Misfits, full Highland regalia, natty suit or straight from the hill in climbing clobber. The club wished to see you, not your wardrobe. That evening in the company were a small group of new members who had joined since my departure and they wore the uniform of the absolute non-conformist. Denim jackets, beads and shoulder length hair. This group held the obvious opinion that the presidential remarks had nothing to do with VS climbing and in the fashion of their cult ignored the president and other listeners and began an intimate discussion on a projected new climb. Some members and their ladies called them to order and requested due respect be given to the presidential maiden speech. The president wisely laid down his notes, then addressing the foregathered company in general and the young members in particular his caustic tones cut through the babble.

'I confess I don't know how I shall lead this club. One thing is for sure, I won't be able to emulate the outgoing president's authority.'

"The word authority brought immediate reaction from the young bloods who growled openly. 'Aye, authority,' snapped Johnny. 'The trouble with you bums is you misinterpret every word in the language. Work to you lot is the most obscene four-letter word in the English language, authority is what we had over the years from the past president and mebbe it's something you have need of.' With that, Johnny thrust into my hand a rolled parchment scroll tied with a red ribbon. I gingerly untied the ribbon, because not only was Johnny an outstanding athlete and mountaineer extraordinaire, he was also world champion Joe the Joker and I half expected a blast of soot in the face or something. The parchment was illustrated with an original hand-painted picture of the Buachaille and Jacksonville, superimposed was the Creagh Dhu crest and these words: 'This scroll was presented to Chris Lyon by his friends and colleagues to mark the termination of his term in office as President of the Creagh Dhu Mountaineering Club. It also serves as a sign of their respect for him both as a person and a mountaineer.' For a bunch that never wore their hearts on their sleeves this was something else again!"

After his abortive sorties in the Himalaya, Cunningham returned to native rock. The 1958 ascent of Bluebell Grooves, as it turned out, was to signal the highpoint of Cunningham's explorations in Glencoe although he did second the thrusting young Great White Hope, John McLean, on two more hard routes on Creag a Bhancair a year later and there are odd scattered gems in Northern Scotland as a legacy to his explorer's eye. Most of his later explorations were to come in the Cairngorms. As for Glencoe, there is little doubt there would have been more first ascents but for a restless spirit which could not confine him to British hills. New Zealand and the Himalaya had been less than successful; the land of Scott, Shackleton and Amundsen proved a different, more fulfilling experience altogether.

GOING SOUTH

In the summer of 1955 Tommy Paul and John had met their old Creagh Dhu friend, Jack Thomson, in Glasgow shortly after their return from New Zealand, a trip that had convinced both there were horizons that stretched far beyond the cranes and derricks of the Clyde. Thomson had just begun a long and distinguished career as an instructor at Glenmore Lodge in the Cairngorms and suggested there might be work for them. The warden, Charlie Cromar, took on the two young Glaswegians on a work-share basis with a wage of £5 a week.

"We were to be instructors and help out with the maintenance," says Paul. "We would instruct, mainly school parties, during the day and help out round the place at other times, taking care of the generators, maintaining the Land Rovers and stuff like that.

"Then a chap came to the Lodge, an Englishman called Tim Allen, nice chap. He was up there skiing and he was telling us he was going down to South Georgia with a party as a mountaineer.

"We had little or no idea where South Georgia was but we thought it was fascinating. Then one night we were up in the room talking about it and Tim told us he was beginning to have second thoughts about it. He said: 'I don't think I will go but one of you two could'.

"The problem was there was only a place for one and we decided to flip a coin for it. John won, Tim Allen dropped out and recommended John in his place and that's how he got on the South Georgia trip."

To this day, Paul remains dubious about the legality of that spin of a coin.

"Cunningham and the lads had me on for years with the short straw trick where I would always end up with the short straw and they would produce the long one, for years they fooled me until I realised they were cheating, the bastards. I mean I wouldn't trust Johnny with the straws so I've no doubt he had a two-headed penny or something. Anyway, he went and I stayed."

The trip south was to consist of eight freelance explorers under the leadership of Duncan Carse, who for many years in the 50s and 60s thrilled radio audiences in his role as Dick Barton, Special Agent. At the time South Georgia, a rugged island measuring 120 miles by 15 lying just to the north of the Antarctic circle was only part-explored and four large gaps existed on the map. It was a British territory (although as is well known by now Argentina disputed this), the only human inhabitants being the meteorologists and radio operators and personnel of Falkland Islands Independencies Survey in the north of the island and those at the scattered whaling stations. Carse's plan was to fill in the missing sectors, departing in late August, 1955, and taking eight months.

Louis Baume was his deputy, an horologist and archivist who later ran Gaston's Alpine Books in Muswell Hill, London, a shop that specialised in early mountaineering literature. Keith Warburton, Tom Price, Cunningham, Stan Paterson, George Spenceley and Tony Bomford made up the rest of the party, most of whom were experienced Alpinists, although Carse was mainly a sailor and Bomford a surveyor. Most were intellectuals, and Baume and Carse definitely establishment, but the carpenter from the shipyards of Glasgow fitted in well and all were later to be grateful that he was on the trip. Price, who was a teacher of English at the time but who later went on to become a distinguished outdoor educationalist and is known to thousands of students and instructors as the warden of the Outward Bound Mountain School in Eskdale, a post he held from 1961-68, says:

"Carse wanted to map the island properly and he wanted some climbers in his party of eight and an old pal of mine, Keith Warburton, suggested me. Then he wrote to all the climbing clubs which is where the others got to hear about it. There were no expenses but Carse promised a gratuity of £100 when we got back to tide us over until we got work. John obviously was a working man but he fitted in very well and was highly respected. He would give Tony Bomford regular beatings at chess, but you always sensed a competitive streak there; if you beat him at something he wouldn't rest until he got you back."

After a sea journey of 30 days aboard the SS Southern Opal, broken only by a 12-hour stop at Dakar for refuelling, Cunningham came on deck on October 4, 1955, to see the north coast of the island of South Georgia free of all clouds and with the snow-covered mountains sparkling in the clear sunlight. It was a mountaineer's paradise and its effect was not lost on Cunningham, helping to dispel the effects of his chronic seasickness. Unloading began at once of the scores of boxes of equipment, tents and sledges, along with 200 gallons of kerosene, into Leith harbour in Fortuna Bay.

A massive upthrust of mountains, South Georgia rises steeply from the Southern Ocean to a height of nearly 10,000ft. and is covered year long with snow and ice with innumerable glaciers. Only along the coast is there vegetation and animal life; a few hundred feet of climb from the sea led to a primeval wilderness of ice and wind. Notorious for its bad weather, the island produced wet and cold in summer and a temperature rarely less than 25° C below. There were fierce winds of 70 knots rising to 110 knots at times. It is only along the coast that there is friendliness and shelter in the company of birds, penguins and the comical elephant – and voracious leopard – seals with the odd scavenging killer whale. Occasionally, an albatross would drift overhead on its long trip back from sea to feed a fledgling. Cunningham fell in love with this strange continent at once, although this first trip was to turn into a major epic that almost cost him and the seven others their lives.

The survey had been organised into four separate journeys with each journey to last 30-60 days. Base camp was at Fortuna Bay on the more hospitable north of the island where, with the expedition mascot Sandra the Panda looking on, Cunningham would fill in time between checkmating Bomford with trawls through a whole arsenal of books, his favourites then and later being Louis L'Amour westerns. From Fortuna the party would venture out hauling heavily-laden sledges – their frames coated with a petroleum-based varnish called Epikote to protect them from severe weather and hard wear – over crevassed glaciers and unmapped cols and peaks. On the Kohl-Larsen plateau Cunningham and Price marvelled at the unnamed and unclimbed peaks to the north-west but most of the time the days were governed by the demands of science, Bomford and others taking observations with a Tavistock theodolite while John and Price wrote down the readings and made sure the 'civvies' didn't fall down a crevasse. There was some climbing done, including a first ascent of Spaaman (6,367ft) in the Allardyce Range and some others further south in the Salvesen range. Throughout those long weeks they lived in a world devoid of life. Nothing stirred and nothing breathed except for the distant roar of an avalanche. The returns to the coast and the sound of terns, gulls and seals were a relief. The sledging undoubtedly tested the teamwork of the party who nonetheless and despite their disparate backgrounds proved a contented mix.

The second journey was mainly along coast, but then they were in the interior, manhauling sledges over glaciers and mountain passes and surveying from small peaks. Life was extremely simple and as a party they were completely self-supporting. At times, storms with winds up to 125mph kept them tentbound for up to eight days at a time, when it was just a case of snuggling into sleeping bags to ride out the storm. It was only on the fourth trip that anything resembling discord surfaced in an incident that 15 years later took Cunningham to the edge of the libel courts. Price says:

"The final journey was not really a surveying trip but an attempt on Mount Paget, the highest mountain of South Georgia and unclimbed at the time. John and I were supposed to be the summit party and when Bomford wanted to snatch another survey en route there was the nearest thing we ever had to a quarrel. The compromise was for the main party to press on while the survey party did its work. They were to follow three hours later to a camp whose exact location was not known. When the weather turned bad Carse had everyone out to guide the survey party in but in the event the survey party found the camp and the others didn't. So it was the divided aims that led to the debacle."

Both Baume and Cunningham's version differed greatly. Baume wrote later: "Now we were in the fourth journey, the last. It had started off with a change of plan made necessary by the damage suffered during an eight-day storm and the resultant shortage of time. The result was that initially we had to cross some difficult terrain near the lower reaches of the Neumayer Glacier, impeded by poor weather and lack of snow cover on bare rock-hard ice. Triple lateral moraines barred the route and a chaos of crevasses and knife-edge séracs across which we had to pass with loads of 60 lbs balancing precariously above the depths. Finally we found a way through and were soon sledging along the upper reaches of the Neumayer Glacier."

At the camp on the Kohl-Larsen Plateau, 3000ft above sea level, a 'mild' blizzard blew up and kept them in their tents for two days and when it cleared Bomford and two of the others set out to take trig bearings while the other five, including Price, Carse and Cunningham, began to move camp towards a 4000ft col. When the weather worsened events spiralled rapidly out of control. Believing that the surveying party could not be far away, the five rescuers went out taking nothing, no equipment, no food. In the hurricane they couldn't find the others or the tents. With blinding snow and 100mph winds they were soon lost and wandered round for a couple of hours or more looking for either the camp or a suitable crevasse for shelter.

Cunningham, in typical understated, tongue-in-cheek style, later told Ken Wilson in a *Mountain* interview: "While the other three were out a hurricane blew up causing a sort of low-level white-out with spindrift being whipped along up to six feet above the ground. When the boys hadn't returned for a full day someone insisted we should go out and look for them. This was a mistake. I stuck some food in my pocket and off we went, with no ropes or ice axes, to sweep the plateau. In the meantime, the survey party were descending a nearby mountain and could see the tops of the tents sticking out above the white-out, so they were able to take a compass bearing and get back safely. We, on the other hand, were swept way off course by the hurricane and eventually we lost the tents. We hadn't got compasses or bivouac gear and the only food was what I had in my pockets. Eventually, when it began to get dark someone suggested sitting down and huddling together for the night. I thought this was crazy; the wind was going about 110 knots and we would certainly have perished if we had stayed out in that. So I looked around, found a depression, bashed it in and broke through to a crevasse. It was bridged about 30ft down. I went back to the others and told them, but they still preferred to stay out in the open so I jumped into the crevasse and was comparatively sheltered. About two hours later they all started to jump into the hole as they were finding it a bit cold outside."

The five spent two days in the crevasse, soaked and without food.

Snow began to be blown in to bury them. They huddled together for warmth and stamped their feet, anything to avoid going to sleep because that would have meant death. On the third morning the blizzard was just as bad and Cunningham took the decision that they had to abandon the others and the camp and make a break for the coast, 16 miles away, a route identical to the one followed by Sir Ernest Shackleton on his epic crossing by sea in an open boat from Elephant Island to South Georgia followed by a desperate trudge the length of the island.

Crawling out of the crevasse, Cunningham and the others were met by an icy blast and with the party in a dangerously weakened condition, things were getting crucial. Cunningham added: "We had to descend a big glacier with lots of crevasses and the only way we could safeguard each other was by linking hands." He went into one crevasse and later implied to Wilson that the other four had been less than diligent in attempting a rescue, although as Price says: "There was nothing we could really do about it with no ropes or ice axes."

Cunningham again: "I managed to bridge out – it took about half an hour – and I took my boots off and climbed in socks, allowing them to freeze on to the walls of the crevasse before making each move upwards. Slowly, I gained height and eventually got out."

Cunningham then caught the others up, took over the lead again and the badly-battered party arrived eventually at Husvik whaling station on the south of the island where they discovered that the missing three had found the tents on the first afternoon and given them up for dead. Undaunted by the experience, some went back to recover the abandoned gear and even finished the survey before they sailed round to Leith Harbour and caught the boat back home.

So ended Cunningham's first trip south, a trek that not only whetted his appetite for more but led to some unfortunate repercussions much later when Carse and Baume read the *Mountain* interview and Cunningham's version of the South Georgia epic. However, as Price said later, it was a typical embellishment on John's part and leaving someone to die was "just the sort of thing the Creagh Dhu would do". The expedition, said Price, ended in an atmosphere of *bon accord* and both Warburton's and Baume's written statements about the debt the whole party owed

Cunningham played a large part in his award of the Perry Medal by the British Antarctic Survey later.

Warburton in his commendation said: "In no visibility over a surface of crusted skavler patterned with deep drifts of powder snow, the five of us set a shaky course for the head of the Neumayer Glacier. At first there was much sprawling in and out of crevasses but this soon gave place merely to tripping or being blown over, a reassurance that we were solidly on the Kohl-Larsen Plateau. Hard put to stop and quite unable to go back we presently found ourselves on a steepening down-slope with more crevasses. This was not at all proper; the accepted descent from plateau to glacier is a gentle declivity without a hole. At this point of crisis the practical leadership devolved on Cunningham who led magnificently in conditions and over ground which were both extremely dangerous."

Baume added: "Got hopelessly entangled in crevasses, decided to try and find some small crevasses for temporary shelter. Goggles, hood and beard one solid mass, situation looking pretty serious. John leading brilliantly and suddenly way down became clear: steep ice slopes leading down, crawling over crevasses on bellies and sliding down on our bottoms."

Price, although later "shocked" by the *Mountain* interview, had remained friends with Cunningham. Three years after the Georgia trip – "When the Creagh Dhu came down to the Lakes in 1959, John rang me and invited me over. It was a drizzly, summer day, so typically they chose Kneewrecker Chimney reasoning that it wouldn't be wet because it was overhanging. I was very, very impressed with Bill Smith who got up with no problem. John, it must be said, had a bit of a struggle. I never thought any the worse of him for the South Georgia thing. I spent the first eight weeks in tent with John there, although personnel were swapped around, and I have never known a more efficient man under canvas and he was a great raconteur."

It was around the early 60s that advertisements, taken out by the British Antarctic Survey, started to appear in magazines like *Climber and Rambler* and in the newsletters of the major clubs inviting applications for 18-month trips – six months were spent sailing there and back – to the coldest place on earth. The Survey needed General Assistants, GAs as they soon became known, to fill non-specific roles as climbers or divers and act as what amounted to minders to the meteorologist, surveyors and geologists staffing the BAS stations of Antarctica. The attractions were obvious: the money was good, there was nowhere to spend it and there was a promise of climbing and exploration on a continent that offered enough adventures for a lifetime.

Parties sailed out from Southampton on the John Biscoe, a vessel named after the retired Royal Navy captain who first discovered Enderby Island in the schooner Tula in 1830. As Bill Smith, who went out in 1964 with Cunningham, Davie Todd and Jimmy Gardiner on what amounted to a Creagh Dhu Antarctic Expedition, says:

"It was just a great opportunity to go and visit the place. It took three months sailing out and three months back so there was no question of having second thoughts. It's one of the most beautiful places you could go to, especially when the weather is good. With the geologists and people like that you just had to make sure they didn't do anything daft and we must have done all right because the time we were there, there weren't any accidents and the year after when we left three or four fell down crevasses."

The continent of Antarctica is five and a quarter million square miles, 96% of which is ice and its vast lonely wastes have been the scene of countless acts of heroism and occasional folly. Initial explorations were carried out in the name of science, but there is little doubt that in the case of Britain in particular there was the occasional political motive. The race to the South Pole and much of the colonisation there was a throwback to the days of the Raj with freelance and wealthy professional adventurers or ex-army officers heading there in an effort to raise the Union Jack before a host of other claimants, Chile and Argentina being the main opposition. Robert Scott's ill-fated attempt to beat Amundsen to the South Pole in 1912 perhaps encapsulates everything both romantically heroic and perversely nationalistic about Arctic exploration. Like Dunkirk and Arnhem it became a defeat to celebrate: the long fight against insuperable odds, the gallant gentleman wandering out into a blizzard to sacrifice himself for his companions, the harrowing last photographs and Scott's final poignant diary entries. There were over 100 applicants to go on Scott's trip and over the next half century there were plenty of other candidates willing to undergo privation, hardship and the misogynistic society in exchange for exploring a new world.

As Cunningham reported: "It's not as unpleasant as you would think. There's lots of booze but no women of course. You just have to grin and bear it. Life isn't too bad, though. There are plenty of books which are renewed regularly and every week we would have a party with booze and lots of good food. Some of the lads developed a remarkable skill in cooking. Most of the people who go out there become remarkably well balanced, taking their pattern of behaviour from their companions. The climate can get on your nerves at times; during storms the snow keeps blasting into the hut and blocking the doorway. You have to dig yourself out regularly."

With up to 30 differing personalities under the same roof in the same base and with the only alternative company being the dogs or an occasional penguin, it goes without saying that the vetting procedure had to be fairly comprehensive. What constituted the right stuff for Antarctica, however, was open for interpretation as Davie Todd's story of his preliminary interview illustrates: "The interview was at the BAS headquarters in Gillingham Street, London and I was ushered into this vast, oak-panelled room by a uniformed flunkey who announced me as 'Mr David Todd'. There was a line-up of old boys there along with Cunningham who was base leader for that trip.

"The interview went all right until near the end one of the guys started shuffling his papers and clearing his throat, obviously with a deep meaningful question to ask. He said: 'Well, Todd, there is just one last thing. You are in the Antarctic and, er, one of the other young gentlemen there starts, er, well, taking, er, an interest in you. What would you do about that?'

"I looked round the room and there is Cunningham with his tongue in his cheek and his head to the side trying hard not to laugh. I gathered he wanted me to go for it so I said: 'Well, I'd just hit him with my handbag.'

'Well, er, thank you, Todd, that will be all.' "

The qualifications for BAS trips were obvious: as well as the practical side of maintaining bases a man needed self-reliance in the face of blizzards, cold and crevasses. He was part of a team and had to get on with that team but in many ways he also had to be used to solitude. The quiet, contemplative nature of life there interspersed with trips out into the fierce environment suited Cunningham down to the ground. For more gregarious characters like Bill Smith one trip was enough.

Cunningham joined the Falkland Island Dependencies Survey as the BAS was then in January, 1960, when a vacancy caused by illness came up and because of his past experience in South Georgia, he was put in charge of Base A at Port Lockroy on the Antarctic Peninsula as part of a five-man team. The salary was £1150 a year – plus full board.

Cunningham swiftly adapted to life down south, leading a number of short ski/climbing journeys on Wienke Island in between surveying trips and revelling in his status as the Governor. Base leaders who, according to the great polar explorer Sir Vivian Fuchs, had to set an example as 'the standard he achieves will set the scene for the year' were first sworn in as magistrates by the Governor of the Falkland Islands on the way down. Bases were also Post Offices, and Falkland Island stamps used for letters home, although in Cunningham's case this was to be the source of some later friction.

Cunningham said: "This was quite a step up from the riotous days of Scotland and New Zealand. Now I had the power to put others in the clink. I never used this power, though and my duties of office were really confined to holding courts of enquiry when aircraft crashed or something like that."

The following year John was transferred to take charge of a base which was to be rebuilt on Stonington Island, Marguerite Bay, in an effort to extend BAS fieldwork south of latitude 70° S. There were light aeroplanes in support and an advance base was set up at Fossil Bluff, 71° S, some 200 miles south of Stonington, where Cunningham's skills as a carpenter proved more than useful.

Willie Rowney says: "I always remember Johnny told me a story when they were building an extension or something on one of the bases and Johnny was working on the roof, hammering in the nails and he noticed this guy coming across quietly and taking the nails out of his box. He thought Johnny had some special nails that didn't bend and every second one he drove in was bending so he thought Johnny must have better nails than him. Johnny seemed to thrive in the Antarctic. Bill didn't take to it at all; the inactivity in winter drove Bill mad but Johnny got right into photography, making it an art form almost and he used to play chess by radio, things like that."

The building of the depot on Stonington Island began in the spring of 1961 with the route reconnaissance for the expedition being over sea. On one of these trips the ice broke up and two tractors were stranded on a small island and again John's practicality came to the fore with a quick revision of his plans. Because their retreat was cut off he was unable to send the vehicles on south and had to find a means of supplying the party with the necessary extra rations. With another companion in the survey he set off on skis and using dog sledges to deliver the supplies, forced a new route over mountainous and heavily glaciated country, carefully by-passing the area of broken sea ice. His own plans to go south had to be abandoned because of the supply position and instead he led journeys east across the Graham Land plateau for geological purposes.

The present chairman of the UK Mountain Leadership Training Board, Iain McMorrin, was on the same trip, arriving in early 1962 on the John Biscoe after stops *en route* at Montevideo and Port Stanley.

Born in Zimbabwe, McMorrin was an impressionable 23-year-old at the time and retains lasting memories of Antarctica and Cunningham.

"We were held up in Stanley, John was already at Stonington, and we spent some time experimenting with a Muskey motor vehicle as they had planned to send one into Stonington for the first time ever. These turned out to be quite lethal contraptions because if they went through sea ice you had a few seconds to exit vertically through a trapdoor in the roof. We all agreed dogs were a lot safer. I hadn't heard of John then and found him a man of few words, definitely not a loquacious sort and not into idle chat. I thought him a fairly tough person, although he did not set out to impress. I was wide-eyed in this new environment and I obviously respected John as a mountaineer and of course he was base leader. His philosophy was that although he was willing to offer advice, a lot of it you had to pick up for yourself. Another new guy on that trip, John Clenell, an ex-army type who had lost an eye in Cyprus, went out for a week's dog training trip with my team, the Spartans. John gave us a tent, a ridiculously small thing and told us: 'That will do for you'. I think he thought 'Well, if you are as good as you think you are, off you go'. That was John's way of blooding you but it was great, you were having fun and were well paid and were very well fed. I had never driven a dog team but soon learned that it would have been hard to do without them. They made the place endurable and were wonderful friends, they communicated with you in a way that humans could not. John's team were the Giants I think, and he looked on them the same way.

"Stonington was a very small base with space for 12 and there were 10 of us and accommodation was in a little alcove of bunks, so you were quite close to everyone else. On one trip across the North-East Glacier there had been a lot of crevasses and it was quite frightening, so much so that I had nightmares for weeks afterwards, waking up in the middle of the night shouting and thinking I was dropping into one. One night after that John produced this loaded pistol from under his pillow and told me: 'No more screaming in the night, McMorrin. This is for you if you get out of control!' "

"A lot of the time was spent reading or playing chess and cooking. The rota was for two days cooking and two days as assistant cook which meant basically you washed up. This turned into massive sessions of one-upmanship and John was competitive even at that. The idea was to dry faster than the guy who was washing and reject anything that wasn't sparkling clean. John would do his best to find a spot, it was a game he liked playing. The competition spread into wrestling bouts which of course John would win easily because he was inordinately strong; he would just put a hold on you get you in a locked position and that was it. I think there were a couple of guys John didn't take a shine to on that trip and he could be very sarcastic, or ironic depending on who was getting the brunt of it, at times. I also found him a very private sort of person. He told us stories about the Everest trip and some of the yarns about the antics of the Creagh Dhu, but the rest was a closed book. To this day I couldn't even tell you if he had brothers or sisters or what background he came from. But there was a civilised air about him, he had an awareness of the world."

McMorrin and others at Stonington also heard the disturbing echoes of

Cunningham's aversion to water.

"We took it in turns to empty the toilet which was just a bin basically. If you were on gash for the day it was your job and you would take a sledge and a couple of dogs and drive down to the sea. If there was a gap in the sea ice it would go down that, otherwise in the open sea. But on your own there it was all extremely vulnerable. If you went in the water it was almost certainly curtains and there was no one to help you. I remember John was always very worried about this. I could see he was quite frightened of the water."

Because of the accident with the tractors and the aborted mission south and, typically feeling the job he had started incomplete and because he wanted to recover the ground lost, Cunningham volunteered to remain for a third year south, an invitation swiftly taken up by his employers.

This time his team succeeded in getting two more tractors over to Fossil Bluff where they assisted in survey work throughout the season. With an aircraft in close support he achieved a large amount of triangulation of George V1 Sound. During 1961 and '62 Cunningham covered about 1,000 miles on skis driving a dog team, and his exploits won him a recommendation for the Polar Medal. Cunningham came to love the polar huskies – the brave, independent and occasionally vicious animals who became the normal means of haulage in the Antarctic. Originally imported from Labrador they were bred at the individual bases and the men there soon took a fierce, covetous pride in their own teams often unwilling to let other drivers use them. Unlike tractors they rarely broke down, although as Cunningham explained, they had to grow up to know who was top dog.

He said: "That is how I trained my team. I made it clear to them all that I could beat them all and that I was King Dog. I used to yell great Scottish war cries when I beat them. After a while they associated the war cries with beatings but of course the beatings didn't come. After that I had no trouble controlling them but when I handed them over to someone else there was chaos because they didn't know the war cries."

It was the year of the Creagh Dhu in 1964 when John returned as base leader to Adelaide Island with Todd, Bill Smith and Jimmy Gardiner and 18 others.

Smith recalls: "One of the trips we did, we left Adelaide Island and we sledged out over sea ice. We were heading down to a place called Fossil Bluff to pen up a small base for the aircraft to land. We called in at Stonington on the way and from there it is 300 miles to Fossil Bluff on sea ice most of the way. What we wanted to do was get there and mark out a sort of landing place because there is an awful lot of crevasses and we didn't want them dropping in. They used small single engine things. We did most of the work with dogs and people were out there learning how to control the dogs and guide the team. John was responsible for all the field work; he organised them, told them what areas they were going to.

"There were hardly any accidents although Davie Todd seemed to have drawn the short straw with one guy called Mike Ayling, one of the geologists. He just seemed totally accident prone. Davie was worried about him a lot, he was the type when he would be getting aboard a boat and he has his hand over the side and of course the motor boat rubs along the side, it doesn't do his fingers any good. He wasn't a good skier, never skied before and we were unloading the boat and I had got the skis down and he wanted to come. I said 'with snow like this it's not very good, you know', but he insisted on coming anyway. The first thing he does is fall and twist his knee and I had to ski back to base with him on my back. He was that type of person but then he told Dave he would do exactly what he was told and everything was all right after that."

The highlight of the 1964 trip was the first ascent of Mount Andrew Jackson, the highest mountain on the Antarctic peninsula and an exclusive all-Creagh Dhu expedition, the remainder of the party having been persuaded to stay behind. Davie Todd's diary extract of 23/11/64, Cunningham's 37th birthday, read: "Today's entry must rotate around what has been the greatest event in my mountaineering career – the ascent of Mount Andrew Jackson, the highest peak in the Antarctic peninsula (11,700ft). The last 1500 feet of the climb which took us up the NE Ridge, saw us executing superb severe crampon work over magnificent ice formations past two cornices and up knife-edge of ridge overhanging the 4,000 ft high East face. A truly wonderful lead by Johnny on the final section saw us on the summit, in mank, at 3.50 pm. Descent made in white-out, at -10° C temperature and camp reached at 6.30 pm."

And in a letter to Kirsty, Shauna and Paul Cunningham on November 7, 1980, Todd wrote:

"At your current ages it possibly sounds strange that you could waken on the morning of your birthday, surrounded by friends, and not receive a greeting or acknowledgement of the fact that you had just chalked up another year of your life. Your father wakened on the morning of this birthday to such a situation. But then after the age of 21 birthdays do not have the same appeal. Six of us, members of the British Antarctic Survey, were camped that day on the eastern edge of the ice covering Dyer Plateau located in the central, southern end of the Antarctic Peninsula. Our camp was placed at the base of Jackson. We were engaged in an exploratory topographical survey of the region which had only been observed from the air on one previous occasion around 1948. Apart from the survey, we wanted to make the first ascent of Jackson. However, the weather was poor and deteriorating with thick mist and the temperature around minus 10° C.

'"Shortly after midday there was a break in the cloud mantle. For a short period, at least, the weather looked reasonable; reasonable that is to tackle the mountain but not good enough to work! Within ten minutes of making the decision to go for the peak the Antarctic chapter of the CDMC (JC, BS, DT and JG) was on its way. A surveyor and a doctor, the two other members of the party 'agreed' to remain at the camp ... I suppose to protect it from vagabonds. Wearing crampons it took us an hour and a quarter to slog up the 1,000 feet or so of approach into the northern cirque of the massif. As we laboured we gradually rose above the thick carpet of cloud which enveloped the entire plateau as far as the eye could see. Only the mountains above 8,000ft showed above the carpet. Apart from the blue sky overhead and the bright colours of our windproof clothing, the entire scene was painted in hospital white: ice white peaks and the fleecy cloud cover through which they protruded combined to magnify and intensify the white sunlight. Without snow goggles we would have been blinded in minutes. We stopped for a breather, and our first talk since leaving the tents, at the base of the clearly defined north-east ridge.

"Your father, a man of few words when facing mountaineering problems, uttered a statement with which I became familiar during our climbs together: 'We'll solo (climb unroped) until it becomes difficult.' Then with a mischievous glint in his eye and an infectious chuckle, his trademark, he went on: 'OK, a one twenty fifth at F8, let's go.' That was his way of saying the climb would be a Sunday stroll, a photographic tour, for the Creagh Dhu team. For fully 1,500 feet the ridge was a mountaineer's dream; a sharp ice arête upon which nature had freeze-dried precipitation into formations which appealed aesthetically to the ice climber whilst simultaneously touching something in that area of the brain which struggles with abstract concepts of life. The ridge was out of this world. With only the front points of our crampons and the ice pick of our ice axes making contact we drifted up the arête bordering the intimidating east face. Glistening blue ice bulges, crystalline white towers, threatening two-way cornices, exposed razor ridges, mushrooms of hoar frost and sculptured ice scoops interspersed with smooth slopes led us on to a ledge beneath the summit.

"Access to the summit, some 60 feet above our small stance, was barred by a unique problem. A huge mushroom of consolidated icy hoar frost, bulging all round and about 60ft thick, sat astride the apex of the four converging ridges of the pyramid named after an American Pharaoh, Andrew Jackson.

"Cloud suddenly enveloped us, the temperature dropped sharply to around -20° Celsius and a strengthening updraught wind reminded us of our fragility. Decisions had to be made quickly as survival superseded success as our number one priority. Sixty feet from the top, surely we could claim the first ascent! But could we truly feel that we had conquered the mountain? As other eyes were drawn towards the line of the descent your father was peering into the swirling mist looking for a break in the overhanging mushroom. He thought he had seen something, a line, a chink in the icy armour. The line that he saw was 70 feet across a 60 degree slope which plunged over 4,000 ft to the glacier below.

"Now to cheer you up, your daddy's birthday did not pass that day without acknowledgement. I remembered it, which prompted me to respond to his discovery of the mountain's Achilles heel with: 'Happy birthday, Johnny. You can lead the final pitch to celebrate the occasion!' He had a typical saying 'Well then what would you have done?' whenever he put one over on someone. Again the mischievous twinkle in his eyes and the Cunningham chuckle as he tied on to the sharp end of the rope. Well then, what would you have done? With an ice axe in one hand and a long ice piton in the other, he gingerly front-pointed his way crabwise across the face beneath the mushroom of ice. Seventy feet of rope ran out and then to a call of 'Wait till you see this!' he climbed straight up into the mushroom. His crampons were the last thing we saw as he inched upwards out of sight.

"One hour later, we were all on the summit after climbing by bridging technique the most exhilarating ice chimney imaginable – What a lead, what a man, what a birthday present!

"On the summit inside emergency bivouac sacks with our boots off, we rubbed our frozen toes and hoped the weather would clear. It didn't, in fact it got even worse. Even with eiderdown duvet jackets beneath our windproof anoraks we were cold. After an hour the consensus was for bailing out quickly in order to survive. Our mountaineering instincts sensed something serious in the atmosphere. Several times on the descent, in complete white-out, we had to use the rope over difficult sections that we had soloed on the ascent. Fortunately our crampon tracks from the outward journey were visible so that with only a couple of assists from the compass we found our tents first time. If we had missed them, the Dyer Plateau, featureless for 100 miles, lay beyond. The ensuing storm, with the temperature dropping to minus 30° Celsius, lasted for four days.

"So there you have it, Clan Cunningham, your father's birthday is a special day in different ways for all of us. I will be thinking of you each on November 23rd, wherever you are. If your memory of me fades in time just think of me as the man who remembered your father's birthday and gave him a special present. Well then, what would you have done?"

Later on the same trip, in a stark reminder of the fine line between death and distinction in the wilderness of Antarctica, Todd had a narrow escape when sledging out for seals to feed the dogs.

Along with a companion, David Vaughan, Todd had sledged a short distance when the accident happened. Vaughan, who was in the lead, had just driven round a thin-looking patch of dark ice and was busy shooting the seals when Todd arrived. Todd's dogs got a whiff of the food and drove the sledge straight for them despite Todd's frantic efforts to steer them round the thin ice. Todd and the sledge broke through leaving the five dogs standing on the thin ice and as soon as they moved they joined their driver in the water.

"Their traces were wrapped round me and I was helpless," says Todd. "The other guy could do little about it and basically I knew I had had it, I couldn't swim. Funnily enough, I managed to stay calm and began to try and set my life in order. All I could think of was reassuring him and I told him what he had to do in the way on contacting relatives etc. He was in tears."

Vaughan tried throwing the handle of his dog whip but that broke and then tried with the lash line which on the third attempt Todd managed to grasp with an outstretched hand. He arrived back at the hut looking like a seal carcass and the whole of his upper body was covered in blue patches but he says: "The saddest thing of all was the loss of the five dogs because I had become very close to them."

Cunningham's final trip down south came to a strange and premature end after a dispute with the BAS over the stamps issued at base. Todd says: "Johnny had this shake of his hand and apparently wasn't stamping these properly and one day he came up to me and told me he wasn't staying another year. Whether he had fallen out with them I just didn't know but in the end there was no rancour."

Certainly, the British Antarctic Survey had few doubts about their long-serving employee. Their later obituary for Cunningham read:

"John's contemporaries in the FIDS will remember him as a complex personality. Essentially, John was a considerate, reflective man but those who knew him will well remember he had his moments. He was, above all, a positive character who was intolerant of the lazy and despised anyone who he felt was not giving their all. He was a good friend to those who got to know him well, being a warm man who was quick to laugh. Everyone who knew him will remember his smiling eyes. He was gifted with a quick turn of phrase which revealed a perceptive, wry sense of humour and a quick intelligence.

"In the field he was unsurpassed and no one could have asked for a better or more reliable sledging companion, particularly when the going became rough. An extremely gifted man who, with a few talented companions, has dominated the British mountaineering scene for the last 25 years or so. The survey is unlikely to see his like again."

There is a more permanent memorial in the southern ocean. At a latitude of 54°12'S, 37°18'W, north-east of the head of Queen Maud Bay on the south side of South Georgia and at a height of 1220m, rises ... Mount Cunningham.

THE LODGE

Although Cunningham had spent years away from Glasgow, in New Zealand, the Himalaya and Antarctica, Duke Street was still home. Even at the age of 38, when he returned from his last trip South, he headed straight for 1252: the idea of a Glasgow bachelor pad was an alien concept in the mid 60s, not only to John but to virtually any other single man in the city, whatever his age. You lived at home until marriage. And as well as a non-starter on traditional East End grounds, it was financial irresponsibility to a man as careful with a penny as Cunningham. In any case, 1252 had become suddenly more spacious. Older brother James had left for Australia a decade earlier and both Bobby and Faye had married and moved out, Faye to Johnstone just outside Paisley and Bobby to Milngavie. John Snr was to die later that year so John's company for the next two years was welcome to his mother Mary, although his life outside the house remained as much a mystery as ever to her.

Bobby says: "When he got the Perry Medal for the first Antarctic trip he didn't go putting it on show. I spotted it once and asked him what it was for and he just gave me a very brief account of what happened in the crevasse. Mother never asked him about his trips, I think in many ways she was happy to see him just getting out of Glasgow, she didn't do much worrying about what he was up to."

Faye remains convinced that her mother didn't even know John had been presented with a medal by the Queen. "It was nothing to him," she says. "If mother had asked he would probably have told her but he wasn't going to boast about it."

John's constant travels meant that in the most part he remained strangers to the neighbours in Duke Street – people he had grown up alongside. Bobby recalls: "He came in once when he heard a commotion from up the stairs. Mrs Bain, the lady there, was shouting 'Stop Thief, he's got my telly' at the top of her voice. John of course goes up the stairs and immediately tackled this guy and puts him in a nice wrestling hold and there's a bit of scuffling and cursing. She's in the house dialling the police when another neighbour came out, someone who had lived there all our lives, and starts attacking John. He just didn't recognise him."

With 40 not too distant and his only career qualification his Brown's apprenticeship, Cunningham had to sit down and do some serious thinking about his future. Although well established as one of Scotland's greatest climbers, the years in Antarctica meant he had missed much of the heyday of the big Himalayan expeditions, invitations to which usually depended on a climber's face fitting on the domestic climbing scene; who you knew was far more important than what you knew. In his own perverse way, too, Cunningham had bypassed the traditional climbing pyramid of easy ascents at home, hard ascents at home, the odd first ascent, a few good seasons in the Alps and then invites to the greater ranges. In any case, his experiences with Hamish in Nepal and later in the Karakoram with the two fruitless Gregory expeditions left him with the distinct impression that Himalayan climbing depended far too much on good fortune, none of which he had been blessed with either on Pumori, Disteghil Sar or Ama Dablam – and they weren't even particularly high mountains. The other traditional outlets for climbers wanting a full-time career within the sport were the travelogue expedition books (à la Bonington) or opening a shop (Joe Brown, Graham Tiso).

Willie Rowney, in fact, tried to persuade Cunningham to take the latter course.

"I was running an office in Glasgow in Royal Exchange Square when Johnny came back from the Antarctic and the lads who were moving around would drop in there to catch up with the latest – who had moved up to Aviemore, who had left home etc. Johnny came round one day and we were blathering away over lunch about what he was going to do next and he said he would like to do something in photography but I thought for a guy well past 30 taking that up and making a living out of it, the chances were not great. Graham Tiso had just started his first shop and that was going quite well and I said to Johnny: 'I don't know if you want my advice or not but if I were you I would go out and get the money and open a climbing shop'. If Tiso, who nobody knew, could do that I thought John would have no bother at all. People would be beating on his door. Some would go there just to see him."

The thought of Cunningham poring over the VAT books during a fine weekend or ordering a new batch of Karrimats from the Karrimor rep would undoubtedly have struck most of his friends and acquaintances as incongruous but Rowney had thought that out, too.

"He said he preferred to have his weekends free so I said 'well I will run it for you and you can climb all you like'. The thing was he knew about equipment. Places like Blacks sold absolutely basic stuff, you couldn't get more downmarket. Tiso started going to these European fairs and finding new gear there. Johnny, I think, would have bought the same sort of equipment.

"A lot of business is timing and luck. Look at Frith Finlayson in skiing. He made a tremendous impact but he couldn't have done the same thing 10 years later. He was in at the ground floor and I think Johnny would have done equally as well. It was years later that Sam Brown opened Highrange Sports in Glasgow and that was part-time and he was a right grumpy character and certainly didn't bring in the punters with his cheery chat. Yet he was able to make it work. Johnny wasn't interested but I ask myself if he had taken that advice he might still be alive and very well off."

The other possible avenue was a job as an instructor at one of the outdoor centres, a taste of which he had already had in 1955 at Glenmore Lodge. But most centres required a teaching qualification; it simply was not enough to be John Cunningham. He also toyed with the idea of embarking and possibly organising a small private climbing expedition to South America, but this would entail self-financing, a return to the shipyards, long spells of work (and overtime) and a lot of self-denial and hard saving. He had done all that before. His mind was finally made up when he went down to Clydebank to see some of his old workmates in Browns and received the final proof that not only were his days as a shipwright numbered, but the futures of the great Clyde yards equally as limited. As a first-year apprentice in 1944, Cunningham had helped put down the deck on Hull 593, a cruiser called HMS Tiger which was completed in 1945, too late for war service and in any case very soon obsolete. When John arrived back in March, 1965, to his horror the boat was back in Browns awaiting yet another refit.

"I think that was what swung it for John," says Bobby. "They had stripped this boat down so many times and started on it again they even called it the Bonus Boat. As soon as the foreman saw John he said to him: 'Thank God you're back, John, I want you to start on the deck again on Monday.'

"I think John had enough of the yard by then but that really decided him. Then they wanted him to look after the apprentices with some sort of outward bound type training, but he refused that, too, which I thought was a bit daft because it was the kind of job that would have given him a lot of leeway. But he had had it with the yards really and I think he had already decided to get some paper qualifications. He had tried before and knew he would never get a job without a bit of paper."

Jordanhill College, close to Anniesland in Glasgow's West End, which offered teacher training and also ran a Youth and Community course, seemed ideal. As well as a grounding in social work the course provided secondment as an outdoor pursuits instructor to Dunbartonshire Youth Service Department on their regional training courses. With two referees required, Cunningham provided the names of Dave Smith, his foreman at Browns, and Chris Lyon. Singing the praises of his younger members of the Creagh Dhu, in fact, had become almost an occupation for the former president.

"With Everest conquered the trustees of the substantial Everest Fund now possessed an embarrassing amount of cash," said Lyon "The Queen's husband, having fulfilled his job of begetting the next generation of monarchy was looking for something useful to occupy his time. It was he that suggested that the youth of Britain be introduced to the character-building outdoor life. Suddenly, what had been the private province of a few zany hard-cases now became the playground for thousands. Everybody wanted in on the act, while personally I still held the belief that if youngsters wanted to climb they, through natural selection, would make the high places. I seemed to spend a great deal of time during that period recommending Creagh Dhu Boys as instructors in the new outdoor centres of recreation."

In August, 1965, Cunningham collected the typewritten paper in the college lecture hall and prepared to sit the entry examination. The

Jordanhill paper didn't seem too taxing, inviting only a discourse in English on a familiar subject and although writing was not John's strongest point – when he was in Antarctica his mum would consider herself fortunate to receive two letters a year – his treatise on 'My Life in the Shipyards' impressed the examiners sufficiently and six weeks later he began the course proper.

He was also pleased to spot a familiar face on the same course, a Lomonds Club member called Jimmy Thomson. Thomson, who until then had worked in a small engineering factory in Glasgow manufacturing small parts for aircraft, now lives in retirement (in a house called Glencoe) on Inverness's Black Isle. A former professional footballer, his career goes back to the Jock Nimlin days all the way up to the Creagh Dhu era of Ian Nicholson whom he first took climbing at Dumbarton Rock when Ian was 16. Thomson remains in touch with Patsy Walsh over in Skye, too, and was spotted on Agag's Groove on Buachaille Etive Mor in the summer of 1998, by then well into his 70s.

Says Thomson: "Most of us on the Jordanhill course were tradesmen and none of us had higher education, so this was a way of opening a door. I saw it as a way out of engineering and John, although of course he never discussed it, I am sure saw it as a way out of the shipyards.

"It was a two-year course and John seemed happy in his skin at college, self-effacing and self-sufficient, he wouldn't try anything if he wasn't going to be good at it. In my days with the Lomonds of course I had come across John and the Creagh Dhu. I had seen him and Hamish working on the Nook at the Cobbler with Hamish banging in pegs and upsetting all sorts of people. John was always very helpful, shouting down if he thought we were off route although he usually was very economical with words. Jock Nimlin would command the company with his conversation, John didn't have time for small talk, it was a waste of bloody time to him. He was definitely a man of action. When he and Mick Noon were up in the Coe in February, 1957, they arrived with a plan of action and nothing was going to sway them from it. They were staying at the Gorge cottage where Hamish used to be based and were going up to do Deep Gash Gully on Aonach Dubh. Well, naturally we all went out and got pissed and came back making a big noise and John and Noon are just lying there in their pits sleeping. When we got up in the morning they were away, doing the climb. That struck me as the big difference between us and them."

Part of the Jordanhill programme involved placement on social work and Cunningham soon found himself back in the East End with a file of casework on disadvantaged families, an aspect of the course he tackled with varying degrees of success. While there was little doubt he could empathise with those suffering hardship and privation in Glasgow he had always despised those unwilling to help themselves. Some of the traditional methods of mediation he found were out of date, too.

Brother Bobby says: "There was a slight hiccup in the course when he and a girl on the same course went to Bridgeton to do some social work and they were given a list of families. The one the girl went to were a bit rough and while John was in the next close he heard this monster giving her a hard time.

"After trying some friendly persuasion unsuccessfully, John did the next best thing, dragged the guy on to the stairs and held him over the stairwell telling him basically: 'No more trouble, or else.' That did the trick but the girl he'd rescued decided this was no way to treat disadvantaged families and reported John to the principal at Jordanhill. I'm sure if she hadn't been there he'd have let go. But John knew the East End and what to expect; the girl had no idea."

The teaching of outdoor pursuits and occasional outings with the Jordanhill climbing club were more rewarding for Cunningham, although like many instructors he swiftly found that it helps if pupils have an actual interest in learning the arts of belaying, abseiling and movement on rock. Some of the juvenile Dumbarton clientele proved stubbornly resistant to the charms of the great outdoors. Jimmy Thomson says:

"Lanarkshire had an outdoor centre at White Craigs in the wastelands of Lanark which we used. There wasn't a house for miles and one week John and I went there with some apprentices from Coalvilles. They were all 16 or 17 and real tearaway types. It was a mammoth task to convince them that when we took them out for a day they had actually done something. There was no cook in residence so John and me ended up doing it all, part of the service. At that time local authorities were rolling in money and the place was groaning with sausage and bacon and eggs and cheese. We would faithfully get up every morning, cook their breakfast and wait for them and this of course in a climate where you couldn't just wade into the bedroom and kick them up their arses. Every bloody morning it was the same: 'Come on, boys, time to get up'. Ten minutes, nothing. We'd go through and they'd be there yawning and scratching, most of them still in their pits. Halfway through the week we'd had enough and started talking it over and thinking, well this is the last day so we won't see these gits again. On the Thursday after another mammoth session of trying to get them out of bed we made the announcement: 'Tomorrow, if you are not there in five minutes, the breakfast goes in the bin'. Next morning we sat there looking at our watches, After five minutes, in the bin. We just sat there, we didn't care, it was the last day anyway. They came through and John just said: 'There's the milk, boys, there's the cereal and there's the bread, just help yourselves'. You should have seen their faces. But I never heard John raising his voice with them. He had a sort of look that didn't encourage people to argue with him. I remember when I was playing football it wasn't the guys who said they were going to get you, you had to worry about, it was the quiet ones who would just give you a look. One day we were up in the Gorms and on a night out and there were some young lads there a bit pissed and we heard them saying: 'That's Johnny Cunningham' and one lad comes over and starts chinning John and announces I have climbed such and such a thing, all proud. And John just turns to him, looks him up and down and says 'Indeed ?' That was all he said, and the guy walked away."

At the end of the two-year course and another written exam there was a diploma for the successful Jordanhill students.

"It wasn't terribly critical," says Thomson. "One or two guys didn't get through, some of them very well educated. So that was it, world here I come."

In the 60s and 70s there is little doubt that the plum jobs in outdoor pursuits were to be found at Glenmore Lodge, seven miles above Aviemore at the village of Glenmore in the Cairngorms and Plas y Brenin close by Capel Curig in Snowdonia. Certainly anyone with any doubts only needed to look in the staff car-park at the Lodge in the 70s and note the MGBs and Lotuses to be convinced of the elitist nature of a job there. Both centres at the time were run by the Central Council for Physical Recreation, both were idyllically situated amid mountain and water and both were staffed by enthusiasts intent on making the most of that environment in their leisure time. On summer evenings at the Brenin keen staff climbers are 20 minutes drive from Llanberis Pass; at the Lodge, Creag Dubh at Newtonmore or the Northern Corries of the Cairngorms are a similar distance away. There was white water canoeing on the Spey or the Feshie and sailing on Loch Morlich at the Lodge while the Brenin had Lyn Mymbyr and an occasionally foaming river outlet literally at the bottom of its sloping garden. A keen skier at Glenmore could be up the ski road and on Cairngorm's White Lady within minutes, while the Brenin had its own dry slope, complete with tow and a token bump. Equipment allowances were lavish, pay on National Union of Teachers scales, complete with generous pensions, and the scale and variety of courses and students ensured that boredom seldom set in. A staff sweater (navy blue at the Lodge and bright red at the Brenin) with the Instructor motif across the chest was the outdoor pursuits equivalent of a green Masters jacket or an MCC tie, with the rights to wear either seemingly just as difficult to attain. Qualifications were strict and, as well as skills in one of the specialist activities, usually involved a teaching qualification. Cunningham, of course, by now had his Jordanhill diploma to wave in the face of any interviewing panel; what he didn't know when he first pulled on the blue Lodge sweater, was that he would have obtained a job there with, or without, that piece of paper.

Glenmore Lodge began life as a Forestry Commission building with the first students – from the Scottish Air Training Corps – arriving there in August, 1947. The CCPR, after those first two experimental courses then took over, obtained a 10-year lease and the Lodge – now Morlich Youth Hostel – became a full-time centre in 1948 with courses offered in the main to the services and the staff employed largely on a voluntary basis and drawn from the major climbing, skiing and sailing clubs. In those days there was no ski road and no lifts – skiing involved a long toil up Windy Ridge carrying skis and sticks – and Aviemore itself was a long way from the Blackpool of the Highlands it has become since. There was a station, a small hotel opposite and a row of shops, but with the Queen's and Rothiemurchus forests spread in front of the village leading all the way to the northern ramparts of Coire an Lochain and Coire an t-Sneachda, a more appropriate place for the nascent outdoor pursuits business it would be hard to find. Loch Morlich, a five-minute level stroll from the Lodge, offered sailing and canoeing while a dry ski slope was constructed on the site on which now stands the Reindeer House. The forest themselves offered abundant practice in what was then known as wayfaring and, later, became the sport of orienteering. When the Forestry Commission lease expired a new, purpose-built complex was constructed half-a-mile further east along the Ryvoan bothy track and the new Glenmore Lodge was officially opened in 1959. With its square outline and glass frontage it was a singularly unattractive building, more like an American motel than a mountain lodge, but some thoughtful planning went into the interior, with a large, functional common room, lecture theatre, stores, dining room and staff accommodation. The new building also inherited the old Lodge's original full-time sailing and climbing instructor, Jack Thomson.

The Creagh Dhu veteran of the Battle of Zermatt, later to become Britain's longest-serving instructor, was unarguably one of the most remarkable men ever to grace outdoor education. His beginnings in Clydebank were as humble as one could imagine but he found his metier in the outdoors with the old Creagh Dhu and although officially one of the club heavies, few people who knew the lantern-jawed Clydesider doubted he had a heart of gold. Many students will recall with fondness the big stern man in a kilt organising the reels at the end-of-course ceilidhs, always with infinite patience. Friends knew, too, that the ultra-straight Glaswegian could be relied on in any circumstances. Tommy Paul had also spent a short period working at the lodge along with John and James Cunningham in 1955 and says:

"When we got back home from New Zealand in 1955 we had only been back a few days when we met Jack in Glasgow. He asked what we were doing and we said we hadn't got a job yet so he asked why we didn't go up to the Lodge. Charlie Cromar was the warden and he offered us £5 a week split between John and me for being instructors and helping out with the maintenance. So we would instruct during the day and do repairs around the place at other times, generators, Land Rovers, stuff like that. Johnny later went off to the Antarctic and my time there ended when a new warden, Murray Scott took over. He decided that one of my jobs would be to check out the footwear of the students for safety reasons before they went out on the hill and report back to him. Well, I did this and he turned round and said the instructor's, meaning me, were not up to standard. I was walking round in these old leather shoes with a suede top and even the sole was flat and tied up with tape. When you are sharing £5 it doesn't go far and things just go downhill so I left just after that.

"Aye, Jack was a hard man all right. There was a New Year's night in the old Lodge and some marines arrived trying to gatecrash the place. They got in and someone called for assistance and Jack went down to sort things out. They never knew what hit them. Someone came running up to me and said; 'Come quick, there's three marines and Jack is putting them out' and I just said: 'Jack will manage, Jack will be fine'. And of course he was.

"Jack had gone to the Lodge one weekend and never come back, he stayed there the rest of his life. Johnny and he were totally different types but one thing he did have in common with Cunningham was his awful driving. I taught John to drive in an old Land Rover with aluminium sides and he kept driving into this wire fence. He said 'I'm drawn to it. It must be a magnetic field'. I had to teach Jack to drive, too, so he would drive into the ditch on the right and Johnny would drive into the fence on the left. Speed and time were things that just didn't register with either of them."

Like Cunningham, Thomson did not slow down with age. A visiting instructor who worked on one of the winter courses in the early 70s recalls being dispatched on a snow-holing mission with him.

"I was terrified of this big gruff guy, but I soon realised appearances didn't count for anything. We were supposed to go up Coire Ciste and dig a variety of holes that the students could come up and view later and we were carrying these big shovels. Jack was in his 50s at the time, I was in my mid 20s, but he was basically burning me off, heading off up the hill at a tremendous rate of knots. It was very windy and then I realised Jack was using his shovel like a sail and catching the wind; rate of knots was right. He was laughing his socks off. Later on he was producing these holes in this bank one after the other like a mechanical digger. I went in one of them and he had even fashioned a WC and washbasin, just sculptured out of the snow, in one of the rooms. The students were very impressed with this and pretty soon they were carving armchairs, things like that, inside their holes."

Thomson, in fact, remained a fixture at the Lodge through an endless variety of wardens, courses and instructors and set a yardstick for staff over the years. Many considered he would have made a good principal or even deputy but his lack of formal qualifications precluded that.

When Cunningham joined the staff full-time in December, 1967, the Creagh Dhu had begun what amounted almost to an exodus from the west coast. As well as Thomson and Cunningham, Bob Clyde had become first manager of the first Cairngorm Chairlift Company and had brought Tommy Paul and Bill Smith up to help. Paul bought what was virtually a ruin in Boat of Garten, rebuilt that and lives there still. Smith remains in one of the old traditional terraced cottages in Kingussie's High Street. Later, Paul took over from Clyde and later still, to keep it in the family, John McLean followed Paul. George Shields and Harry Mackay were already instructors with Frith Finlayson's ski school. A day out on the White Lady would often turn into a Creagh Dhu reunion.

Paul says: "Bill and I had both worked on the first lift at Meall a' Bhuiridh in Glencoe, fixing the lifts and so forth. Then they started the lift at Cairngorm and Bob Clyde was given the job and he wrote to me and asked me if I wanted the job of engineer on the lift and Shirley my wife and I came up here in 1961 and have stayed ever since. Then of course I was looking for an assistant and I was looking for a man who could do all I could do but probably better and the only one I could think of was Bill Smith. People say there is a Creagh Dhu mafia but it was simply a question of saying I need an assistant here who has experience in lift systems and is a good engineer and there weren't many names on that list. So I suppose you could say Bill was head-hunted."

Smith says: "There were about nine of us involved in the lift at Glencoe, running it for the Glencoe Ski Club. Frith Finlayson and me were the first operators. When I went over to Cairngorm, Bob and Tommy were already there and the life suited me down to the ground. We used to get the early squad out at about four in the morning to make sure the road was open. I would take one of the ploughs and go up into the car-park and start working on the ski tow paths and stuff like that. The other machines would follow on behind and flatten the snow behind.. You would get very involved in it. Later, if Johnny brought a party up he would always stop and have a cup of tea with us."

Down at the Lodge, some of the most remarkable innovations ever seen in outdoor education were taking place, the catalyst being the arrival of Eric Langmuir to the principal's office in 1963. An able climber, Langmuir in his days as president of Cambridge University Mountaineering Club, produced the first two ground-breaking routes at Etive Slabs in 1954, Sickle and Spartan Slab as well as early explorations on the magnificent Carnmore Crag near Kinlochewe in the far North-West but it was his abilities as an administrator and motivator for which he will be best remembered, particularly at the Lodge.

After university, Langmuir had spent three years as an exploration geologist in Canada before taking, in 1959, the post of principal at White Hall Outdoor Pursuits Centre on Long Hill, high above Buxton in the Derbyshire Peak District. White Hall, under the auspices of the Derbyshire Director of Education, Jack Longland, had produced a number of innovatory courses in climbing, caving and canoeing for the county's schoolchildren and became the role model for places like Glenmore Lodge and Plas y Brenin. Langmuir was, and still is, convinced that the best teachers did not necessarily make the best instructors and was adamant that any innate ability to imbue children with a love of outdoor sports was as important, if not more so, than formal qualification. His most famous guinea pig in this respect was the great rock climber Joe Brown, the former Manchester plumber who with John Cunningham and another White Hall instructor Gordon Mansell, Langmuir still rates as the best instructors he has ever seen. Langmuir, now retired to a spectacular contemporary mansion just off the A9 at Avielochan between Aviemore and Carrbridge, says:

"I went up to the Lodge when Alec Dalrymple who had just settled into the job of principal, died of cancer. In those days it was run by the SCPR and they had just moved from the old Lodge into a purpose-built place higher up the road. Like White Hall, the Lodge also ran on a system of voluntary help and was orientated towards schoolchildren, but with the opening of the new Lodge we were getting some of the colleges of education, Moray House, Jordanhill and I M Marsh Liverpool, coming up, not just for outdoor sport, but also geography and geology, natural history, even art. It was run as a going concern, albeit on a shoestring and John Cunningham appeared on the scene when it was going through a transformation to courses aimed at specialists. I had my heart set on him long before any job came up. We needed someone like John because I always thought it very important to have people who weren't just teachers, weren't just educational but were top-class performers. I place great store by mountaineering because I considered that the basis for everything else. People could sail or canoe or ski but they had to be mountaineers. One thing that White Hall taught me is that you don't have to be a teacher to be a good teacher and the best teachers I have come across have been non-qualified: Joe Brown, Gordon and John. None of them had any inhibitions about the way they were going to teach. John and Joe had the ability to get something across that made it stick, they were guys people just listened to. I was looking around in my mind as to who could do the job. Like Joe, I basically went fishing for John.

"I inherited Jack Thomson, as did all my predecessors. He was a remarkable man. I think a lot of people were usually frightened of Jack for a while because he could be quite severe. But Jack was a wonderful instructor and how he could keep up such a high quality of teaching and commitment over that length of time astonishes me because as well as being the longest-serving instructor in Britain he was also Britain's first full-time ski instructor and helped get BASI off the ground. He never missed a day's work, cycled from home, always on time and was absolutely straight, embarrassingly so at times. There was such integrity there. For a guy who had been through the mill like he had it was really quite remarkable."

Under Langmuir, the emphasis of the Lodge moved from basic taster courses for children and students to more specialised courses. There were introductory and assessments for the Mountain Leadership Certificate, mountain rescue courses, winter survival courses and specialist rock-climbing, canoeing and sailing weeks. Langmuir's instincts about John were proved right in dramatic fashion on one of the mountain rescue courses. He says:

"There were no fatal accidents in the seven years I was at the Lodge although there was a near miss once on Creag Dubh during a rescue week and a famous avalanche on the Coire Cas headwall. We had set up mountain rescue courses, which was quite a big thing for then, but Creag Dubh was too risky a place to be realistic. The idea was that people had to abseil to a ledge halfway down to help with the lower. John was on the upper ledge and everything had been going fine. John was supervising the abseil point and this bloke came up and just as he was going to launch into space John noticed he hadn't clipped his karabiner in and he was completely detached from the rope and he just managed to grab him and pull him in.

"That made a big impression on John and also a big impression on me and we stopped going to Creag Dubh. It was just too serious for someone to make a little error and too much to watch. The consequences of a slip were fatal. But that was why I had brought in John, someone with an awareness of what was going on. I think John had a rapport with rock basically. I didn't get to climb with him as much as I would have liked but I remember one route we climbed at Creag Dubh. There was light rain and I think we were maybe two pitches up and the next section went up a little corner with the holds all sloping, just pure balance which of course John excelled at.

"He went up and had a look at the move, then came back down and said: 'We'll have to wait 10 minutes', I thought to myself 'He is having me on', but right enough 10 minutes later he went up and made this delicate move across. It was very impressive, almost as if the rock had told him 'Come back in 10 minutes and see how I feel then'."

There were more innovations at the Lodge after Langmuir left in 1969. The Scottish Council for Physical Recreation gave way to the Sports Council and there were a number of far-reaching staff changes. The new principal was Fred Harper, the former chief instructor, with Bill March taking over as deputy. A year or so later, more new mug shots appeared on the staff rogue's gallery in 'Ben the Hoose', the Lodge cleaning and pack-ing and unpacking area from whence led all the dormitories. Allen Fyffe, the formidable pioneering Cairngorm climber arrived in 1971 and the canoeing and watersports were in the hands of Bob Smith, who while never advertising the fact was probably the strongest man there. Smith's party piece was one-arm pull-ups on the garage doors inside which he stored his Lotus Elan. Chris Rawlins, Brian Hall and Reg Popham were fine all-rounders. Smith and the others, however well qualified, soon dis-covered who was the boss at the Lodge.

"When I met John he was in his 40s and I was in my early 20s, a precocious lad," says Smith. " We used to have a 35-seater bus and we used to come off the hill at the Cairngorm car-park, supposedly on the dot at 4.30 when the bus was supposed to leave and invariably John was late for one reason or another, never arrived until nearer five. I had the effron-tery to mention this at a staff meeting. Next time I had someone with a sprained ankle coming down off the hill and got to the car-park at 4.31 on the dot ... just in time to see John driving straight past us. But John really was a super, generous guy."

Reg Popham, who worked at the Lodge between 1971 and 1980, originally studied engineering at Glasgow University, worked as an engineer for three years then in 1970 went to Moray House in Edinburgh just as Eric Langmuir arrived from Glenmore. He says: "In 1970/71 three jobs came up all at once at the Lodge and me, Fyffey and Bob Smith got them. John was given the task of assessing me for climbing and we went to Creag Dubh to do Jump so High. It was extremely nerve-racking but John just told me to relax, and gave me a good report. Fortunately."

This formidably talented group of full-timers was backed by a small army of temporary and voluntary instructors. Cunningham brought in Creagh Dhu members Rab Carrington, Ian Nicholson and Davie Todd to help with climbing courses, Fyffe's great East Coast climbing buddy, Jim McCartney, also spent time there and mountain rescue weeks would find leaders of the country's main teams in residence including Taff Tunnah from RAF Leuchars and John Hinde from RAF Kinloss. Captain Mike Wright appeared from time to time with army courses and some extremely tough officers and NCOs, while most weekends Ben Humble, the stone-deaf SMC and mountain rescue archivist and a long-term Lodge habitué, could be found tending his beloved alpine garden by the entrance drive (now in a sad state of neglect). On the winter and summer assessment courses there were invariably other famous names seeking qualification for their Mountain Instructors Certificate and there were also the teachers who arrived with the courses, again all committed to the concept of outdoor education. Dunfermline College had Joe Jagger, father of Mick, I M Marsh the formidable Miss Jamieson and before them Bobbie Brown, the former Rangers and Scotland goalkeeper proved a dedicated and popular visitor in his then role as Glasgow PE teacher. These diverse personalities produced an incredible variety of ideas and opinion all channelled into the Lodge; it became a forum for advancement and change in outdoor pursuits, a development recognised and nurtured by Harper when he took over.

"When I arrived we were coming into the golden era of outdoor education. The Lodge was booked up all the year round and was developing a much higher profile. The SCPR had relinquished control and the Sports Council had taken over, we were well-paid civil servants in effect, but we also had a whole building of people passionately interested in climbing. John's effect on the Lodge was immediate and startling. He allowed new courses to be run and contributed greatly to the quality of the existent ones. His talents as a mountaineer were well known – his development into a first-class instructor was wonderful news for the Lodge. I had met him a long time before at the bridge by the Biolay camp site in Chamonix and I had come across the Creagh Dhu, although as an intimidated novice, before that. I knew you had to ask to get anything from John, if you did ask he would give it but over the seven years together at the Lodge we gradually became friends and I don't think in that time we had one cross word, which is amazing in a place that made as many demands as the Lodge."

On the surface Harper was a stern and unsmiling character who took his job extremely seriously, an opinion reinforced by the sight of him motoring through the Lodge corridors at high speed intent on some undefined mission while students and staff backed into the walls and out of the way. But appearances in Harper's case were deceptive. A serious nicotine addict, before the Lodge became a no-smoking zone he would roll up with impunity in his office; a visit there would be a fight through a dense evil-smelling clag while his ashtray overflowed alarmingly on to his rotas and Sports Council minutes. A former member of the Squirrels, the anarchic Edinburgh club that included Dougal Haston, Fred had also helped pioneer some of the harder climbs of the 60s at Creag Dubh and most intimidated temporary instructors could console themselves with the thought that while Fred looked and acted what was commonly known in the early 70s as 'square' he had once ascended and named routes like Cunnulinctus, Gang Bang and Strapadicktaemi barely eight miles down the road. He earned even more plus points after one night when students and some of the newly-arrived voluntary instructors had been waiting in the lecture hall for Harper to arrive and deliver a lecture on mountain safety only for a smirking Cunningham to appear after a long wait to announce that the lecture was cancelled – the Principal had had an unfortunate accident. Harper, wearing flip-flops, had cut his big toe off with a Flymo on his lawn: he was one of the Boys after all.

Harper was officially Cunningham's superior, but in fact, despite some later friction over the regular stays at the Lodge of John's girlfriend, Alison, the men became firm friends and spent two holidays together.

Harper, who now guides private climbing and ski-touring parties and lives just on the outskirts of Kingussie, says:

"We had two trips together, once to St Anton, Austria, skiing and once to Yosemite. He was of course a much better climber and skier than me but it didn't seem to matter, we just had fun. In Yosemite, he and Bob Smith and I were camped alongside Davey Agnew and wife and big dirty dog at Camp 4. I had a healthy respect for bears, Davey Agnew and Bob Smith had no fear whatsoever and John was absolutely petrified by bears. In any case, Agnew and Smith and the dog were not far off the bears' size. John would sleep in the middle and every night there was the same scenario. Agnew's dog would start barking, we'd hear this sniffling and John would dig Bob in the ribs and tell him: 'Bob, the fur coats are here'. Outside it was chaos with Bob and Davey in their Y-fronts hurling rocks at the bears, to a great bedlam of shouting and grunting and dog barking while John and I timidly peeped out of the tent door, out of our bags and ready to do a runner if our protection failed. Then we went up to do Snake Dike on Half Dome and we were bivvied with a huge fire to keep the fur coats away. It was big enough for me and I was half-dead with exhaustion anyway but John kept piling on bigger and bigger logs and it became so hot we had to move out into the wilderness – and closer to the bears – to avoid it.

"After a week the Camp 4 grapevine discovered that John was in the valley and they dispatched young hotshot, Jim Donini, along to climb with him. The clear intention was to burn John off. Most of us would have found a way of avoiding the confrontation as it was the type of climbing, like off-widths, that we were not used to and we had only been there a short time.

"But John was not going to back off. This would be about 1975 and he would be 47 or 48 but still very athletic and very mobile. Donini would be in his 20s but I think I can state quite categorically that he more than held his own with Donini. On the same trip we headed down to Taquitz Rocks and met Yvon Chouinard in Ventura where he gave a party with his famous and much-advertised octopus salad. John had been sandbagged by Yvon in the past when he came to the Lodge with his marijuana-laced cookies. Chouinard prepared this salad himself and unknown to us it was heavily spiked and John, Bob and I – who liked octopus a lot – were transformed from honoured guests to the live entertainment for the evening by a mixture of the deadly salad and California Red. It wasn't all beers and skittles, though. Snake Dike, the Braille Book, South face of North Dome, Nutcracker, Lost Arrow Spire, Traitor Horn and Open Book and many other climbs gave us some of the finest routes of our lives, some of the best days, nights and times. I'm glad we did it then because we can't do it now. After John left the Lodge to go down to Liverpool, I saw him occasionally when he came up to the Gorms and found him same as ever, young, warm and gentle under the 'Glesca' skin."

While Harper appeared, on the surface at least a total introvert, March his deputy was the exact opposite. A graduate of King's College in London and Loughborough, 'Big Bill' was a very large, very strong and outgoing six-footer with a huge toothy grin and a formidable appetite for climbing, drinking and occasionally fighting. People either loved or hated

March, although few could resist his enthusiasm and days out with him were invariably unforgettable.

An evening on Dinas Mot in North Wales' Llanberis Pass included solo ascents of Western Slabs and Direct Route followed by more conventional ascents of West Rib and Diagonal, seemingly in hectic competition with Rab Carrington and Jimmy Gardiner of the Creagh Dhu who we had raced us up the scree from the road. Later, in the Pen y Gwyrd on the way back to Plas y Brenin, the beer went down almost as swiftly before the appearance of the equally large Mike Wright, an army captain with a fearsomely scarred face, prompted a huge wrestling match between him and March over the bar tables, much to the consternation of the hotel residents.

March was rightly proud of his strength and fitness but once came unstuck in spectacular fashion. A student called Tim Hawkins, a former junior army officer turned outward bound instructor, was at the Lodge on a mountain leadership training course and, unlike most students, had showed a disinclination to follow meekly in the footsteps of the Lodge instructors on expeditions. He had, in fact, given most of the staff a hard time and was obviously very fit. Bill, who as deputy principal remained desk-bound for much of the week, had got wind of this in the staff room and decided he was going to come out and 'burn the little bastard off', appearing next day with a light pack for the walk up to the Fiachaill Ridge from the Cairngorm car-park.

To everyone's amazement, Bill and Hawkins, as if hearing a starter's gun, disappeared at high speed up the Coire an Lochain path for all the world like Coe and Ovett on the last lap of the Olympics 800m final. What Bill didn't know was that Tim Hawkins was the army cross-country champion and the 'race' could have only one outcome. When the rest of the group arrived on the Coire an Lochain ridge 20 minutes later Tim was happily puffing on a Benson and Hedges, admiring the view and chatting away to the scowling and silent runner-up.

March had also upset the Creagh Dhu in the past, one night bursting drunk into Jacksonville to avenge some pub slight and brandishing a broken tomato sauce bottle at the assembled company. A serious incident was only averted by the diplomacy of Davie Todd who for his pains was clobbered on the side of the head with a rock by a Creagh Dhu member seeking redress from the invading Englishman. Later still, March threw two of the younger members of the club out of the Lodge after they had been caught consorting with two girls from the domestic staff – and obviously expecting a free doss for the night.

A more unlikely climbing partner for Cunningham it would be diffi-cult to envisage but gradually, whether by accident or design, the brash southerner and the quiet, laid-back Scot found themselves on the same rope.

Fyffe, who on the face of it, seemed the more logical choice of climb-ing partner at the Lodge for Cunningham, says: "These things sometimes work out quite well. They were both wanting the same things. They were both keen to do the same sort of routes and Bill's enthusiasm had to be tempered by something and I think that is perhaps what made a good combination. I got on well with Johnny mainly I think because when I came to the Lodge in 1971, I'd just done the north face of the Eiger and that was one of the routes Johnny really wanted. I think that made a difference to how he viewed me."

Fyffe did get to climb with Cunningham, on the first winter ascent of Gaffer's Groove in Coire an Lochain in February 1975 when Cunning-ham was 47 years old.

"It was like climbing with your hero," says Fyffe. "When I was growing up in Dundee and later when I was at Aberdeen University, Cunningham and the Creagh Dhu routes were held in a bit of awe, Gal-lows things like that. Gallows is still E1 5c and that was done in 1947, the year after I was born. Gallows was a leap ahead of its time as was Guerdon Grooves. I remember when Johnny came up here I was dying to ask him what Guerdon meant and he explained it was some sort of biblical gift, although who it was a gift to I don't know. He had a bit of a revival when he was up here and not just in the Gorms. He did things like Twitch at Glen Nevis which is an E1 slab route, a pure slab and totally unprotected, although I don't know if the guide gives him credit for that. So when I got to climb with him there was a wee bit of that hero worship around when John said: 'You have this pitch.' and you knew if you don't get up it he certainly will. The pitch on Gaffers Groove we did was really very good.

Pretty hard and Johnny just made a superb job of it, no going up and down or anything like that – he just seemed to be pretty definite when he started on it."

March himself, in a letter to Jimmy Marshall two years after Cunningham's death in 1982, told of their first climb together: "I knew Johnny between 1969 and 1974 and in the time I climbed with John I never saw him retreat or back off a lead. The first time I met him he was so quiet and unassuming yet there was a certain presence. I was an aggressive young climber eager to climb for the sheer joy of it. It was the classic mentor/apprenticeship relationship and I was to learn more about the business of climbing than any other person.

"Our first route together was Hell's Lum Direct [in the summer of 1970]. It was a classic gully route and the crux pitch was normally climbed by the left side up a steep crack. The guide also mentioned a fierce looking crack on the right side and John decided it would be a good first ascent for a wet day. It was lashing rain as we tramped across the plateau and we soloed to the foot of the cave. I looked up; it looked awful, a narrow slit streaming with water."

March knew it was his lead; and also knew he was being tested, but he was on ground that suited him since the gully puts more of a premium on brute strength than good technique.

"As it happened I need not have worried in spite of the fact I gave a rather dismal performance. The crack succumbed slowly to some desperate thrutches until I found myself stuck next to a chockstone with my feet dangling, rather like a man stuck in the neck of a bottle.

"John expressed concern about lack of runners, I got a leeper in and John uttered some muffled words of praise. He must have been getting wet and cold but never complained. I didn't want to go down and hand over the lead, not for a reason of pride, but because I wanted his respect. I pushed upwards against the chockstone, which was the size of a TV set, and suddenly it broke loose."

March managed to hold the boulder in place and then threw it, over his shoulder, missing his second by a foot. Cunningham's rationalisation of what had been a close shave was typical: "Aye, well there should be a bit more room now the wee boulder's gone." Later, over a drink, March asked him: "Would you have gone up if I had come down?"

"You didn't," said Cunningham with his quizzical smile.

Despite this unpromising beginning, Cunningham adopted March as his climbing partner, rightly reasoning that the Englishman's youthful vigour could give some impetus to what was his third decade in climbing. Certainly after several years when he had stopped pioneering new routes in Scotland, March and the large, untapped areas of the northern Cairngorms proved rejuvenating. Both men had staff flats at the Lodge and Karen March, Bill's Canadian wife, recalls: "Bill and John were great climbing buddies with tremendous respect for each other's abilities. I came on the scene in 1971 when their friendship and partnership in climbing were established. They were always having great planning sessions down in our flat over tumblers of sherry."

There was little doubt, however, who was the senior partner in the alliance. March would introduce Cunningham anecdotes into his course lectures and his hero worship could sound faintly embarrassing, while Ken Wilson, in his outspoken way, often wondered about March's motivation. Wilson says: "I met Bill when he was at Kings College and he was a very pushy sort, very upwardly mobile, very ambitious and very able but I wondered how keen he actually was on climbing, although he was interested in getting his standard up. Some of his behaviour could be a bit bizarre at times. I was on the management committee at Plas y Brenin when Bill got the principal's job there after leaving the Lodge. There were some feral goats in the field opposite which Bill took exception to and one day he just had them all shot causing a huge outcry among the locals. People like Esme Kirby [wife of Thomas Firbank of *I Bought a Mountain* fame] were absolutely outraged."

Exploration in the northern Cairngorms had accelerated after the Coire Cas ski road was completed in July, 1960, although far from dramatically. The cliffs of Coire an Lochain and Coire an t-Sneachda could be reached within an hour from the car-park and access to the hitherto remote crags in Loch Avon was made relatively easy with a ride up the first ski chair of the morning and a descent from Cairngorm down Coire Domhain or Coire Raibeirt into the massive basin encircled by Shelter Stone Crag, Carn Etchachan, Hell's Lum and Stag Rocks. Robin Smith,

who climbed his first snow route on Coire Cas as an Edinburgh schoolboy on a Lodge Christmas course in the 1950s, had found the Needle on
the Shelter Stone in 1962. But even this, the first extreme in the Cairngorms, had failed to spark the stampede for new rock usually associated
with other areas. Exploration was spasmodic although there was manifestly plenty of unclimbed rock around. In the case of the embryo
Cunningham/March partnership any new routes had perforce to be attempted in between courses. There were summer rock climbs on Shelter
Stone – Postern Direct, Consolation Groove and Threadbare – but as the
name of Consolation Groove suggests, they had been beaten to the main
prizes. Fyffe says: "They always seemed to be pipped at the post on things
that they really wanted to do. They were after things like Haystack on
Shelter Stone and never got it, they had to be content with Consolation
Groove instead. The same with Pin and Snipers, they just never got these
routes."

At least Cunningham could console himself with another thought: that
Haystack (Nicholson and Carrington), The Pin (Carrington and Gardner)
and Snipers (Carrington and Shields) all fell to Creagh Dhu members.

A winter attempt on Citadel, the big prize on Shelter Stone, proved
to be another frustrating near miss, the pair being benighted after running
out of ice close to the top. A Lodge rescue party, including Bill Smith who
was working on the maintenance of the Cairngorm ski tows by then, met
them coming back across the plateau and as Harper says: "I never saw
Bill move as fast in his life when we got to the chairs and told him John
was missing."

Until his arrival at the Lodge, Cunningham had shown only a marginal interest in snow and ice climbing. True, he had attempted Point Five
and Zero gullies on Ben Nevis with Mick Noon several times and had
made the first ascent of Deep Gash Gully on Aonach Dubh with the same
partner. But compared with the likes of Marshall, Smith, Patey and Fyffe
his contribution to Scottish winter climbing was minimal, although
Marshall, whom many would unhesitatingly place as the greatest British
ice-climber of all time says:

"John when he put his mind to it was undoubtedly one of the best
ice climbers ever although I have to say I was amazed by his lack of

prowess in the Alps. He always kept his crampons razor sharp, Jimmy Stenhouse and I once hammered them two inches into the Jacksonville floor for a laugh. He was very tidy and methodical on ice. In the late 50s he wanted to climb Zero and Point Five with Noon and would have climbed it given the conditions but they just kept missing it. I did Ravens with him and McLean and we did it old style. McLean stood on a boulder and Johnny stood on him. But then when we got higher I couldn't see how he got up. I struggled up eventually then asked him: 'How on earth did you do that.' And he said: 'Ha ha! I found this wee hole for my ice axe hammered it in, then just did a handstand on it.' He was like that, would always withhold a vital piece of information!"

Normally, however, when the snow fell Cunningham went skiing, although he was by no means outstanding at this.

He had been among the first in the club to try skiing back in the 40s and in fact helped introduce Frith Finlayson to the sport, but over the years his improvement had been only marginal. Both Finlayson and George Shields (although, it must be said, their standards as top-class instructors are extremely high) had scant respect for Cunningham the skier.

Finlayson says: "I failed Johnny when he took BASI and he didn't take too kindly to it. But I always gave him a hard time with skiing. I think it was my revenge for all the hard times I got when I was behind him on a rope. I used to lead him a merry dance on the skis."

"Johnny was a crap skier," says Shields. "Really crap. No rhythm or anything, you just wouldn't recognise him at all, this guy who could move so well on rock. It was just like his bike riding, no feel for it at all."

Mike Wright remembers Cunningham trying to pull a practical joke on Ali Ross, the well-known instructor, when Ross was working for Finlayson on Cairngorm.

"That smoothy Ali was taking a ski school and John was trying to sneak up and push him over in front of his class. However, just as John was about to shove Ali he tipped over himself and fell at Ali's feet, much to everyone's amusement, including his own. I can also picture John on one of the T-bars hopping up the slope on one leg which was no problem with those fit thighs of his."

Cunningham's skiing was hindered by a locking cartilage in his knee, a legacy of his wrestling days, which could occasionally be embarrassing.

"One day he was skiing at Meall a' Bhuiridh," says Davie Todd, "when he went into a tuck and the knee locked and he couldn't get up. So he's hurtling down towards a ski line and totally unable to get out of this tuck and has to go into a hockey stop. But his edges stuck in and he flipped, right on to his head and back on to his feet whereupon the knee unlocked and he landed on the end of the line. So John just shuffled forward as the next in the queue and trying to look as though that was normal routine and of course everyone is looking at this and saying 'That ... was... incredible, that guy is some skier!' "

When Cunningham did belatedly throw himself into winter climbing it was with the passion and dedication of an addict. Most Lodge personnel can pinpoint the start of the snow and ice front-pointing era almost exactly; the winters of 1970-71, when nights in the staff wing were made hideous by mysterious comings and goings and the sound of hammering late into the small hours. It was the time when everyone's favourite ice axe underwent a metamorphosis; first a softening by heat, then some bending and shaping to the required angle (the degree of slope of the head occupying hours and hours of discussion and occasionally argument) followed by some tempering. Cunningham, March and others went out into the Cairngorms armed to the teeth with every conceivable size and shape of shaft, hammer pick and serrated teeth. Most were tried, rejected or retained. What satisfied the activists one week was *passé* the next as new and even more bizarre tools appeared on the market. The use of crampons with two projecting front points to kick or balance a way up ice was not new; the Austrian and Germans had used the technique throughout the 60s (and even prewar in the case of Willo Welzenbach), and Cunningham himself in between survey trips on his second spell in Antarctica had experimented on ice walls near the Marguerite Bay base, eventually discovering that he could climb some quite steep walls in balance and without the use of hands, arms or axe.

Iain McMorrin remembers some of Cunningham's early experiments with front-pointing at Stonington in 1962: "There was an ice cliff close to base on the North-East Glacier and John would take me out to practise ice-climbing. I had these Grivel 10-point crampons, heavy lash-on things with vertical points, and an expensive Simond axe which I had taken down south with me. John looked at this disdainfully and told me it was useless, I had to cut it down. A long axe was OK for walking but pretty useless for that type of climbing and John had one of his cut down so the hand was closer to the pick. This was 1962 and I could see even then he was thinking and brooding about this technique. When I heard about the advent of front-pointing later on, I realised John had taken this from Antarctica all those years before to Glenmore Lodge."

In the famous interview in *Mountain 14*, Cunningham told Ken Wilson: "I used to practise on some big lumps of ice for about an hour a day and soon got tired of chopping steps so I started to see how steep I could climb just by knocking the front points in. I found that eventually I could climb up to 80° ice with no support for my hands just with my nose on the ice. When I came back to Scotland and started using the new Salewa type of crampon this improved things even more and since then I have hardly had to resort to step cutting."

The Cunningham concepts were greeted with scepticism in some cases and in others outright hostility by the traditionalists weaned on the old method of fashioning a ladder of steps up steep ice for hours at a time.

Fyffe admits he took a deal of persuading: "I had been with Jim McCartney over in the Hutchison Memorial Hut in Coire Etchachan. It was late December in 1969 and we had just done the first winter ascent of Architrave.

"The plan was to walk out of there and over to the Lodge for Hogmanay because Jim was sure that was the place to be, he had his leather jacket with him and thought he could cut a dash there. Anyway we came over and met Johnny and Big Bill and proceeded to get very drunk on cheap sherry in Cunningham's room and the next thing I remember the conversation had moved on to front-pointing. At that time Jim and I had done some very good routes in the traditional style, Parallel Gully B and Zero and things like that. Jim was making a name for himself at that time but I was a young lad and just stayed quiet in the background. Johnny and Bill had just moved on to front-pointing but Jim didn't go along with this concept. We were using the old Grivel 10-point crampons and Johnny was insisting we had to get 12-point crampons with front points but of course we couldn't afford a second pair just to experiment. There was what you would call a heated discussion, a lot of which I am sure was down to the old East/West divide before it just fizzled out into drunken ramblings. Later I realised what a good grasp Johnny had of anything technical like that. He really understood climbing gear, perhaps it went hand in hand with being a joiner."

For Cunningham the worth of front-pointing was irrefutable and as he told Wilson somewhat testily: "I haven't the time to justify something that I know works perfectly."

With March, and using front points, he did a very quick repeat of Zero Gully, but the problem of gripping tools for the hands remained. Conventional ice axes without a raked pick invariably pulled out when weight was applied and on Zero and, later, their most famous route The Chancer on Hell's Lum, the pair had used ice daggers which as well as needing considerable strength to apply and pull up on, proved very limiting in other ways. On The Chancer – their attempt in January, 1970, to find Scotland's first Grade Six – the ice on the main vertical icicle dinner-plated as Cunningham was pushing down on a dagger and he was luckily held on an ice screw.

It was plain that a new breed of ice tools would be needed but they need not have worried; the US Cavalry was riding to the rescue in the shape of a young climber from Maine born to French-Canadian parents and called Yvon Chouinard. Chouinard, arguably the greatest innovator in most forms of climbing (his Great Pacific Iron Works, as well as rigid crampons, curved hammers and axes also produced the first chromolly-steel rock pitons) had arrived in Scotland with his friend Doug Tompkins in the winter of 1970 midway through an eight-year mission to write a book called *Climbing Ice*.

Chouinard had spent a lot of time travelling and taking in various techniques for his book. Originally planned for publication in 1973, such was the pace of change in ice-climbing that constant revision meant it did not hit the bookshelves until 1978, when it at once proved the definitive work in its field.

He had first started making ice-climbing equipment in the mid-60s and had visited Chamonix in 1965 and 1966 where he front-pointed the

North Face of Les Courtes, an experience that left his calf muscles 'wrecked' and he himself determined to find an axe that would take some weight off the lower limbs on steep ice. Chouinard, who between fishing trips is still a major player in the innovative gear and clothing Patagonia factory in Ventura, California, says: "Les Courtes was a horrible experience and I went straight from there to the Charlet factory in Chamonix and persuaded them to make me an axe with a bent pick, which took them by surprise to say the least. I had researched *Climbing Ice* for something like eight years and tried to assimilate every technique from around the world. It was like skiing and every country had its different systems. The Germans had front-pointing, the French had the flatfooted technique and the Scots had step cutting so I was pretty well read up when I went over to the Cairngorms."

In February, 1970, a month after the Cunningham/March ascent of The Chancer, Chouinard and Tompkins, using rigid 12-point crampons and new curved axes, caused a major stir with the first winter ascent of the direct finish to Raven's Gully on Buachaille Etive Mor. This was a much-discussed, much-coveted but seldom in-condition line and, although its ascent owed more to Chouinard's stunning lead up the desperate final chimney on thin verglassed rock and with minimal protection, than the magical properties of the new American tools, most saw this as a breakthrough. The meeting between the 32-year-old Chouinard and the 42-year-old Cunningham at the Lodge later that season later took on all the significance of Rodgers' introduction to Hammerstein. Cunningham, for one, immediately recognised the worth of Chouinard's curved axes while the American was later quick to acknowledge the debt he owed the Scot "for revealing to me the subtleties of front-pointing".

Chouinard and Tompkins followed a Cunningham snow and ice course over to Hell's Lum, whose Alpine character – in some winters a bergschrund appears at the foot of the initial slabs – impressed the two Americans. They also had a narrow escape soloing when a section of windslab broke away just in front of them. Later still, they watched as one of the students was caught in a small avalanche on the way back to collect the pack he had dropped, fortunately he stayed on the surface.

Chouinard says: "We went off and did some steep little routes on

Hell's Lum. John was very interested in the new axes and we hit it off pretty well. I enjoyed his company but of course he didn't have the right gear. But he was very open and keen to take in new techniques."

Cunningham also took Chouinard back to Glencoe for an introduction to Jacksonville and the Creagh Dhu, an experience the American would never forget: "We were there in this, well hut is probably too kind a word for it, and John trapped and killed this rat. When some other guy arrived at the door later that night John asked him if he fancied a sandwich and presented him with the rodent ... between two slices of bread."

The experience failed to dim Chouinard's enthusiasm for all things Scottish and he returned in 1976 after being handed the finance for a National Geographical film on Scottish winter climbing, part of a major travelogue which unfortunately has never seen the light of day. Chouinard recruited a number of leading British climbers including Cunningham, Nicholson – who three years earlier had soloed Point Five and Zero in a morning – and MacInnes and filming began on Ben Nevis in almost perfect conditions, although perilously close to spring.

"Part of the film was supposed to be fictional," says Chouinard, "with John playing a hard case from a rundown part of Glasgow. He rides on his motor bike across Rannoch Moor, solos something and then slips and falls but no-one knows if was it real or imagined, it was kinda surreal. The film never got to be seen because later on in another section, filmed in China, half the film crew were caught in a terrible avalanche. The director was killed and I broke a couple of ribs. I was not very lucky with those sort of things. On the first day of spring on the Ben I was caught in a soft-snow avalanche when a cornice broke on Number Two Gully and I was tangled in rope but stayed on the surface, fortunately. I can remember John and Hamish sprinting on their crampons for safety while I caught the brunt of it. I remember John thought it all highly amusing. But we got some great climbing, there was rime ice everywhere. I got to do Point Five with John and it was great. I would say without a doubt he was the best ice climber I came across in Scotland, catlike and very natural, he just moved so well."

Cunningham's earlier debut as a climbing film star did make the small screen – when John Cleare, the celebrated mountain photographer and a crew from London Weekend filmed him and Tom Patey in Coire an Lochain in the Northern Corries in 1970. This production, too, had its teething problems and while Cunningham probably thought the Nagar porters on his Disteghil Sar trip the ultimate in stroppy indolence, he had to revise his opinion after his exposure to the ACCT, the film technicians' union.

"The first problem surfaced when the crew arrived in Aviemore and discovered their hotel wasn't licensed," says Cleare. "It was Easter and quite busy so they had to be moved to somewhere like Grantown which of course with the extra driving lost us precious time. When we did finally get on the hill, Tom in his usual fashion was striding ahead into the coire with the tripod – Ian Clough was helping out too – and when we got to the big snow slope up to The Vent he jokingly said something to the crew like: 'Don't slide off here, boys, or you'll finish in the loch.' There was a stunned silence, then one of them said: 'Right lads, all out' and they basically just sat down in the snow. The producer was Alex Hamilton-Brown who had walked in with his suede coat with fur collar, and they told him they wanted danger money for carrying on. So he had to walk out to the car park, drive down the road – the phone in the car-park wasn't working – and ring London to negotiate their 'danger money'. By the time all this was sorted out of course the light was gone. And all this time the crew were sat in the same spot in the snow. I really hoped they got piles."

Cleare and his reluctant helpers eventually filmed Cunningham and Patey in the Left Branch of Y Gully, a Grade III on which Cunningham demonstrated unsuspected step-cutting skills. Cleare was struck by the contrast between the two men, both firmly ensconced in Scottish mountaineering legend by this time, but who had rarely climbed together.

"Johnny was so neat, competent and meticulous in his climbing; Tom would go for it, punching holes, forcing it with his head-down style. Johnny of course was always immaculately turned out, too, always with the latest climbing wear while Tom would invariably have odd socks on. But they obviously got on very well together."

It was the advent of front-pointing that prompted Ken Wilson to travel north from London to interview Cunningham for a special edition on Scottish winter climbing in *Mountain* magazine.

Wilson, who can probably be best described as the Marshall MacLuhan of the climbing world, an acerbic theorist, opinionated chronicler and the recognised guru on every aspect of the sport, was into his second year as editor at the time and, he admits, not very experienced in the techniques of interview journalism.

The article, in fact, caused a lot of soul-searching for both men.

After regurgitating for Wilson's benefits most of the major Creagh Dhu myths – including the Battle of Zermatt – Cunningham went on to describe his first trip to Antarctica and the crevasse incident. Unfortunately, and obviously in an attempt to introduce some black humour into the tale, he then implied that the rest of the party had left him to die in his icy tomb. Within weeks, Wilson had nasty letters from Louis Baume and Duncan Carse and had to publish a humbling retraction.

Tom Price, who was on the same trip, rationalises it into 'Johnny's embroidery' and says: "When the interview with *Mountain* went in we were quite shocked. I didn't take much notice really putting it down to John's sense of humour but others took strong exception and they had to publish a retraction. I thought John was a bit of a fool to say it. What is certain is that he was not left by his companions but it is true that if he had not been able to climb out himself they could have done little to help him, for the party had left camp without rope, axes or food intending to be away only a few minutes.

"The expedition had ended in an atmosphere of *bon accord* and when several years later the article appeared everyone was amazed and incredulous and two, Baume and George Spenceley, very much incensed. I shrugged it off as a joke that rather misfired and it did not seriously alter my good opinion of Cunningham. He could always make a story a bit more dramatic or comic and leaving behind someone who could not keep up was, according to him, the kind of thing the Creagh Dhu would do; it was a way of vetting aspirants to apprenticeship."

The incident left Wilson with a somewhat jaundiced view of Cunningham, the Creagh Dhu and most things Scottish and he says: "I wanted to do a winter climbing issue and Robin Campbell and Jimmy Marshall pointed me in the direction of Cunningham. In retrospect he was probably the wrong person because he and Bill March were into this short, very steep ice climbing and it was considered a bit avant garde. But it went down great and he was an interesting character and a force in rock climbing in competition with Brown and Whillans. I found him a discursive sort of guy but he dropped me right in it. I got very tart letters from Baume and Carse leaving me in no doubt what would happen if we didn't retract. A more experienced journalist would have seen the potential trap and got the other side of the story, but I was a bit green in those days. Baume owned Gaston's Alpine Books in Harrow on the Hill in London and was a relic of empire, very preppy. I screamed at Cunningham, 'retract say something, anything', because it could have turned nasty."

Cunningham himself was extremely concerned about legal action and Harper remembers: "It was a very bad time for John. I don't think I ever saw him so worried about anything."

Early in his stay at the Lodge, Cunningham had renewed his climbing acquaintanceship with another old Creagh Dhu colleague, George Shields, then resident in Aviemore. The pair discovered the possibilities of Stac an Fharaidh, which although in a prominent position above The Saddle at the head of Strath Nethy, had been totally overlooked by passing climbers.

Stac an Fharaidh is like a mini-Etive with reasonably difficult padding up glaciated slabs and Cunningham had first discovered them with a Lodge party in the summer of 1969. He took Shields back to produce four more routes, much to the surprise of Shields, who believed the pair had had an irreconcilable falling-out the year before.

Shields, who has worn out several sporting careers – all at the highest standard – including gymnastics, rock-climbing, skiing and cycling, still lives in Aviemore and works part-time at the Loch Insh sailing school whose proprietor Clive Freshwater also worked at the Lodge. (Freshwater won a famous legal battle in the 70s with the landowners along the Spey over the legal rights to canoe the river.)

Shields says: "I became very active climbing wise in the late 60s and early 70s and John and I did a route together in Coire an Lochain in 1968 called Procrastination. While we were doing that we spotted this other line parallel to it and Johnny said 'We'll keep that for you and me and come back and do it together'. I said OK but time went on and I was up there one day with Brian Hall. We had another climb in mind but then I saw a load of folk in Savage Slit and thought we had better go and do the Johnny line before someone else spotted it. So we did it, Daddy Longlegs, but unknown to me Johnny was watching me through a telescope from the Lodge, he had a fix on me. When I got back I could tell he was in a huff and I could also tell he knew what I had been up to but he asked me what I had done and I told him.

"He said: 'You know we were going to do that route together'. I started to explain but then he just cut me off and said: 'Well I don't think very much of that, in fact Big [John] McLean would never have done that and he's a right bastard.' So what did that make me? We climbed together after that but then he started with Bill March and I think he always held Daddy Longlegs against me. Bill used to come to our house a lot and socialise but he got awful childish about climbing, childish in a competitive way. It was if he was a bit jealous. I am not competitive at all and neither was Johnny in that sense but this is something I have noticed in English climbers, they are all a bit like that. I think Johnny in the end got fed up with Bill. Bill would get him up in the middle of the night and say we will go and do a great Grade Six over at Shelter Stone or wherever and John would be up and ready in the morning and Bill would still be in bed saying: 'Oh, I won't bother going up today'. He got pissed off with that. Johnny to me was a climber's climber, your sort of Stirling Moss. Moss never actually won the world championship and Johnny never did any huge faces but he was acknowledged as the best technically and he was capable of anything. I'd put him alongside Brown or Whillans although he never had the fan club or the publicity they had. But Johnny and Bill Smith could always go down south and do anything they were doing."

Cunningham settled into a comforting routine at the Lodge. Rock climbing with students at Chalamain Gap or in the northern corries; training and assessing potential instructors and occasionally longer forays to Glen Nevis and the North West. Unlike most gifted climbers, he was a fine instructor and impressed most of the students he came across. George Kemp from Penicuik, Midlothian, attended a week's assessment for the summer MLC in September, 1973 and recalls: "On the three-day expedition we were in the wild country between Loch Laggan and Loch Ericht. John obviously had very strong thoughts about walking on the hill and insisted we all walked in single file. I was made tail-end Charlie with John in front of me and he said I was to look out for anyone stepping out of line. Not long after that he himself drifted a couple of paces off line and I did exactly what he had told me to do and yanked him back. He looked a bit sheepish at this but then explained he liked to walk on ground that had never been trodden before. That made a big impression on me. Next day we were having a drum up near Ben Alder when along the track came a Land Rover with four guns and a gamekeeper. The keeper asked John where he was bound and he mentioned a route which seemed to satisfy the keeper who said he and his party would be shooting near a certain corrie and it would be appreciated if we would keep away in case we frightened the deer. John agreed – but we still finished up in that corrie."

In the winter the Lodge ran skiing courses, BASI assessments, winter survival and snow and ice climbing weeks and John also found time to become a competent sailor and canoeist, although water was not an environment he was comfortable with. Bob Smith, now the principal at the Sports Council's Cumbrae watersports centre near Largs in Ayrshire, says: "John was never a canoeist. There was one day on the Feshie when he and Allen Fyffe were heading down in a C2 and it broke up on some rocks. John hopped out straight away while Allen carried on with half the boat wondering why he was having to do all the work. He had to take the British Canoe Union qualification and for that you needed a bronze medallion for life-saving and basically we just cheated him through it, talking to the assessor at vital moments."

Reg Popham says: "John got into canoeing when we did staff training and got the basic proficiency but he was never happy. When we did the bronze medallion we trained in the pool at Aviemore baths and took the test at Inverness baths. John was teamed with Stuart Anderson who was Olympic standard, very strong and he was flipping hands under water and keeping Johnny up. "

Cunningham, however, did have other uses on canoe courses.

Smith says: "We were out on the Insh when we were having problems over access and this guy called Brigadier Curtis comes marching up to confront us. John of course says: 'Who are you?'

'I'm Brigadier Curtis.'

'Are you in the army then?'

'I was, yes. Who are you?'

'I am John Cunningham. But since I was a magistrate in Antarctica you can call me John Cunningham ... JP.' "

John also discovered table tennis in a big way, and would commandeer the table in Ben the Hoose after dinner for prolonged and fierce sessions with his girlfriend Alison or, when she was not there, anyone else who fancied their chances. It was a sport whose subtleties appealed to the more devious side of his nature and like anything he tried, he went into the fine detail of penholder grips, crafty spin serves and strangely-layered bats. The well-known Lake District climber Des Oliver worked as a voluntary instructor at the Lodge in the early 70s having suffered the usual introductory Cunningham put-down several years earlier.

Oliver says: "I first met John at Lagangarbh Hut in Glencoe in 1952. We had just come back from climbing Red Slab on Rannoch Wall and as I hadn't done many VS routes I was feeling pretty chuffed. As I entered the hut Cunningham was sat at the table writing something in the hut log. I didn't know who he was at the time and it was only after reading the book later I discovered who he was. Anyway he asked what we had done and when I said Red Slab he said 'Aye, an average VS'. My ego came down a few notches.

"Later I was working as a voluntary instructor at the Lodge in the early 70s and John of course was there, too. We went out together a few times on the plateau but the thing I remember most about him was not the mountaineering but the table tennis in Ben the Hoose. In the evening we would have an occasional game. I played a bit but I could never beat John; he used the penholder grip and that accentuated the spin. He used to take great delight in seeing your attempted returns fly all over the place."

Other visiting instructors suffered more severely at the hands of Cunningham and his humour which some, usually not on the receiving end, would find extremely funny, and others quite painful. In their mildest form, his practical jokes would consist of unscrewing the salt cellar so that your dinner was covered in a mound of salt when it came your turn to use it; at the other extreme there were some very dodgy sandbaggings, as the teenage twin brothers who arrived at the Lodge to work as voluntary instructors over the summer of 1973 found out to their cost.

Both were able climbers, but very young, occasionally brash and of course English, a combination Cunningham would find irresistible. One day one of the twins announced he was going down to Newtonmore to climb The Hill at Creag Dubh, an E2 on the main face notorious for its minimal protection, and approached Cunningham for advice about placements.

"What did you take when you did it." he asked.

"A number four hexagon," replied Cunningham.

Off went the young aspirant. At the crux, however, he discovered not only was there no crack to take a number four hexagon, but precious little for anything else and, after a serious epic he took a long fall and although held by his second, his brother, sustained moderately serious injuries, including a broken pelvis. It was some weeks before he returned to The Lodge, complete with plaster and crutches and the first thing he did was confront his climbing advisor:

"I thought you said you took a number four hex?"

"Aye, that's what I took."

"But I couldn't find anywhere to place it."

"Funny that." replied Cunningham, "neither could I."

On a mountain rescue course, Allen Fyffe witnessed another example of the Cunningham quiet put-down: "They were doing an improvised lower and Johnny set the scene for this guy: 'You are on a climb together and halfway up your mate feels ill so what are you going to do?' This guy thought about it for a bit then rigged up this incredible haulage and pulley system and basically pulled his mate up the cliff. He got him onto the ledge and of course was absolutely knackered. Johnny just turned to him and said: 'That's very good, but what did you do that for?' And the guy says: 'Well, I was trying to rescue my mate'. So Johnny, and here you'd have to imagine the sort of earnest look and puzzled voice he'd put on in situations like this, asked him: 'Strange, I thought it would be easier to lower him'. "

Like many in high-risk pursuits, Cunningham and other Lodge staff found humour a way of confronting near-death or injury.

Mike Wright was a career army officer who had narrowly missed out on SAS selection when he met John at the Lodge. Wright was a hard case but a gentleman and he hit it off with Cunningham right away although it cost him a bad injury. Wright, now an electrician in Helmesdal, Norway, says: "I was on a survival course at the Lodge in 1968 where I first met John. I'd be about 29 and he really epitomised everything I wanted to be, but couldn't. He had charisma and I even copied his style of dress with the tight climbing breeches. He took me under his wing and I owe a great deal to John both as a teacher and a friend. In many ways I should describe him as my hero – he did things in a way I should have loved to have done but I didn't have what it takes. I respected him as a climber and I think he respected me as a canoeist. We tried to help each other improve. I had many laughs with him, but I also had what could have been a serious accident with John. We were climbing unroped in the gully to the right of Aladdin's Mirror in Coire an t-Sneachda. It had a huge cornice which we had to tunnel through and it was I who was given the honour of going out on top first. John's final words as shouted up to me were 'Don't lean back' which of course I did, bringing down the cornice and everything, except John's favourite axe, down to the valley floor. It was painful and I ended up in Raigmore Hospital, Inverness for eight days alongside another group from the Lodge who had been avalanched off the Coire Cas headwall. But the first words John spoke to me when he reached me were: 'Where's my axe?' As pained and shocked as I was I had to laugh. I was very friendly with Bill, too, but later on I sensed a schism between them. Out here in this valley there is one of the biggest waterfalls in Norway and it freezes into an icefall in winter. I told John it was something he and Bill should try but he was very keen that he would do it with me. He didn't want Bill to find out about it. But I mentioned it to Bill and he was all for the cameras and TV coming out; John couldn't stand that sort of thing."

Because of its location, the Lodge was in the front line for mountain rescue in the Northern Cairngorms, much of it involving searches for walkers and climbers lost on the plateau between Cairngorm and Ben Macdui. In fact, the Lodge was an official mountain rescue post complete with radio in the small office next to Harper's, and instructors invariably carried Pye handsets even on the most mundane of expeditions.

Says Harper: "When I arrived at the Lodge we were part of the Cairngorm team, which I didn't like, and we withdrew. The Glenmore Lodge team were involved in a huge amount of rescue, there was a moral obligation because we were so highly skilled and the best placed. But it became a rod for our backs and I became used to waking people up in the night to call them out to look for a lost soul. It eroded into their own time and there was terrific pressure on the Lodge instructors."

Despite their rounded and benign appearance accentuated by their easy access via the Coire Cas car-park and the trappings of a skiing centre, its lifts and mountain restaurants, the northern Cairngorms are in fact a carefully baited trap. The top chair lift lands customers within 400 feet of the Cairngorm summit at the Ptarmigan restaurant while midway along the popular walk from Cairngorm to Ben Macdui was what appeared on the map to be the haven of the Curran bothy, a scruffy but serviceable shelter. In bad weather, however, the plateau swiftly closes its jaws and Lodge principals over the years had always been circumspect about winter trips up there.

In normal conditions it's a reasonable walk across the plateau; under snow and with the few landmarks like Coire Domhain and Coire Raibert often covered and impossible to find, pinpoint navigation is required. In severe winters the Curran bothy would disappear all together, its tin chimney, sticking out of 15 feet of snow, providing the only clue to its whereabouts. Add to all this winds of up to 100mph – even in summer – and you have the most lethal mountain area in Britain.

On the early evening of Sunday, November 21, 1971, the Lodge staff had just finished dinner when Harper called them together for a briefing. With him were a worried-looking Ben Beattie, a teacher at Ainslie Park Secondary School, Edinburgh and John Paisley, principal of the Edinburgh Education Authority outdoor centre at Lagganlia, three miles south of Aviemore close to Feshiebridge. Harper told the staff what he knew: a party of six children and two female instructors from the school were missing on the plateau having set off from Lagganlia a day earlier. Their probable location was between Cairngorm and Macdui although there was a possibility they had found their way down into Loch Avon or even the Lairig Ghru. Outside the Lodge, it was classic call-out weather with the first blizzards of winter sweeping the hills. On the summit of Cairngorm temperatures were well below freezing while winds of 50mph battered the plateau. Harper recalls: "When Beattie and John Paisley appeared at the Lodge at around 7 pm I knew the minute I saw them we had a tragedy. Nothing was more certain."

It was a tragedy that was to change the future of outdoor pursuits irrevocably and leave a lasting impression, not just on Cunningham, but on most of the Lodge staff involved. The seeds of Scotland's worst-ever mountain disaster were sown weeks earlier at Ainslie Park where, like many schools under Edinburgh Education Authority, outdoor pursuits were considered a key part of the curriculum. Some children, as well as various expeditions in Scotland, had canoed Grade Four rivers in Austria and climbed in the High Tatra in eastern Europe. Beattie ran the school's mountaineering club and had planned a tough winter outing for his charges that weekend. They were to head for Lagganlia on Friday, spend the night there and then set off over Cairngorm to Ben Macdui – another 4,000 footer – on the Saturday morning. If all went well there was the possibility of crossing the Lairig Ghru, the 10-mile defile leading from Coylumbridge almost to Braemar, and climbing Braeriach and Cairn Toul the remaining two of the Cairngorms' four 4,000ft mountains. The itinerary was virtually out of the question even in the best of conditions but optimism is the fuel of most mountain adventures and Beattie's high objectives would be considered fairly routine among climbers. As it was, Beattie modified his plans as soon as he heard the weather forecast on the Saturday morning which foretold deteriorating conditions after a bright start. Plan B was to head over Cairngorm, spend the night at the Curran bothy midway between Cairngorm and Ben Macdui and then descend into the Lairig Ghru and from there back to the pick-up point. Because of the large number in the party (17), Beattie split the group into two, with himself taking the stronger group and the weaker one coming under the leadership of his girlfriend Cathy Davidson, a 21-year-old third-year student at Dunfermline College of PE, a keen climber but with limited experience of Scottish winters. Davidson's group consisted of herself, another student teacher, 18-year-old Shelagh Sunderland, and four girls and two boys aged between 15 and 16. Sunderland, who had gone on the trip of part of her teaching practice, had as it turned out, even less experience than most of the children and is arguably the most tragic figure in whole misadventure.

Beattie and his group were one hour ahead of the Davidson party in passing over Cairngorm and Lodge instructor Steve Mitchell, repairing a radio at the summit, recalls them going through. The weather conditions at the time were of a westerly wind blowing into their faces at around 30 knots along the proposed route. Visibility, too, was down to about 50 yards and from then on, events began to spiral horribly and swiftly out of control. The hour's start that Beattie's party had proved crucial to them. Although they ran into the winds and snow they arrived safely at the Curran bothy at around 3.45 pm, spent the night there and descended via the March Burn to the Lairig Ghru and from there to the pick-up point at the western end of Loch Morlich where Paisley was waiting. It was there that they discovered that Davidson's party had not returned and the two men hastened round to the Lodge to raise the alarm.

Harper, realising that little could be done in the prevailing conditions that Sunday night, nevertheless sent three two-man parties out into the blizzard. Allen Fyffe and Reg Popham headed over the plateau down to the Shelter Stone in Loch Avon – a huge boulder and a traditional doss for climbers and walkers for over 100 years – via Coire Domhain, Chris Norris and Bill March took a parallel course down Coire Raibert with an abortive attempt to find the St Valery Refuge, another bothy perched above Loch Avon, and Cunningham and another instructor made a low-level sweep up Strath Nethy as far as The Saddle at the western end of Loch Avon in the hope that Davidson and her party may have found their way out there. The search swiftly turned into a personal battle for survival for the Lodge staff.

"It was a vicious night," said Fyffe. "It was a hell of a struggle all the way down to the Shelter Stone and Reg was in a bad way. On the way down we set off flares which, it came out eventually, the kids had seen."

Popham says: "We floundered about for ages looking for the Shelter Stone and eventually it was Allen who found it. We sent up a Schermully flare. Chris Norris and I were both pretty knackered but by 7 am next morning the wind had died down. But there was deep snow everywhere and it took the four of us hours just to get the two miles to The Saddle."

The four Lodge instructors were almost into Strath Nethy when Harper's voice came on the radio; Davidson had been spotted staggering in the snow close to the Feith Buidhe, a river inlet above Loch Avon. Harper recalls: "Bill didn't want to go back up. I believe he knew what he was going to find."

Popham adds: "There was only two pairs of snow shoes so Fyffey and Bill went back up from there via Cairngorm and contoured round. Chris and I carried on out. There were helicopters flying round but no ground to air contact and we just had to carry on walking out totally knackered. At one point I remember we saw a Pye radio and picked it up reluctantly because of the weight, that's how done-in we were. Then, finally, a chopper picked us up halfway down Strath Nethy. Six days later all the snow had gone."

Meanwhile, as a part of the massive search mobilised for the Monday morning, Cunningham, Beattie and Paisley had driven up to the ski car-park and were heading up the Fiacaill a' Choire Chais ridge on to the plateau, arriving there at 9.08 am at about the same time that the Whirlwind from RAF Lossiemouth, with Brian Hall on board, found Davidson. Conditions were so bad that at one point Hall had had to climb out and lead the helicopter over the plateau on a rope. Cunningham later told Mike Wright what happened next: "I think John had an instinct where he would find them because of his familiarity with the plateau but in the end there were just six mounds fairly close together covered in snow."

Fyffe and March arrived in time to join the probe line and Fyffe says: "I remember – and it was the first time I had ever done this – my probe hitting one of the bodies."

Gently, Cunningham scraped the snow off the faces of the dead children but something about one of them made him check again. Jabbing the boy gently in the eye he got a response to stimuli and 15-year-old Raymond Leslie was discovered to be still breathing. A few minutes later Cunningham radioed in the news to the Lodge that Harper had been dreading, but expecting. Of the party of eight that set off from Lagganlia on the Saturday morning, only Davidson and Leslie were found alive. Big strong Bill March wept as the snow gave up its victims: Cunningham reserved his emotions until later.

"It was hard to come to terms with at first," says Fyffe who retired from the Lodge in 1998 after 25 years there and is now secretary of the Scottish Mountain Leadership Training Board – with an office annexe in the Lodge.

"I had been on rescues before, but this was different. They were mainly climbing accidents and this was basically a walking accident and it was a group of kids. It affected Bill very deeply I know, but I remembered feeling a slight bit of optimism that we had found one of them alive."

Bob Smith, was among the party deputed to go up and collect the bodies and he said: "You still couldn't see a thing on the Monday afternoon. We threw snowballs ahead to navigate but you couldn't even see them.

"John didn't say much at the time, unlike Bill, but the anger came out later and the sense of waste. He knew he would have got those kids off the hill. You don't bivvy on the plateau in winter. They may have been tired but John would have cajoled them down, kicked them down even. Cathy only did what she had been trained to do."

The six-day inquiry under the Principal Sheriff of Banffshire later pieced together exactly what had happened.

Heading down off Cairngorm on the Saturday afternoon, Davidson and her party ran into bad weather almost immediately and were soon struggling against high winds and fresh snow. To add to the problems, their attempts at navigation in the poor visibility, as it usually does in these circumstances, took them further downhill. It began to get dark and with a tiring party, Davidson took the textbook decision and decided to bivouac. But on the open plateau there was no shelter and fresh powder made it impossible to dig snow holes. In the chaos of the bivvy itself vital equipment like flares and the one pair of snowshoes were lost. At the time they were within half a mile of the bothy and safety and did spot the flare in the distance from the Fyffe/Popham sweep. On the Sunday, after a devastating night, conditions grew worse and Davidson, after one attempt with one of the boys to force her way out, could do little more than go round and dig the children out from time to time. Another night out in the open proved fatal for five of them and Shelagh Sunderland. Harper, an expert witness at the inquiry along with Eric Langmuir, said: "The worst thing was the folly and stupidity of the whole thing. At the inquiry I stayed in an hotel in Banff and the parents of the dead children were there, folks basically with no understanding of what had gone on and how something like this had come about. They had no notion that their kids would be put in a position like that. At one point Lothian Regional Council tried to blame us for not finding the kids on that first night, but the Sheriff said: 'I hope I'm not hearing what I think I'm hearing' to their counsel."

The Sheriff in fact praised the six who went out while the jury, resisting counsel entreaties to censure both Beattie and Paisley, finally delivered formal verdicts of misadventure.

Harper insists, however: "I think John in the conversations I had with him later felt that Ben and Cathy were being left to carry the can, dumped on by people higher up the chain neglecting their responsibilities. They should have been held more accountable than they were. Ben and Cathy were sacrificed in effect."

Smith agreed: "They [Beattie and Davidson] were hung out to dry. Others had set the policy. At one time kids at that school were doing Grade 2 or 3 rivers, the next thing 4 and 5, they were being more and more extended. Ben had done 10 weekends on the trot at time of accident, but that clobbered him. I don't think he ever recovered."

Alison, John's girlfriend and later his wife, remembers ringing him from Liverpool when she heard about the accident.

"I asked him if he wanted me to come up and he said 'No, there is too much going on here'. He was shocked by it all but basically he would just get on with his job. He knew the people who had caused this very well, of course, and it had all been rather foolish. But he was the one who found them as well. It was this ability to just cut off. He had seen it all before, he had lived longer than Bill and seen a lot of tragedies in the mountains. He had helped with a lot of rescues and bodies and things and in the end his feelings and his anger was directed towards the ones who were the cause and he would just cut them completely. He wouldn't say that but the way he treated them in the future would reflect his emotions towards them."

Like the Ibrox football disaster just 10 months earlier, the repercussions from the Cairngorms tragedy were to last for a long time and cause a massive rethink about the way outdoor leisure was approached. In both cases (66 fans died at the Rangers football ground on January 4, 1971, when the terrace stanchions collapsed on Stair 13) several groups of Scottish parents had blissfully seen their children off on a weekend's adventure only for those children never to return; in the manner of the council who will only sanction a pelican crossing after 2.8 fatalities on a road crossing, it took their deaths to hasten change. While Ibrox was totally rebuilt, the Lodge, for one, ended its schools courses and most of the Cairngorm bothies, including the Curran and St Valery Refuge, were demolished over the next few years on the assumption that their presence would cause other parties to extend themselves. Greater liaison was urged between parent and school bodies about outdoor trips and it was recommended, too (although this was impossible to enforce) that certain areas of Scotland should be designated no-go areas for school parties in winter. Beattie, after a spell in the wilderness was offered, in a surprising gesture by Harper, a full-time job at the Lodge which he accepted. "It was time to rehabilitate him." said Harper. "It was a bold step, but justified, I thought."

That Beattie could be assimilated into the life of the Lodge and become friends with Cunningham and other members of the staff says virtually everything about where they, in particular, believed the blame lay for the tragedy. Cathy Davidson also returned to the Lodge to pass her Mountain Instructor's Certificate. Mike Wright, who was on the same assessment course, says: "She was a tough little girl with badly frostbitten hands I remember. But she impressed both John and myself when she managed my fat lump on the mountain rescue carry."

Beattie was later killed on an expedition to Nanda Devi while Davidson married a climber, and later emigrated to Canada where she lives now. Raymond Leslie, the 15-year-old survivor found by Cunningham, later went on to become a top-class canoeist and represented Britain.

Cunningham's final first ascents in the Cairngorms were some of his best. In February 1973, he, March and Roger O'Donovan – later to become principal at the Lodge but at the time an instructor – spent a weekend under the Shelter Stone in Loch Avon and ascended Salamander and Devil's Delight on Hell's Lum Crag on consecutive days, the latter a now classic Grade Five. The photographs of John on it have been published dozens of times and one in fact appears on the cover of this book. Cunningham and March later flew up Point Five in under three hours to finally usher out the era of step-cutting in Scottish ice-climbing, but marriage later that year to Alison and, for the first time in his life, responsibility to someone else, took the edge off his pioneering spirit.

There is little doubt also that by that time his love affair with the Lodge was beginning to pall, although it was to be three years before he finally left.

Davie Todd remembers a letter from him at the time: "I think the Lodge was becoming a routine. It was like map and compass the first day, climbing the second, expedition on Thursday and Friday. It was like the shipyards, he was back in the Big Factory in the Sky."

There were other factors in his disenchantment. A Lodge voluntary instructor who had been in Cunningham's company at an I M Marsh end-of-course ceilidh remembers: "John came over and sat next to me as I was watching Big Jack trying to organise a Strip the Willow or some-thing. John asked me: 'Where's your lemon?' (lemon curd, burd, bird). I had in fact fallen for one of the students in a big way and we later married. Fred had found out about this illicit liaison, mainly because the college principal Miss Jamieson had been staying in the room next to mine and had lodged a formal complaint that one of her girls was being molested by a member of staff. The outcome was I was hauled in front of Fred and sent down the hill so I was keeping well clear of the girl that night. John was outraged and incredibly (incredible because up till then he had always kept his personal life to himself) he spilled out this obviously long-held resentment about Lodge rules and how he had been treated like a child in the case of Alison by Fred, having to keep her at arm's length and so forth. He then lent me a quid (I made very sure I paid it back) and told me to go and buy 'the lemon' a drink. But I knew then he wasn't going to stay at the Lodge."

The friendship between Cunningham and March had turned chilly, too, after the publication of March's Modern Snow and Ice Techniques, which went on to become one of the best-selling climbing books in Britain and which many thought should have been titled John Cunningham's Modern Snow and Ice Techniques. The book, along with another March effort on Mountain Rescue had been published by Cicerone Press. Not to be outdone, Cunningham later also wrote Winter Climbs in Cairngorms, Creag Meagaidh and Lochnagar for the same company – but without the same commercial success. Walt Unsworth, the Cicerone publisher, recalls: "At the time we were going through a stage of bringing out Scottish guide books really in an effort to get the SMC to pull their fingers out and update. Ian Clough had done one for Ben Nevis and Glencoe and John, I think, had similar ideas for the Cairngorms. With John as author I would think it sold around 3,000 copies, reasonably successful, and has continued selling in various different guises since."

Fred Harper says: "Bill's two little books have proved very valuable over the years but I do know that John was the originator of a great deal of the material in it. In saying this, I don't mean that Bill plagiarised something that John had done, he was simply the man with the drive and the energy to get these things down on paper and felt that the publication of them was sufficiently important for him to devote time to this sort of work.

"I never saw any evidence that John had any similar drive to publish or write, perhaps partly because he would not have been in the least interested in any enhancement to his reputation that might have resulted from publication."

When March left for the principal's job at Plas y Brenin in 1975, Cunningham applied for, but failed to get, the job as deputy at Glenmore, a decision that devastated him at the time. The Rhodesian/Scottish climber Rusty Baillie was given the post instead, but it was the awareness of another arrival that finally caused Cunningham to begin thinking about leaving the Lodge for good.

Tommy Paul says: "John appeared at the house in Boat of Garten

Above: South Georgia party on board the SS Southern Opal. Right to left: George Spenceley, Stan Paterson, Tony Bomford, Cunningham, Louis Baume, Duncan Carse, Keith Warburton, Tom Price.

Below: Cunningham drying out after a big storm

Photos: Tom Price

Above: Scraping ice from the sledge runners. Clockwise; Price, Warburton, Cunningham, Bomford, Baume, Carse.

Below: Crossing a large crevasse on the Novosilski Glacier

Photos: Shell Photographic Unit

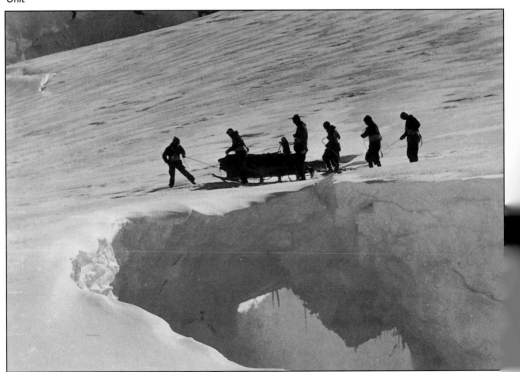

Above: The Lodge staff in 1974. Standing left to right; Jack Thomson, Roger O'Donovan, Reg Popham, Rusty Baillie, Fred Harper, Bob Barton, Adrian Liddle: kneeling; Martin Burrows-Smith, Steve Mitchell, Sam Crymble, Ingrid Kristofosson, Cunningham, Allen Fyffe.   *Photo: Ben Humble*
Below: Cunningham leading Y Gully, Coire an Lochain, with Cunningham and Tom Patey shown in the insert.   *Photos: John Cleare*

Left: How to do it – Bob Smith on the Spey.

Below: How not to do it – Allen Fyffe and Cunningham with their 'double' canoe.
Photos: Cunningham coll.

Above: Cunningham on the Catinaccio d'Antermoia after the 2nd ascent of the NE Face.
Below left: Cunningham climbing artificial on the Civetta   *Photos: Cunningham coll.*

Above right: Cunningham on the top of the Badile after a fast ascent of the Cassin Route.

Davie Todd at the Solvay
Hut on the Matterhorn
Photo: John Cunningham

Below left: Swanning at Zermatt in 1967. Left to right; Alec Fulton, Davie Todd, Cunningham.

Photo: John Cullen

Below right: Cunningham reading in the tent at Alpiglen

Photo: Davie Todd

Alison Waters, Cunningham and Bill March at the Lodge in August 1970

Below: John and Alison's wedding at Rothiemurchus Chapel in 1973. Best man Duncan Ross is partly hidden coming out of the church door.

Above: The doting father with Shauna

Left: Alison Quatermass with Paul Cunningham
and Natalie Quatermass

Below left: Kirsty Cunningham

Below right: Shauna Cunningham

one day and I was chattering away and I knew there was something on his mind. I could always tell with Johnny, he would take his time to get round to it – Bill Smith was more direct, he'd just come straight out with it. If you told Bill you were going to walk off a multi-storey Bill would just say 'Aye, OK, if that's what you want'.

"So I just waited and Johnny eventually said: 'Have you still got my tools?'

"I said 'Aye, do you want them back?' and he said 'Maybe a couple of items.' So he went in the box to lift something out and I asked him: 'What do you want these for, John?'

"And eventually after a lot of humming and aahing he told me ... he wanted them to build a cradle."

DEAR FATHER

In 1970 Cunningham was 42, still single and had just told Ken Wilson in the *Mountain 14* interview: "At times marriage seems like a good idea, especially when you are having a hard time. Then you look round at your friends and wonder about it again. I think I will get married eventually but when I don't know. I still have a lot of things to do and a lot of places to go."

There had been relationships in the past, but most of them had foundered on his insistence on putting climbing before the prospect of true love and from his days at Duke Street, through shipyard, expedition, Creagh Dhu, Antarctica and now the Lodge, Cunningham had spent most of his life in almost exclusively male society.

Willie Rowney recalls the end of one beautiful friendship: "Johnny was very sensitive to any degree of ridicule. He had a girlfriend at one time and he brought her up to Jacksonville for a weekend. Bill Smith and I were the only others there so it was an awkward grouping. We started jesting with him when we caught him doing little jobs around the place as he wasn't famous for doing little tasks and we began to wind him up about this. Eventually he was even washing the dishes and I said to Bill: 'Look, he's washing the dishes now!' and he did not like that. That was the end of a great romance, it stopped that day. I was sorry for a wee while – about 10 minutes. Poor lassie, she must have been ready to knife us. But he was sensitive. When he was in Antarctica one year his mum did a Christmas message and she must have said something like 'I hope you are well, Johnny son' which is how she would speak to him but I think with all the people sat round in the base listening he didn't like it. He had a sort of girlfriend at the time – he was more her boyfriend that she was his girlfriend and she took it upon herself to organise a Christmas message but of course she didn't dare send it herself, she knew he'd be mortified so she got me to do it and I told him how things were in the Coe and all that. That was fine but he didn't like his mum doing it, it was if she was talking to a wee boy. None of us could understand, I don't think he had been out with a girl till he was 23. He would never mention the subject then one day he spotted there were women around and then he made up for lost time. He certainly had a lot of girlfriends after that but how somebody with his appearance escaped for so long I just don't know. At one dance he got slightly tipsy – John was a very average drinker, a comic drunk – and there was a dreadful looking girl there and Johnny decided he was going to do her a favour and dance with her, he had decided he was going to make her evening and he said something to her about seeing her home and she didn't exactly jump at the chance. He told her: 'You are lucky having a presentable young man like me asking to take you home' and she said straight back: 'You should go and get a spoon and lap yourself up'. He came back and told us this and we loved it. That was the comment of the night."

George Shields says: "Johnny, although a very good-looking guy, always resisted women up to a certain stage. We used to call him Second Hand Rose or something like that because he was always moaning about the other married lads and how they were under the thumb. It was a long time before he noticed there was such a thing as girls, probably into his late 20s."

"Girls weren't part of our scene at all," says Tommy Paul. "It was very much a bachelor thing. In many way it cramped your style because people like Smith, Cunningham and myself would never swear in front of a woman and if women appeared at the weekend the boys would feel restricted because of them. They weren't really welcome and it was said to people's faces sometimes. Johnny could be very blunt, very unreasonable at times."

Most of his friends, in fact, considered Cunningham would remain a bachelor all his life until, in May, 1970, thirty-two I M Marsh College first-year students arrived at Glenmore Lodge for a fortnight's outdoor pursuits sampler. The all-girl PE specialist college whose campus was on Barkhill Road, in the leafy suburb of Aigburth in Liverpool, had sent students to Scotland for many years – probably due to the Scottish principal, the formidable Miss Jamieson – and was undoubtedly one of the highlights of the four-year course there. There were introductions to basic navigation, rock-climbing, canoeing and sailing as well as a two-night expedition under canvas, most of which, in the idyllic surroundings of early-summer Badenoch, left a sometimes lasting impression on the teen-agers. If it was a highlight for the girls, however, it was also unarguably a month – the IM Marsh courses went up in two batches – that was antici-pated with some relish by the single staff at the Lodge, most of whom had spent a few long months digging snow-holes or navigating through white-outs with bearded, hoary-handed aspirant instructors on the winter courses.

Cheltenham Ladies College and an amazing institution in Chiches-ter called Bishop Otter – most of whose students were of a staggeringly high standard of good looks – sent girls to Plas y Brenin on a similar course, and however strenuously a succession of principals at both the Brenin and the Lodge may have denied any 'goings-on' there was little doubt that this was one of the perks of a job at both centres. For many, the memories of the Lodge in early summer in the 70s were not of tiptoeing up the granite of Shelter Stone or rolling down the white waters of the Feshie but the sight of dozens of bikini-clad teenagers basking in the sun or playing volleyball during dinner breaks on the large grassy area in front of the staff room. The routine treks up to Chalamain Gap for rock-climbing introduction or the often limiting sailing on Loch Morlich sud-denly became more bearable in the company of 12 students in T-shirts and shorts (even the weather seemed better in those days).

As Allen Fyffe puts it so succinctly: "It was Big Bill who offered me a job at the Lodge and he said it was £25 a week for teaching rock climb-ing to 64 female PE students. I said I didn't think I could afford £25 a week."

Not that liaisons between staff and students were encouraged. Fred Harper admits now: "There were quite strict rules about that sort of thing, but I know also that girls would arrive surreptitiously and I knew also matters like that were generally hidden from me."

In fact, quite a few long-term relationships were formed initially at the Lodge. Davie Todd met his future wife Mhairi when she was domes-tic bursar there and Todd was helping Cunningham out on the climbing courses. Chris Rawlins married a ski teacher.

There was also the 42-year-old John Cunningham and a 19-year-old IM Marsh student called Alison Waters.

Born in Leeds, Alison was a county-class table tennis player and although she admits her personality had been submerged by college life she retained a native bluntness that appealed to Cunningham from the start, although she insists she fell in love with Scotland before she fell in love with him.

She says: "Some of us took to the outdoor life more than others, remember we were only 19 at the time and some of us were quite impressionable. I loved it. When I finished the course I went straight back down to Leeds, changed my clothes and went straight back to the Lodge to work three months of the summer as a skivvy – that's what I did, cleaning the spuds and veg. I think I blossomed then because I had been quite downtrodden at college, not downtrodden perhaps but my personality just hadn't developed.

"I just loved Scotland, I loved the loneliness and I was quite taken by it spiritually. I couldn't believe there was a place like that, I used to wander through the woods on my own at night just taking it all in. I wrote to my mum and dad to tell them how taken I was with it all."

In the same letter Alison told her parents of 'this fantastic man', an instructor at the Lodge. She says: "But it wasn't in a romantic way. Nothing happened at first with John, we were just friends and he had a girl at the time and I had a boyfriend in Leeds although on the way home I rang him up and told him that was it after three years. John was to be admired from a distance because although he was very friendly he treated everyone the same. I think our friendship developed over the table tennis table; he was so awful at it, so I taught him how to play. In return for him teaching me skiing.

"Typical, the day we clicked John was off to the Alps for six weeks the day after so I started trying to get used to the idea that I wouldn't see him for a long time. Anyway, three weeks later I was in the Lodge cleaning and saw the blue mini coming down the road to the front entrance. Big Bill had fallen off something and they were back early. I remember saying to him: 'Gosh, you're back early' and he replied: 'I was quite glad to come back, anyway' and that was that. It was as if it was meant to be."

For the three years before their marriage in June 1973, the couple pursued a long-distance relationship – with Alison doing most of the hard work.

"IM Marsh was very strict, it was like a girl's boarding school. You were not allowed to skip lectures and it was 8.30 in the morning to 5.40 at night. There was no way you could get out of the last lesson. I was a student and the trip used to cost £13. I used to have a taxi waiting, straight down to Lime Street and arrive at Aviemore at four in the morning. Usually John would leave the little blue van there and have a room ready for me and I'd be in the little room with my heart going like this and then he'd wake me at eight and announce we were going to Edinburgh. Off to Edinburgh and back in a day to Tiso's climbing shop in that damn blue mini with holes in the floor and watching the white line whizzing past. But I thought 'Oh yes, I'm in love, I'll put up with all this'. I remember going to one of the Creagh Dhu dinners. I was very young and there was all these hardened Glasgow women there and I was this young bimbo really. I was out of my depth and of course they all wanted John to themselves and I got a bit fed up. They talked a different language really. The men were just quiet Glasgow men, men's men and they certainly weren't interested in me. We hardly thought about the age difference, I didn't anyway. In front of his climbing friends I think John was a bit embarrassed and introduced me as 'a friend' and the others were obviously used to John and female friends and non-commitment, But I wasn't going to be fobbed off. I wasn't pushy or anything but they could tell, this was it. There was never a question that this was going to end, it was just there.

"He wasn't very good on the phone either, it was like a new invention for him and the Lodge had the old button B ones. I'd get two letters a term if I was lucky. Pretty short: 'I must be going now' or 'off skiing this morning'."

Cunningham eventually proposed by letter, saying something like: "How about getting married?" but the strictures of male/female relationships within the Lodge caused a delay to the eventual wedding. Alison had already decided to move to Scotland in 1972 and said: "I rang the director of education in Inverness and told him I was coming up and could he give me a job. But I couldn't teach secondary because the qualifications were different so I finished up teaching primary in Inverness, I used to follow the snow plough down from the Lodge at 8 am on Monday morning. I think John rented me a room in the Lodge because it was all very strict then. We got married the summer after that and had the big three-bedroomed flat in the Lodge. So it was a funny situation. John couldn't live out, he had to live in so we couldn't get married until they built the new houses because there was no co-habitation allowed, Fred was very insistent about that. I left college in 1972 and we got married a year later so we had to wait a year."

The wedding was in Rothiemurchus Chapel and one of the few occasions Cunningham set foot inside a church. Duncan Ross, a senior instructor at the Lodge, was best man and Faye Ogilvie arrived with her mother, husband Bill and her son, George.

Faye remembers: "It was nice wedding, all the crowd were there, all the Boys. Some had their partners and they were all the same, just enjoyed what they were doing. Talked about climbing all night."

Alison says: "John's mum was great, I just called her mum. She was an old lady then but she was lovely. She was obviously very fond of him and he of her although he had never been a great one to keep in touch. Our honeymoon was a disaster. We went up to the Mull of Kintyre and stayed in a little hotel, there was a jug of water on the table when we were having the meal and apparently it was straight off the hill, though we didn't know it at the time. It went straight through me clean as a whistle but John got dysentery and it wasn't very nice and I had to drag him to the doctor who put him on a drip to get the bacteria out of his stomach. Not very romantic. As for married life we were very happy and with me being young and innocent to the world. But life at the Lodge was like being among a family anyway. John had to adjust, though. We'd be up in the Trossachs and he'd pull the van in and expect to sleep in the van, in the snow in January, he was used to it of course."

There were more adjustments to make after Kirsty Cunningham, the first daughter, was born on December 12, 1974. If many of his friends and family had found it hard to picture Cunningham as a married man, the thought of him changing nappies and rocking a cradle astounded them.

"A lot of folk could never imagine Johnny with kids," says Davie Todd. "I could and I knew he would just talk to them like he did the husky pups in the Antarctic". The news left John's sister Faye flabbergasted.

"John was a strange type to be a father because I never ever thought he would have kids. Not so much getting married but having children. He just didn't like them. Don't get me wrong, he loved my son George but my son was mine and he could hand him back you see. When George was just days old, John came to see him and I lifted the baby up and gave him to John and John was sitting there mortified; there was nothing there at all. When he said Alison was having the first one I thought 'In the name of God, what kind of father are you going to be?' But he turned out to be a very good father, very protective and I think loving."

Alison says: "John would think he was still going skiing on a Saturday morning on his day off and I would be there with Kirsty and say 'hang on a minute, what about me going skiing?' He wasn't selfish, he was just doing his own thing. He had to adjust to this other woman in his life. When he was up on the Ben making the Chouinard film for the National Geographic they were up there for ages in an hotel because the weather was bad and I insisted he came down to Yorkshire and picked me up. This didn't go down too well with some of the others. Hamish was there talking in riddles as always and Ian Nicholson and others were there and the sole topic of conversation was climbing, they were all up there in the clouds somewhere, but I just wasn't going to be ignored. He'd say 'Yes but none of them have got their wives there' and I had to remind him that he had two people to look after now. He said: 'Don't start getting fed up with me you are all I've got', but he couldn't express it in words. He had to start thinking about two other people He didn't mind me being there, he had just never thought of it."

Paul Nunn, a massively popular figure on the British climbing scene for three decades, also recalled the change in Cunningham during the Ben Nevis film: "He was in great form during the Nevis filming. He was in his element and talking about his young daughter, Kirsty, he seemed like a man 20 years younger."

When Bill March left the Lodge for Wales, Cunningham applied at once for the vacancy of deputy principal. The interview was at the Scottish Sports Council office in Edinburgh and did not go well.

Alison drove over with him and she says: "John had a very bad interview and I think he knew when he came out he wasn't going to get the job. When Rusty Baillie got it he was very, very disappointed. To make matters worse when we got back to the car we had a parking ticket and we had the nearest thing we ever had to a row. Over the years the Lodge at the staff had become like brothers and it really was a very happy and comfortable climate but when the time came we had to move off from that side of things. I think if he had got the deputy's job I think we would have still been there today and not getting it really was the catalyst for us to move."

Ironically, the job that took Cunningham away from Scotland was at IM Marsh, where a new outdoor education course had been introduced open to both male and females. In charge was Ron James, the North Wales guide who had for many years run the Birmingham Education Authority centre at Ogwen Cottage. The vacancy had appeared after the death of two IM Marsh lecturers, Rick Scott and Dave Bland, killed by stonefall at the foot of the Gervasutti Pillar on Mont Blanc du Tacul in the summer of 1976.

James' then deputy, Jim Lyon, says: "I had met John in the early 70s at the Lodge when I was up there doing my winter MLC and when Rick and Dave were killed we were faced with finding a successor for the autumn term. John had applied and both Ron and myself were very keen to get him on board. We thought it was a golden opportunity to get someone with a name and reputation."

John and Alison moved to a house at No 2, Hillside Road, West Kirby, on the Wirral and within sight of North Wales. She says: "It was pure coincidence that I had happened to be a student at IM Marsh and I knew the area a bit and where to look for a house and a nice area. But it was a bit of a culture shock having lived in the mountains for four years. I used to walk around the Wirral looking for the hills. People insisted there was a hill nearby but it wasn't – it was just a common. I used to walk around in a woolly hat looking a right twit. John could still get to the hills on his courses. I couldn't."

Cunningham maintained a high standard of climbing, spending evenings at the outcrops and was also elected a vice-president of the British Mountaineering Council.

Dennis Gray, the BMC secretary at the time who had spent a lot of time with the Creagh Dhu in the 50s, says: "We used to go for a pint after the BMC committee meetings. John was very quiet but what he said was usually worth listening to. He laughed when he told me he had been at Pex Hill quarry and had been burned off by some of the young lads there. He said he would have to start training again."

Although Cunningham's climbing standards remained consistent, despite middle age, he never managed to improve his driving. That remained consistently bad. On a trip to North Wales, Alison remembers: "We'd gone down in the little blue mini traveller. I think we were at Plas y Brenin and John said he was going for petrol. It was only a mile down the road but by 7 pm he hadn't come back. I was in a panic and rang the police and the police were out looking for him. What had happened was the accelerator jammed and he didn't know how to stop the car, he had to keep going down all these narrow roads and he had finished up in Bangor. In the end he had driven the car into the side of the road to stop it. He was hopeless, absolutely hopeless. Later we had a Fiat estate and I always gave him a box of food to go down to Wales. He rolled the car and the eggs all broke and he thought his brains were leaking there were eggs everywhere, he thought he'd cracked his skull. I used to get postcards from abroad saying 'I want you to hear this before it gets back to England, I skied over a cliff yesterday and I'm in hospital but I've only got 80 stitches'. He was sort of lackadaisical, and I remember someone telling me that away from climbing he was the vaguest man they had ever met."

As at the Lodge, Cunningham made a big impact with the IM Marsh outdoor education students. Lyon says: "He was held in awe by the students but he was not really at home in the college environment. He was far better when he got out in Wales or the Lake District. We had a big camp up in Langdale with about 150 tough Liverpool kids and John dragged me up a few extremes. I was smoking at the time and we were doing Deer Bield Buttress when the matches ignited in my pocket; John was pissing himself as I swung about on the rope trying to put this fire out."

Mark Shrimpton, a former IM Marsh student now living in Sydney, says: "My memories were always how few words he spoke, but by god when he did speak everybody went quiet and listened because you knew that for a man with his judicious and economical use of words every sentence would be full of wisdom. We had this guy on the course called Big John Conville who was a hard man from the Paras and said to be involved in Bloody Sunday in Northern Ireland. He wouldn't listen to anyone but he would take John's advice. Ironically, he was killed at Xmas 1979 on the North Face of the Matterhorn just a month before John. Then there was the Robin Hood's Cave bivvy we did in the Lakes on Helvellyn when all of us keen students had freeze-dried foods and reconstituted stuff and John came out with a frying pan, a bottle of wine, a cut glass and fresh bread rolls. The sizzle of bacon made us think that maybe all this backpacking nonsense was a con spread by manufactures of lightweight foods."

Mike Dales, now the Conservation Officer for Mountaineering Council for Scotland based in Perth, was on an Environmental Education course at IM Marsh in 1979, a part of which took in outdoor pursuits.

He says: "I knew John for one term, a quiet personality and a quiet sense of humour. When you are 19 and wild he was totally the opposite to that. The Glenridding trip was in November, 1979 and we walked up the first day and settled in the cave. There was this quiet Scotsman who wouldn't push into the conversation but when the conversation went quiet he would come in with some real gem of wisdom and really witty, funny stories about the Creagh Dhu, Hamish MacInnes and things like that. He sort of lived as if life went on forever. He was looking at that trip with a group of new students and the main thing over the two days was to get to know those students because we would spend the next three years together. He would walk alongside me and have a chat for 10 to 15 minutes, what I had done in the past, where I was from.

"By this time I was pretty well aware of what he had seen and done and I was thinking 'there you go, I have told you about the canal I used to canoe on when I was 15 now you tell me about the Himalaya', but no he just wanted to talk about me and get to know me. He was a very good lecturer with incredible experience to draw on and the one that stands out was in the last week of term before Christmas. I think it was the traditional winter one and someone once described it as 'The Don't Go Out and Get Yourself Killed at New Year Lecture' and it was very witty and very hard hitting but someone walked out of the lecture afterwards saying 'I hope I will never be counted a friend of John because all through it he would say 'A friend of mine ... ' and it was an illustration of someone having a nasty accident.

"Of course Big John Conville then went and did exactly that on the Matterhorn, so the two John Cs were actually killed within five weeks of each other and they never found his body, either. He had a memorial service in Hampshire.

"He was due to go in the SAS but he wanted life as an extreme mountaineer, too, I remember how enthused he was at the thought of being taught by John for three years, The thing was with John Conville around everyone thought that to be a mountaineer you had to be a big hunk of a chap with massive muscles, but there was this slight man showing students the way up impossible ice bulges and things like that. When Noel Hulmston came round and did his lecture and slide show to raise money for John's family there was this recording of John as he was ice-climbing and you heard this line or two of his voice and everyone had forgotten it. Goose bumps. A presence was suddenly in the room again. Even now there's a strong sense of nostalgia and loss and there were education cutbacks at the time and John was never replaced. So there was something about what John had done in Scotland and what he had done elsewhere never came our way. That was a loss to us as students. I work in Scottish mountaineering and one bit of Scottish mountaineering history I have had contact with was knowing John and for that I'm very grateful."

Shauna Cunningham arrived on August 12, 1977 and Cunningham began to consider his and the family's future again.

Tommy Paul, who stayed in touch after the Cunningham move south, says: "We were joking with Johnny that he would be getting his old age pension. He told me there was an opportunity to get early retirement at 55 from that job and he reckoned he could manage just fine because he could still go to the Alps with private guiding."

"I think that was what he was going to do," says Alison. "He wasn't particularly enjoying himself at college, there was a lot of politics in it.

They were going for a degree course and it was all changing. At the Lodge it had all been free and easy and it wasn't down in Liverpool. He wasn't as happy as he had been at the start."

Cunningham had obtained his BMC guides certificate in 1973 (asked for a list of climbs done, his written reply included 44 first ascents) and there is little doubt he could have swiftly built up a year-round clientele. Jim Lyon, however, had already begun a business called Mountain Ventures run during summers away from IM Marsh and with an office in Liverpool. The obvious choice to lead these was seated opposite him in the IM Marsh staff room.

Lyon says: "John was interested and I think he saw this as a way of getting out of the humdrum of teaching. Being John though, he wanted to change the way we did things, he wanted to take clients out and do the big three, the Eiger, Matterhorn and Mont Blanc in just two weeks after driving all the way out from Liverpool, Typical Cunningham. Then when we got to the Matterhorn he had this other plan; instead of the usual Alpine way we were to go up in evening, stay illegally at the Solway Hut and on from there next day, coming down while all the rest were on way up. But that scheme ran into a snag straight away when a client fell ill on the way up the Hörnli and John finished up having to nurse him down. I can still see John cajoling this bloke down and then our chagrin at seeing him running down the snow slopes with this guy, who suddenly seemed as right as rain. But John was behind him egging him on and he was running down trailing a rope. Unknown to him, John had just untied. I was the big boss of course and went around wearing a suit and with a briefcase and John used to take the piss, calling me the Man in the White Suit. On the first trip with Mountain Ventures we were in Alpiglen camped there and we had some great times in a café there where a lot of the people there remembered John from his attempts on the North Face a lot earlier.

"John certainly had his moments on those trips, some of it was very funny. Me, another instructor Mick Quinn and John were taking another party up to the Rimpfischhorn and we were pushing on even though it was obvious the weather was changing. Both Mick and myself thought it was time to turn back but John leading the first rope gave no sign whatsoever that he intended turning back. All of a sudden there was a clap of thunder and a flash of lightning and that stopped John's rope. A bolt hit a rock about 20 feet away and as one the whole party turned round and started heading back down. John's remark was something on the lines 'Well if they want to go down, we'll let them make the decision!' Then as we were going down this snow slope the static electricity was so great you could hear it in the air. One of the clients had a spare axe on the back of his sack and the tip of the axe was fizzing and buzzing and you could see the client pricking his ears up thinking it was some sort of insect. Cunningham was walking down with his hands in his pockets, the rest of us were quite frightened.

"There was a hard side to John's character, too and it came out whenever anyone tried to give out any bullshit about climbing ability. There was an American client on one of the courses in Grindelwald and we were doing an Ecole de Glace. John was giving a typical session on the glacier and séracs when this guy pipes up: 'When are we going to do something hard?' which of course was a very foolish thing to say to Cunningham. So he picked out this 90 foot concave ice wall and soloed up it placing ice pegs for other people to clip into if they wished to, a very impressive piece of climbing. John Whittle, himself a top-class mountaineer who was working on the course, reckoned it was harder than anything on the Ben this tongue of ice. John came down and handed his Chouinard hammer and axe to the Yank, tied him on the end of the rope and invited him to have a go at that. The client of course couldn't get past the first peg."

Lyon was also struck by Cunningham's measured attitude to death.

"There were two IM Marsh students who had come over independently and one of them was killed on the approach to the Breithorn, just tripped over his crampons and fell. John packed his sack, struck the tent and put the other lad on the train home, practical, objective and unemotional."

Kathy Murgatroyd, another client on the Alps trip, had first met Cunningham in 1974 when she had been at the Lodge for a ski party training leader and she says: "I remember his attitude to this day. Everything was precise. His explanations. His demonstrations. He expected no less of his students. He sought perfection in us and his enthusiasm for the sport was infectious. I will also remember his knowledge of mountain flowers which came to me as a surprise at the camp at the Schwarzsee below the Matterhorn."

In all there were three trips with Mountain Ventures with another booked for the year of his death. He was also due to run an Easter course in snow and ice mountaineering for the college, the course finally going ahead under the leadership of ex-students as a tribute.

"They made a great job of it." says Lyon. "It was a marvellous course. It was run for John and in John's name and the money went to Alison, I think."

Alison says; "John was doing the Mountain Ventures thing to get cash for us, but honestly I think he was starting to slow down a bit. I mean if you think he went to the Alps and was going up the Eiger or something every day he would have to get himself fit for that. He would run on the roads round here but it wasn't his scene really. He wasn't climbing on a daily basis like at the Lodge so I think his fitness might have slowed down. I think he was ready to become involved more in family life. He would have still skied, would be retired and he was talking about retiring when he died ."

"John was into jogging for a time I remember but I think it was all a bit tongue-in-cheek," says Lyon. "It was the running boom at the time and I think he just wanted to see what all the fuss was about."

Paul, John's son, was born on December 3, 1980 and Alison says: "John was very settled just before he died, very settled. I remember sitting there pregnant with Paul and him saying won't it be nice to have another. Then Paul being born was the icing on the cake because it was a boy and he was a really nice little lad. We went through a list of names for the kids, most of them Scottish of course, Kirsty and Shauna obviously but in the end we settled for Paul Michael John. John was very proud, it didn't stop him dashing off climbing and skiing but he was very proud in a quiet way. He was a big softie really."

On January 26, 1980, John sat down at Hillside Road and wrote one of his rare letters, this time to his brother James and sister-in-law Pat in Australia:

"Dear James and Pat,

First of all thanks for the present of three bottles of Australian wine, they were really great.

We used the sparkling wine to celebrate when Paul was born, the white wine at Christmas and tonight we finished off the red. Hope you had a lovely time over Xmas and New Year.

I had Christmas at home with the family and New Year was spent in the icy depths of the Cairngorms, much to Alison's annoyance. Up there, I met the usual crowd, Big Jack, Tommy, Bill, Harry, Bob, Iain and Frith. In fact, I had Hogmanay dinner with Iain and first-footed Frith, who is on the wagon by the way. So I joined him in a New Year's Eve drink, a bowl of soup. Quite a change! The weather over here is pretty cold, fog and ice everywhere and snow and ice in the ski areas.

I go back to the Cairngorms mid-February for ice climbing and a little skiing. Unfortunately, Alison and the family can't come up with me as Kirsty is at school.

The girls have colds at the moment, or should I say never-ending colds and coughs, I suppose it's usual for this time of year. Paul is OK, he hasn't caught anything so far. I am enclosing a photograph of Paul and the girls which was taken at Xmas time. Kirsty has started collecting stamps and if you could help her with some Australian stamps she would be really pleased. She only has a couple from down under.

I hope all of the photographs which you took out here came out all right. I noticed when I was in Tommy's office that his ice climbing poster was gone, he said you had taken it back with you, it is quite a good shot. I was actually fiddled when I sold the rights of that shot. I was paid £50 for it. If I had known then what I know now I could have made quite a bit marketing it myself. Anyway, I will close for now and hope to hear from you fairly soon.

Best wishes and love from everyone,
John, Alison, Paul and the girls."

News of John's death, as it turned out, arrived in Victoria before his last letter.

Alison knew at once when she opened the door to the policeman.

"I had just fed Paul. He was sat on my knee It was about midnight and there was a knock on the door. A policeman was there I just looked and said: 'It's John, isn't it.' I was in shock but I remember trying to tidy the house because it was such a mess. They said they hadn't found him which was the awful thing, then they said he might be sat on a ledge or something and I thought 'don't be silly if he was on a ledge he'd have climbed out'. I said 'No he's gone', it was an instinctive, a gut sort of reaction. The worst thing you can ever do is tell the kids their dad has died, especially aged 5 and 2. You can't explain fully at that age. They produced a list of reasons why it shouldn't happen. Shauna said 'Why didn't someone reach out for him and why wasn't there a handle there?' It went on like that for two or three days

"Of course the other thing that happened was that because there was no body, they were going to have an inquest and until then wouldn't give me a death certificate. The money was all frozen and there was a mortgage to pay. So eventually my father who is a legal executive went down to see the coroner and convinced him it wasn't suicide or anything like that but it was a good six months before they issued the death certificate. They had to wait a certain length of time."

At IM Marsh, Cunningham's death was accepted as an accident, the nearest thing to an in-house enquiry being a written version of events on the fatal day from the students involved.

The memorial service was held just down from Hillside Road at St Michael's Church on the Wirral and along with a large section of the British climbing community, there were colleagues from the Lodge and the Creagh Dhu.

Fred Harper, who had earlier broken the news to a stunned Lodge staff meeting, remembers being struck by the contrast between some of the climbers in casual gear and the "traditional west coast thing of black tie and white shirt in Bill Smith, Tommy Paul and the rest".

An eulogy by Davie Todd was read which "was very moving" said Allen Fyffe who had driven down with Harper. "It was a superb letter from Davie saying basically that after Johnny they broke the mould. There were a lot of people I didn't know there. It was the first time I had met Big

McLean and Jimmy Marshall. I remember talking to Alison, and of the people who were there – who knew Johnny – I was probably nearer her age than anyone else. She was really upset as you can imagine. But we were all in a state of shock. I remember after Fred broke the news, I was due up on the hill with a Lodge course and forgot my crampons, the first time that had ever happened."

Tommy Paul had heard the news from Iain Finlayson and he says: "He phoned me and said: 'My dad's just heard that Johnny Cunningham's died'. I said: 'Died?' 'Well, been killed' and I said: 'Killed?' He said: 'He was drowned' and I thought it would have to be drowned. I went swimming with Smith and Johnny and he kept to the side, he would do three strokes and then head for the side. Same with Smith. It was a big turn-out. It's always difficult when there isn't a body to bury. It happened with my nephew, he was drowned in a school party and it destroyed my brother and his wife, they kept wondering if some day he was going to show up and this was 20 or 30 years later.

"To have a service is a formality, there is no coming back and I think it was a good thing to do, although Johnny wasn't a church man, far from it. Whillans and Brown were there and people like that, they could recognise a quality climber. Johnny was a big influence for a long, long period. A lot of people took up climbing because of him. With scores of people, if nothing else, he taught them there was a way of life that was worthwhile."

"I remember supporting his mum," says Alison, "down the aisle of the church. The other thing was I'm a methodist and I'd asked the methodist minister to come to this catholic church and he never turned up so at the last minute this 80-year-old curate had to step in and do his best and he didn't know John from Adam and he was giving it 'and the going out and the coming in'. I expect John would have had a good laugh at that. But finally it was all over and it was a relief to get it all over with. It was time to get on."

Alison remarried in 1988 to Barry Quatermass who was playing rugby union for Fylde and was a patient after she started a physiotherapy business. They have a daughter, Natalie, who gets along famously with Kirsty, Shauna and Paul. John Cunningham's name still comes up after 18 years.

"I've come across people he has taught skiing and things like that. One bloke was talking about being at the funeral of a famous climber, John's of course. I said that was my husband actually and he is looking at me and this always happens. Even Barry. He has a very good pal at work, a keen skier and outdoor type and he went to the Alps with a guy from Yorkshire, who it turned out had been skiing with John. Kirsty has been on teaching courses and was down in Conway for an English weekend. Of course she is still Kirsty Cunningham and someone says to her: 'You are no relation to John Cunningham, are you?' She said: 'Actually, it's my dad'."

Cunningham would be proud of his three children. Kirsty teaches languages at a school in Chester while Shauna is at Nottingham University doing law and Russian and has a contract, starting in the millennium, with a firm in London specialising in commercial law. Paul went up to Glasgow University in September, 1998, to study English and psychology, the decision to return to his father's home town leaving him, as he said, "very excited".

"The girls are not into climbing, though some of it has come out in Paul," says their mother. "He is not sporty but goes cycling and camping so it's in his blood."

Kirsty, although just five in 1980, retains vivid memories of her father: "I have little snapshots of him, like him smacking me when I was naughty, although never too hard, the presents he would always bring home from wherever he had been travelling and meeting him at stations. The day of the accident is so clear; I can remember the police arriving and for weeks on end after that I kept thinking he would come back. I'm cross in some ways that I never really did get to know him; I talk to other people who knew him so well and I feel a bit envious."

"The students came round to see me after the accident, they were smashing lads really," says Alison. "A couple of them in particular had been badly affected by it and they were actually married. I finished up trying to make them feel better about it. The one who had first gone in the water couldn't take it all in, I don't think. We had actually booked a holiday in Yorkshire when it happened and of course I had to ring this lady up in the Dales and tell her we wouldn't be coming and she said;

'It happened to me five months ago, my husband was run over by a trac-
tor but it was just an accident' and I thought 'Yes, you are right it was just
an accident' but at 28 and with three little kids that was quite a big thing
for you to accept."

There are other reminders, too. In the Quatermass home on the Wirral
stands a coffee table fashioned by John out of a centreboard from a sailing dinghy at the Lodge and Alison says: "He was a very good carpenter
and we are still using that coffee table. I tried to give other people things
to remember him by. I gave Jim Lyon and Ron James a lot of the climbing
equipment to pass on to the students. Tommy, I think, has his shipyard
tools. John and Tommy were very close, like brothers really. I think Johnny
in married terms was more a late developer, Tommy married much younger.
Yes, Johnny was a late developer but as far as life was concerned he had
done an awful lot.

After he died they brought back his rucksack and all the bits and
pieces and I put in an insurance claim for a watch which had cost me
£140, very expensive in those days. Then we found it wrapped inside a
sock in the bottom of the rucksack, he must have taken it off for climbing.
I will probably give it to Paul when he's 21.

"The funny thing is, I keep it in a drawer by the bedside and it has
never stopped going. It has never been worn but it has never stopped. All
these years ... "

EPILOGUE

"Och, that boy got me in a lot o' bother." Bill Smith and sentimentality do not go together but the verdict on his younger partner on so many adventures is delivered with a chuckle. There is no disguising the fondness the old man retains for John Cunningham as he sits in his Kingussie cottage and looks back over 50 years to the day when he and a 16-year-old East End Glasgow boy first appeared on to the Scottish rock climbing scene. Smith remains an iconic figure in what is left of the Creagh Dhu. When this book was first started I was left in little doubt that while many of Cunningham's contemporaries would have preferred to have kept their memories of their friend private, if Smith agreed to co-operate the rest would follow. "If Big Bill says OK then that's all right with me," said one.

Ian Nicholson, who with Con Higgins put up the E3 Apocalypse on the Buachaille's Slime Wall in 1969, was born the year after Cunningham and Bill Smith first crept their way up that forbidding precipice to find Guerdon Grooves in 1948. Conversations with him are laced with strong feelings about the traditions of the Creagh Dhu and there is little doubt he regards Smith as the club godfather.

"He is the one we all respect," says Nicholson. "Everyone looks up to Bill, he is the one who set the standards for the club."

Bill Smith was 74 on June 12, 1998 and his climbing is limited to very occasional trips to the Etive Slabs, usually behind the rope of John McLean but on still respectable routes like Spartan Slab. Like so many of the club from the Cunningham era there is no evidence of dotage here. As George Shields, who at the age of 62, fathered his sixth child, a son, and after many years as one of the top ski instructors in Europe now contents himself with mountain biking, says: "The thing is it's not as if we all got to 50 and then started putting on the medallions and jogging. We have carried on with the sport most of our lives, it has become a part of our lives."

Smith, who has a handicap of eight, plays golf virtually every day.

Willie Rowney says: "Bill's terrific. When the weather is right he skis in the morning and plays golf in the afternoon and will occasionally have a curling match at night. I think Bill really decided that his Cunningham days were over in his early 40s and was looking around for something else to take up. It was golf and he is very competitive you know. He curls seriously and plays golf seriously, not in your face competitive but he likes a game. He doesn't like just to go out and mess about and he very quickly caught on. He is a very well co-ordinated guy, everything he does, he does to a high standard. Three or four years ago someone discovered he had a bike. He kept it a secret. Bill did his own thing in his own time and really has never let himself go."

Faye Ogilvie remains convinced that most of The Boys have never grown up; they remain delinquents at heart. "I remember when my first husband and I bought a car and Bill and John came down to see it. When I looked out of the window they were shaking it, seeing if the suspension was all right. I said: 'I'll kill you two'. They haven't changed. I met Tommy Paul, Smith and MacInnes in my mother's house. I think of them now as I thought of them then. They are all nuts."

So what became of the other Boys of Yesterday?

John Cullen, who lives in Milngavie within a couple of miles of the site of the Craigallion Fire and Rowney, who retired to Lenzie, are still handsome, active men and avid golfers playing the occasional round with Smith on his trips back to Glasgow. Cullen, before his retirement from civil engineering, planned the Glasgow section of the M8. Hugh Currie, who ended his journalistic career as managing editor of the Daily Record, is a champion veteran runner. Shields works part-time for Clive Freshwater at his Loch Insh watersports centre, and at 68 he still instructs mountain-biking. Tommy Paul, having completed over the years his idyllic cottage at Boat of Garten, enjoys frequent trips across America with his wife Shirley in their motor home, often with stays at the Davey Agnew home high in the Tetons.

In the summer of 1998 Dave and Mhairi Todd drove up to the Yukon for the centenary celebrations of the Gold Rush. They spend every available minute away from teaching in the wilderness of Canada. Pat Walsh has a croft on Skye while Charlie Vigano, probably the only hardcore Creagh Dhu member to die in an actual rock-climbing accident, was killed in Calpe, Spain on March 25, 1998. He was 69.

Visitors and clients at the Cairngorm chairlift will find it hard to miss the burly figure of John McLean on his rounds there. A fervent and occasional pugnacious supporter of the Cairngorm funicular, McLean was 60 in 1998 and still climbs at a high standard. Some say he has mellowed, although there are occasional glimpses of the recalcitrant hardman who once "asked" Sir Chris Bonington to leave Jacksonville. Mick Noon was back in Glasgow from his home on Huntly Beach, Los Angeles to suffer through a part of the atrocious summer of 1998. He brought over his son, Stephen, who was born in America and as well as an ascent of Ben Nevis with Cullen enjoyed a weekend in a bothy complete with open fire. "It was just like old times," he says.

Jimmy Marshall, too, sneaks his old PAs into a sack for the occasional weekend away. Alongside pictures of his dead son Colin in his Edinburgh flat, is the framed proof of his honorary membership of the Creagh Dhu, dated May 30, 1987. He is massively proud of both: "I'd always been big pals with McLean and one weekend he invited me up for a smoker up at the ski doss at Bridge of Orchy. I took the son-in-law because he had never met these people and my own son came along, too. The steam team were there and it was like a western; the cork came out of the bottle with a plop and there was a tremendous thrash. I'm not a great drinker – after three I usually fall down – and I was lying between two bunk beds unconscious when several of them appeared and dragged me downstairs, stood me up and said in sort of grand, official tones: 'We are offering you membership of the Creagh Dhu Mountaineering Club, you must accept it or reject it.' I accepted. I was flabbergasted and highly honoured but Johnny would be turning in his grave if he knew."

It is the Boys' shared experiences, backgrounds and affinity with the hills that left them with friendships that have lasted – for five decades in some cases. There is still that sense of humour laced with determined lifemanship, too.

Paul, Smith, Shields and McLean were on a skiing holiday in Courchevel in 1995 and Paul recalls: "We were on the bus on the way up to the ski slopes and the rep was taking money and organising the ski passes. Bill qualified for an Over 60, so did Shields, and McLean was getting a bit miffed about this because he was only in his 50s then and had to pay the full amount. Then we found we could get another reduction for over 70s and of course Bill qualified for that, too. McLean was getting desperate and said: 'Can we no put them all together and split it.' but of course we said no way. So then Shields asked: 'Is there anything for a BASI instructor? and they said 'Only if you have a group' and George looked round at us and said: 'This is my group' so he got a pass for free. Then the lass says to these four old guys: 'I'll come and ski with you and show you round if you like' which gave us a huge laugh because George had taught out in the Three Valleys for years. But we said nothing and she came and skied with us and I could see her eyes opening at these geriatrics. She was totally knackered at the end of that."

Time hasn't been so kind to some of John Cunningham's other friends.

Iain Finlayson, the three-year-old who had opened the door of the Glencoe ski doss to find his Christmas apple tree, collapsed and died at his home in the French Alps in 1990 at the age of 39. His father Frith and mother Jeannie live in a small house on the outskirts of Aviemore where Frith is a popular if occasional high-risk presence in the local bars. Frith's memories of Cunningham and the Creagh Dhu are rich – "I have walked with giants" he is fond of saying – but most of his friends will inform you that many of those memories are seen too often through the bottom of a whisky glass for his own good. Pat Walsh has had to wrestle similar demons. But after two heart attacks, problems with cataracts on both eyes and a lifetime of fighting the odds, the little Clydesider remains as irrepressible as ever.

"Where I live on Isle Oronsay I can still see the mountains and the sea. I have had a great life. I think if there was such a thing as reincarnation I would still come back as Patsy Walsh," he says.

Duncan Ross, John's best man, and Roger O'Donovan who spent the memorable two days at Hell's Lum with Cunningham and March in the winter of 1973, both died tragically early of cancer. Don Whillans, who never forgave Cunningham for robbing him of Carnivore, died of a heart attack in 1985 Chris Bonington, of course, became Sir Chris, although perhaps some credit for this should go to Mick Noon who saved his neck all those years ago on Tryfan.

Jack Thomson and Bob Clyde both passed away in the early 1990s, the boyhood friends now lying side by side in the same Insh churchyard with a fine view across Rothiemurchus Forest to the Cairngorms. Chris Lyon, who for many was, and still is, the Creagh Dhu, died in December, 1994, aged 72. Many of his marvellous writings survive, unpublished.

Bill March outlasted his friend Cunningham by only 10 years. After his short spell at Plas y Brenin he and Karen emigrated to Canada where March took up an associate professorship at the University of Calgary. He is remembered there with much affection and earned the Summit of Excellence award for his pioneering from the Canadian Alpine Club. John Amatt, who himself left for Canada from Manchester 23 years ago and now organises the Banff Mountain Film Festival, says: "Bill did a lot of new routes out here and proved a big inspiration to a lot of people. He led the first Canadian expedition to Mount Everest in 1982, but he also had a lot of personal difficulties. Karen had breast cancer and had to suffer through chemotherapy for a long time, his mother-in-law had a stroke and Bill at one time had to have back surgery."

Just two days after Karen had been given a clean bill of health by doctors on September 8, 1990, March was in Panorama, British Columbia, when he collapsed and died walking down a trail. A full autopsy was performed but no-one could pinpoint the exact cause of death. He was 49.

Amatt adds: "He had just been talking with Bruce Hendricks who was with him at the time. They were discussing death and Bill had said something on the lines of 'Well, if I have to go it would have to be in the outdoors doing something I love'. An hour later he was dead. There were lots of tests but they came up with nothing. We just have to think it was Bill's time."

March had remembered his days with Cunningham to the end, telling Jimmy Marshall in a letter: 'I shall always treasure the happy days of comradeship I had with John'. And Karen March, who still lives in Calgary, says: "The world is missing two great guys and great climbers, too."

Mary Cunningham died in 1990, 14 years after the bulldozers came in and demolished Number 1252, Duke Street. After years of pounding by Glasgow Corporation trams and the heavy machinery at Beardmores the corner tenement was finally condemned in 1976.

Faye Ogilvie says: "I dare say Parkhead Cross has changed completely. It is a right den now. I get lost going down there. I remember my mother she took dementia in later life and she wanted to go home but we could never find out where home was. So we took her to Duke Street and of course she could recognise nothing because there was nothing there so it didn't satisfy her. So home ... I don't know where home was, but I think it was Duke Street she wanted."

It is 18 years since John Cunningham died in those alien seas off Anglesey, but his legacy of hard climbs and inspiring deeds remain. It's always tempting to look back on one's own youth and pontificate about the golden age but there is little doubt that climbing has changed. Whether for better or worse will, as always, be in the eye of the beholder. Editorials in climbing magazines employ four-letter words, ropes and rucksacks disappear forever from the foot of climbs and climbers are paid to wear free equipment. One full-page advertisement in one magazine featured a bronzed god posing as 'Arguably Britain's Greatest All Round Climber' and personal trainers offer their services for climbing improvement. A close friend of the author's who in 1997 went on a rock-climbing course at Glenmore Lodge spent, with the whole of the Northern Cairngorms a 20-minute drive away, most of the week on the Lodge's newly-opened indoor climbing wall. Chris Bonington's version of the Jacksonville incident came via e-mail and satellite from his 1998 Sepu Kangri expedition and concluded with the words: 'It seems funny writing of these distant times by a lake below a great mountain in the heart of TIBET.' If anything illustrates how horizons in climbing have shrunk it is surely this.

And while the Creagh Dhu once employed its apprentice blackboys without any fears of a Politically Correct backlash, an article in Climber, six pages in front of an obituary featuring the smiling features of Charlie Vigano, informs us that a Women's International Symposium at Plas y Brenin had produced 'new guidelines for federations on equal opportunities for women in the sport'. All this is not stated as criticism, simply fact, but certainly many can picture the cynical grin on John Cunningham's face and hear an echo of that cackling laugh if he had lived to read that one.

Says Willie Rowney: "It has changed. Cunningham and the gang, absolutely straight. You never had to worry about gear going astray, there was nothing devious about them. That was one of the things that was so great about those days. I don't have any friends that I could put at the same degree of closeness as the lads from the club. We went everywhere together and I think that is why were are still friends even though we are scattered about a bit. We all go back a long long time – I was 17 when I first met them and that's 48 years. I think those days will be with us forever."

"We were all good friends," says Mick Noon. "All that gang were tarred with the same brush. We knew and understood each other and I think we would do a good turn for anyone."

John Cunningham's, for all its brevity, had been a remarkable journey, but there was a sense of the inconclusive about its end, almost as if he had decided to leave us all with one final enigmatic statement, one last leg-pull.

Tommy Paul, for one, has never accepted his death, and George Shields, quite independently, said: "I was talking to Bill Smith the other day and we were saying that if John walked in here now we wouldn't be in the least surprised. Some people reckon he's trying to set the underwater record to the United States."

Faye Ogilvie sits in her living room in Greenhills, East Kilbride, and talks about her long-dead brother almost without a sense of loss.

"You know," she says, "if our John came up the garden path now and knocked on the door I wouldn't bat an eyelid."

There's hope, said Shakespeare, a great man's memory may outlive his life half a year. Inside a bedside table in a house close to the Irish Sea, an expensive watch ticks away. For all the world like a heartbeat.

APPENDIX

THE CREAGH DHU

By Chris Lyon

The despair of industrial depression
Rots a man body and soul
Ragtag, broken, beaten soft hand outstretched for the dole
This is the masses I speak of
The mob that is so easily beat
Who cheer for the flag that is winning
Then crumble when thrown on the street
Tis of individuals I wish to speak of
Rough diamonds that always gleam through
About those who sought high adventure
Like the club they call the Creagh Dhu
Parish boots crunched the unknown by-ways
Heather the bed for the night
Twas pease-brose or porridge for breakfast
For dinner just pull your belt tight
They followed the cascading river
Lifting a fish, a rabbit a hare
Till they came to the towering mountain
And wondered what is up over there?
Steep slopes fell to their parry
Ridges and tops to their thrust
Then they turned to the virgin rock face
To sate their insatiable lust
Escape found on time-worn ledges
Freedom balanced high up above
Then followed pure understanding
An all-consuming passion. Then love.

Far below at the Fire of Craigallion,
The eternal flame that never burnt oot,
Faces now glowed,
Few round the fire, there was plenty of war work about,
The philosophers told the high wanderers,
The rest have crawled back to the slums,
Exchanging their dreams of freedom,
For a handful of material crumbs.
In the shadows beyond the embers,
Sat a boy in the circle of dreams,
Mind baffled with book talk learning,
Grasped the truth of the mountain and streams.
'Where is this Highland of Freedom?' he asked eyes shining bright.
A granite hand clasped his shoulder,
Spun the boy round to the night.
'O'er there is a cliff called Creagh Dhu,' boomed a voice banner unfurled,
'Climb that if you can my wee laddie,
Tis first pitch top the roof of the world.'
Sixty years on they still climb to the sky,
Leaving the legend of triumph and skill,
Part men, part gods and part devil,
Paying homage to their mistress, the Hill.

FOR JOHNNY

By Davie Todd

So Johnny, you have finally completed the big climb. What an out-standing one it was.

From below, it appeared that as you pushed on leaving a trail of lesser mortals behind each pitch was better than the one before. Of course, boldness and vision, which ranked highly among your qualities, reaped the rewards they so justly deserved. I wondered how many of your climbing friends regretted their relative frailty and wished that they could have hung in there instead of baling out for the security, and obscurity, of the valley.

It would be easy to say that you always had an eye for a good line. But that would be an over-simplistic observation on a life that will never be repeated. Of course it will be attempted and claimed by the types whose careers are devoted to personal glorification through the mountaineering media. No doubt they will gloss over the easy variations which they elect to take whilst simultaneously failing to mention the conditions along the way. I can imagine your typical grin as I ask: 'How many winter ascents are claimed in summer conditions?'

As for Ali, Kirsty, Shauna and Paul, it is sad that they could not have shared some of the climb with you. However, they will in time draw strength from your example. And of course there will be no shortage of friends and relatives to offer the security of a psychological rope as they face the pitches ahead.

Having had the honour to share a number of notable pitches with you on the big route, from the Clydeside shipyards to Antarctica I can only say thank you for the encouragement, the warm friendship and myriad memories.

Au revoir,

Davie.

LIST OF FIRST ASCENTS

Sron Na Ciche, Skye.
July 16, 1956: Bastinado. E1, 90m. JC, John Allen, Bill Smith.
Climbed during club trip. On the same day as Pat Walsh and Harry McKay did the first ascent of Trophy Crack.

Craig y Castell, Tremadog.
July 12, 1951. Creagh Dhu Wall, 70m, Hard Severe. JC, Bill Smith, Pat Vaughan.
An all-time classic. Nobody has ever owned up to the carving on the rock at foot of the first pitch!

Ben Nevis,
August 1965. Rolling Stones. HVS, 135m. JC, Con Higgins.
Cunningham's only recorded first ascent on the Ben.

Beinn a'Mhuinidh, Kinlochewe.
Summer 1971. The Creep. HVS, 85m. JC, Bill March.
Vertigo. HVS, 85m. JC, Bill March.
Stoater. S, 90m. JC, Bill March.
During a Glenmore Lodge rock-climbing course. The pair added an unnamed VS to the same crag.

Tollie Crag, Loch Maree
May 9, 1970. Stoney Broke, HVS, 90m. JC, Bill March.

Carnmore Crag.
July 22, 1966. Abomination, HVS, 100m. John McLean, A Currey, JC

Creag Dubh, Newtonmore.
Sept. 1967. Trampoline, VS, 25m. JC solo.

Coire an Lochain. Northern corries of Cairngorms.
Summer 1968: Procrastination. S, 70m. JC, George Shields.
Ventricle. HVS, 95m. JC, George Shields.
Summer 1969: Puffer. S, 70m. JC and party.
Auricle. HS, 90m. JC, Bill March.

Coire an Lochain ctd.

Never Mind. HVS, 60m. JC, Bill March.

A bizarre and incident filled first ascent involving two pegs for aid, a
tension traverse (still needed) and a slide down an arête to a foot
hold.

February, 1975: Gaffers Groove. V, 60m. JC, Allen Fyffe.

Shelter Stone Crag.

August, 1969: Postern Direct Finish. VS, 255m. JC, Bill March.

Consolation Groove. HVS, 150m. JC, Bill March.

Beaten to the line of Snipers by fellow Creagh Dhu members
Carrington and Shields, this was the 'consolation'.

Summer, 1970: Threadbare. VS, 280m. JC, Bill March.

Six pegs for aid.

Hell's Lum Crag.

Summer, 1969: Hell's Lum Direct. S, 150m. JC, Bill March.

Climbed on a pouring wet day as the March 'initiation'.

January, 1970: The Chancer. V, 90m. JC, Bill March.

Ice screws were used for tension to get out onto the main icicle.
Cunningham also took a fall onto a Salewa ice screw, which held.

February, 1973: Salamander. 1V, 155m. JC, Bill March, Roger
O'Donovan.

Devil's Delight. V, 165m. JC, Bill March, Roger
O'Donovan.

Two big plums snatched during a weekend under the Shelter Stone.
A poignant guide book entry as all three were to die prematurely.

Stag Rocks.

Winter, 1970: CM Gully. III, 135m. JC, Bill March.

Stac an Fharaidh.

Summer, 1969: Pushover. HVS, 140m. JC.

A Lodge voluntary instructor declined to follow.

Whispers. VS, 135m. JC, George Shields.

Aprés Moi. VS, 150m. JC, George Shields.

June 14, 1970: Pippet Slab. S, 135m. JC, Bill March.

The Cobbler.
June 1947: Chimney Arête. VS, 25m. JC, Ian Dingwall.
Cunningham's first new route on The Cobbler and photographed by Ben Humble while working on a guide book revision.
Summer, 1948: Direct Direct. HVS, 130m. JC.
    Incubator. HS, 80m. JC, Ian Dingwall.
    Deadman's Groove. VS, 90m. JC, Bill Smith, Sam Smith.
    Ardgarten Arête. VS, 55m. JC.
    S Crack. VS, 40m. JC, Bill Smith.
August, 1949: Echo Crack. HS, 40m. JC, Charlie Vigano.
August, 1949: Punster's Crack. S, 45m. JC, Bill Smith.
May, 1951: Porcupine Wall. Aid route, 45m. Hamish MacInnes, JC.
September, 1951: Whether Wall, VS, 40m. JC, Hamish MacInnes.
May, 1952: Cupids Groove, VS, 15m. JC, Hamish MacInnes, Bill Smith, Hugh Currie,
Summer, 1955: Nook Direct. Aid route, 60m. Mick Noon, JC, Bill Smith, George McIntosh, Pat Walsh.
A much-attempted line up the huge overhanging nose on North Peak. Now a free climb.

Buachaille Etive Mor.
June, 1946: Crow's Nest Crack. VS, 85m. JC, Peter McGonigle.
Cunningham's opening salvo on the Buachaille and graded severe in rubbers at the time.
October, 1946: Autumn Slab, VS, 25m. JC, Bill Smith.
The first new route from the Cunningham/Smith Steam Team.
    Curving Groove, VS, 80m. JC, Bill Smith.
October, 1946: Grooved Arête, S, 65m. JC, Bill Smith.
An interesting day with Chris Lyon and Kenny Copland climbing Juniper Crack while W H Murray was round the corner on Waterslide Wall.
June, 1947: Gallows Route, E1, 25m. JC, Ian Dingwall.
Scotland's first extreme and still rated a 'chop route' by the current guide writers. Smith was away on National service at the time.
    Great Flake Route, V Diff, 45m. JC, Ian Dingwall.
    Sunset Groove, V Diff, 40m. JC, Ian Dingwall.
    Sunset Rib, V Diff, 30m. Ian Dingwall, JC.
May, 1948: Ravens Gully Direct, E1, 50m. JC, Bill Smith, Tommy Paul.

Buachaille Etive Mor ctd.

June, 1948: June Crack, VS, 60m. Bill Smith, JC.
Climbed on the 12th, Smith's birthday.
                    Guerdon Grooves, HVS, 160m. JC, Bill Smith.
The first route on Slime Wall.
July, 1948: Domino Chimney, S, 50m. JC, Bill Smith, Tommy Paul.

June, 1951: Dalness Chasm Left Fork, VS, 350m. JC, Hamish
                    MacInnes, S Jagger, C White.
Another good route for a wet day.
August 3, 1954: August Crack, VS, 50m. Bill Smith, JC
                    Trident Crack, S, 45m. Bill Smith, JC.
August 4, 1955: Garotte, VS, 30m. JC, Mick Noon.
                    Pendulum, E2, 40m. Pat Walsh, JC.
September 16, 1956: Whortleberry Wall, HVS, 115m. JC, Bill Smith.
The pair had already climbed the first pitch (Autumn Slab).
August, 1958: Bluebell Grooves, E4, 50m. JC, Frith Finlayson.
A phenomenal lead. One peg used on the overhang on Pitch 2.
Finlayson was finally lowered off "hanging 15 feet out from the rock".

Creag a'Bhancair.

August 9, 1958: Carnivore, E3, 160m. JC, Mick Noon.
Earlier attempts had started in the middle of the central wall until
Don Whillans found the entry pitch over on the left. Cunningham
then 'jocked off' Whillans who returned with Derek Walker in 1962
to force the Direct Finish.
August, 1959: Cayman Grooves, E1, 70m. John McLean, JC.
                    Piranha, VS, 70m. John McLean, JC.
The 21-year-old 'Great White Hope' on top form.

Aonach Dubh.

September, 1951: Deep Gash Gully, VS, 40m. JC, Willie Rowney,
                    Bill Smith
August 2, 1955: Boomerang, HVS, 90m. JC, Mick Noon.
                    Little Boomerang, VS, 65m. JC, Mick Noon.
The first breaches in Aonach Dubh's Lower North-East Face.
September 15, 1956: The Gut, HVS, 75m. JC, Bill Smith.
February 24, 1957: Deep Gash Gully, 1V, 40m. JC, Mick Noon.
July, 1966: Hesitation, HVS, 60m. JC.

Aonach Dubh ctd.

      Tightrope, Aid route (now Bannockburn) 130m. JC,
      John McLean.

August 23, 1966: Stumblebum, E1, 115m. JC, Bill Smith.

The valedictory route of a great partnership.

Etive Slabs, Beinn Trilleachan.

April 6, 1957: Agony, E2, 155m. JC, Mick Noon, Bill Smith.

The first big corner on the slabs, some aid used.

April 7, 1957: Hammer, HVS, 150m. Mick Noon, JC.

*With Swastika, probably Noon's finest contribution to Scottish
climbing. Some tension used on Pitch Four.*

May, 1958: The Long Walk, E2, 340m. JC, Mick Noon.

A high-level girdle of the Slabs that required some aid.

September, 1959: The Long Wait, E2, 255m. JC, Robin Smith.

*A mega pairing, probably the one and only time. Cunningham had
done the early pitches with Whillans before. Smith led these,
Cunningham the final four pitches.*

INDEX